Trust Your Wings and Touch the Sky

A Strategy for Success based upon the quotations of Ralph Waldo Emerson

by

John V. Madormo

TABLE OF CONTENTS:

Introduction

Accountability

Attitude

Awareness

Beauty

Character

Confidence

Conviction

Courage

Diligence

Friendship

Humility

Ingenuity

Kindness

Knowledge

Leaving a Legacy

Living in the Now

Opportunity

Overcoming Fear

Passion

Patience

Perseverance

Purpose

Service

Wisdom

Wonder

Epilogue

References

INTRODUCTION

Trust Your Wings and Touch the Sky. An Emerson quote? A book title? Or sound advice for those looking for answers? How about all of them.

Over the years, hundreds of self-help and advice manuals have been written to help us become more well-adjusted human beings, better able to overcome adversity. Like you, I have perused my share of these seemingly life-altering self-improvement guides, and in fact have found some very helpful. But I have also discovered, because of the sheer numbers, that many of these texts begin to blur after a while. Upon investigation, we find that many thought-provoking strategies are no more that regurgitations of previous efforts. For years I have been in search of the universal, all-encompassing manual that would lead to a happier, healthier, and more prosperous life.

Little did I know that *it* had found *me* years ago. As a longtime devotee of the writings of author-philosopher-transcendentalist, Ralph Waldo Emerson, I had never stopped to realize that hidden within the complete works of this nineteenth century master was a bounty of knowledge — advice and counsel that could easily be applied to help cope with today's most pressing problems. In fact, if you were to identify and catalogue specific Emerson quotations, you would find yourself with a wealth of wisdom — a virtual road map for a successful life. Rules to live by — tenets to follow.

If you're wondering when you'll have the time to digest the complete works of Emerson and compile such a list, fear not. All the work has been done for you — in this very text — ready for your perusal. But don't think that this was some selfless act on my part. I had good reason to do so. You see, I am always in search of inspirational quotes for my own personal motivation. And I am assuming there are many others out there like me. Regardless of our lot in life, we can always use insightful words or phrases to help us make critical decisions, to determine which path to follow in a given situation, or just to get off our butts and do whatever it is we've been putting off. And so, this compilation of Emerson quotations is my personal owner's manual for a successful existence, and one I hope you will find helpful.

I want you to think of me as a fortune hunter who has stumbled upon the treasure of a lifetime, and one who is more than happy to share this amazing find with you. In actuality, I have been a college professor for more than thirty years, and a student of Emerson for nearly that long. In this book I have identified 100 of Emerson's most inspirational quotations. I have broken them down into twenty-five categories — Accountability, Character, Conviction, Ingenuity, Patience, Purpose, Wisdom, to name a few. I have then provided an analysis of each quotation, with suggestions on how we might apply these Emerson principles to our own lives.

I encourage you to read this book cover to cover, and then to place it in a location that will be easy for you to remember. My hope is that you will refer to the 100 quotes and essays contained within this collection in the same way you would refer to a dictionary or a thesaurus or a search engine. Sometimes all you need to address a problem and right the course is a single short reading. I've tried to select quotations that are simplistic on the surface but yet much deeper when you reflect upon them. My ultimate goal is to see you apply the wisdom of Emerson to your daily life, and to enable you to make more prudent, more insightful, and more enlightened choices — and to instill in you the courage to face your demons, and ultimately overcome adversity. Ralph Waldo Emerson put it best, "It is the fear of the young bird to trust its wings." Are you ready to soar? Our journey is about to begin. It's time to trust *your* wings…and touch the sky.

John V. Madormo

ACCOUNTABILITY

> "Shallow men believe in luck...Strong men believe in cause and effect."
>
> Ralph Waldo Emerson
>
> (from "Worship," *The Conduct of Life*, 1860)

Around our house when difficult circumstances present themselves, it wouldn't be unusual to hear, "Things happen for a reason." I know that my kids are tired of hearing those words. One year my youngest daughter, for her birthday, asked that she not have to hear that phrase for an entire day. I was happy to accommodate her — for a day.

For the most part, I believe that the saying, "Things happen for a reason" has been unfairly relegated to some unseemly list of trite, overworked, meaningless phrases — ones that adults use when they can't come up with a reason for a particular outcome. But it is really a much more powerful statement. As Emerson suggests above, it's all about cause and effect. Simply put, there are consequences for our actions. And usually, they are appropriate.

When we honestly examine the happenings in our daily lives, and try to remain objective, more often than not, we have to admit that most outcomes are logical in nature. Things *did* happen for a reason. We may not have liked the reasoning. We may have a hard time accepting it, but if we think through an event in a methodical fashion, we can see why something occurred the way it did. And luck had nothing to do with it.

There...we've said it. That dreaded word — luck. Or more aptly put, the reason behind everyone else's good fortune. When good things happen to rivals, we call it luck. When good things happen to friends, we still call it luck. When are we willing to admit that someone actually deserved a promotion, or a prize, or whatever else they happened to earn? I'm not suggesting that we are never happy to see someone else succeed, but when was the last time you watched a news story about someone winning a multi-state lottery, and didn't use the word *luck*? Didn't they actually earn it? Didn't they have to purchase a ticket in order to be eligible? By doing so, they put themselves in a position to win. Sure, the odds were against them — terribly so. But by buying the ticket, they earned the opportunity to succeed. It may have been a million-to-one shot, or more likely several million-to-one shot. For this argument, the odds don't matter — only the rules. Buy a ticket—earn a chance to win. In the lottery, as in life, you can't win if you don't play.

Now please don't think I am advocating that you throw away your hard-earned dollars on lottery tickets. But isn't Emerson talking to both winners and losers when he says, "Strong men believe in cause and effect." If you buy a ticket, based on the odds, you are likely to lose. Cause and effect. If you buy a ticket, regardless of the odds, someone has to win, and that could just as easily be you as anyone else. Cause and effect. If you play and lose, you deserve it—because of the long odds. If you play and win, you deserve it—because you followed the rules—and because someone must win.

We've beaten the lottery analogy to death. The point is this we tend to attribute luck to someone's good fortune not to some skill they possess. If we examine the circumstances, we can make a pretty good case that lucky people prepared themselves for the moment, and gave themselves an opportunity to succeed. Is that luck or is that foresight? Let's give the other guy a little credit.

If you aced a test, received a promotion, or were presented with an award, and you happened to overhear someone say "Why can't I get lucky like that?" you know it would bother you. The individual who makes a statement like that seems to be dismissing your talents, and is attributing your windfall to luck. But it wasn't luck. Because there is no such thing as luck.

There is only cause and effect. And although we may not want to hear it—things do happen for a reason.

> "Don't say things. What you are stands over you the while, and thunders so that I cannot hear what you say to the contrary."
>
> Ralph Waldo Emerson
>
> (from "Social Aims," *Letters and Social Aims*, 1875)

There are a number of quotations throughout history suggesting that people learn more about us from what we do rather than what we say. Emerson is saying precisely the same thing. We can talk all we want, but people will judge us by our accomplishments or lack thereof, not by what we say we will do.

There are a lot of big talkers in our society. Politicians, ad pitchmen, company spokespersons — but how often do they actually follow through? It would be nice to see political ads, not those purchased by political parties, but rather those paid for by an impartial independent agency whose sole purpose is to determine if the promises made by incumbent candidates are indeed kept. The problem is that there is no one to pay for those ads. But wouldn't it be a refreshing alternative to the scores of negative ads we must endure every four years.

It's easy to judge those running for public office so before we throw the first stone, we had better examine our own track record. Think about the things we have told others that we will do someday — from remodeling a room, to planting a flower garden, to writing a book. There are certainly a great many people who have accomplished these feats, but there are far more who just say that they will do so someday. Which camp are you in? The doers or the talkers?

Over the years I have tried to surround myself with doers — people who don't need to announce their next project, but those who roll up their sleeves and get to work, without fanfare. These are some of the most pleasant, most optimistic, most enthusiastic people you will ever meet. They possess a serious work ethic. We know this, not from what they tell us they have accomplished, but from what we can see with our own eyes. If you hang around people of action, you will soon become one yourself. Hang around talkers and in no time you'll become a card-carrying member of their fraternity. It's your choice. Hard work and procrastination are both extremely contagious.

I once read that you don't need to remind your boss of everything you are doing. If you are responsible and diligent at your place of employment, these traits will shine brightly. Your superiors will notice, as will other co-workers and friends. If you are a student, the same principle applies. I have been around students for the last 30 years. It doesn't take long to spot the talkers—they're the ones with pressed jeans, with every hair in place, and with poor listening habits. They position themselves to get in the next word, and of course, the last word. The doers, on the other hand, are too busy accomplishing their next goal to talk endlessly about it. Time to them is precious. They have learned to manage time, to prioritize, and to inspire friends and co-workers by their actions alone.

Emerson's quote also helps us identify the people of character. If we watch someone's actions for one hour, we will learn more about them than had we conversed with them for a day. Observation—it is the way to discover which individuals will become ideal employees, future leaders, and for that matter, faithful mates and partners.

Individuals who act, rather than boast, recognize the true meaning of accountability—answerable, responsible for one's actions. These are the same people who believe that life is fair, that you reap what you sow, that we get what we deserve, and that luck is self-made. And if these folks stumble along the way, they resist denial and excuse-making. They don't point the finger at someone else, or claim bad timing. They recognize the fact that we are far from perfect, and that we are not infallible. Those who embrace accountability are not afraid to admit failure. They don't beat themselves up, nor do they alibi. They take responsibility for a failed action and vow never to repeat it. But they know that they are human, and that they may slip again. It gives them something to strive for.

So, like Emerson, it seems even the Nike Company had the right idea when they advised consumers to "Just Do It." As did St. Francis of Assisi who recognized the value of actions: "Preach the gospel at all times," he said. "Use words if necessary."

"No change of circumstances can repair a defect of character."

Ralph Waldo Emerson

(from "Character," *Essays, Second Series*, 1844)

Most professional athletic teams at one time or another have had a disciplinary problem with one of their athletes. This is nothing new. And at some point when the coach or manager or general manager or owner has had enough of the off-the-field distractions, the player is traded away, and the athlete becomes someone else's problem. And following the transaction, someone will invariably say, "The change of scenery will do him good."

Based on the quote at the beginning of this section, it is doubtful that Emerson would feel the same way. If you are a person who follows sports, and troubled players, you know that for the most part, he's right. These malcontents float from team to team never seeming to find an organization or city that will embrace them. Teams try to justify their decision by suggesting that the player was misunderstood by his former owner or coach and that a new home will resolve all of those problems. History tells us that it rarely does.

Emerson points out that if the problem is a character flaw, it will travel with the individual from city to city from team to team from league to league, and for a while the problem may be masked, but ultimately that defect will surface and nothing will have changed. It's really no different than moving an ugly piece of furniture from room to room. For a short time, it seems to add a new dimension to its surroundings. But in time, the unsightliness shines through and you're back where you started.

Then what is the answer? Is this a hopeless situation? Are the player and the unfortunate piece of furniture doomed? Well, if all you do is move them around—from room to room or city to city—then yes. But what if you addressed the real problem—the defect. What if you had the couch or loveseat or whatever it is reupholstered? Then a change of scenery is no longer required. And can't the same thing be done with a human being? We're not talking about dressing up someone with new fabric or slip covers. We're talking about addressing the problem of character defect. Surely counseling of some kind would be in order. And it certainly would cut down on moving expenses.

This section isn't about problem athletes or ugly furniture. It's about being accountable. It's about admitting to yourself that a change of scenery is not the answer to a problem. It goes deeper than that. Are you the kind of person who can't seem to get along with anyone, who flits around from job to job, who is always misunderstood? At some point, you must accept the fact that it's not *their* problem…it's *yours*. And if you continually search for a new community or work environment with the type of neighbors or co-workers who appreciate someone with your talents, then you're just fooling yourself.

Whether it's Alcoholics Anonymous or Gamblers Anonymous or an anger management group or some other organization helping you beat an addiction or personality flaw, healing can't begin until you admit the problem—take ownership of this *defect,* as Emerson points out. Treatment can't begin until you want it resolved. And what does relocating do for you? New environs maybe, but same defect.

Some folks are stubborn however. They believe that by altering the external forces around them, they will find contentment. And so they keep trying to change their environment, not themselves. The answer isn't in another state, it may be down the street at a nearby church, or counseling center, or even at the local library or bookstore in the form of a self-help book or CD. It's a lot closer than you think.

Ralph Waldo Emerson has been referred to as a writer, a philosopher, even a transcendentalist. But he may just have been one of the greatest psychotherapists of his time. Who can argue with his message—when the change takes place within *you* (not the circumstances or venue), then and only then will you find peace.

> "Let me never fall into the vulgar mistake of dreaming that I am persecuted whenever I am contradicted."
>
> Ralph Waldo Emerson
>
> (from "Concord and Discord," *Journals and Letters*, 1838)

Can you remember the last time a boss, a teacher, a co-worker, a friend, a spouse, or whomever, uttered the words "Hey, can I offer a little constructive criticism?" Can you remember how you felt? What you heard was not an *offer* but rather a *criticism*. The individual offering advice may have been very sincere. He or she may have genuinely wanted to help. But when someone uses the phrase "constructive criticism," we only hear negativity. We don't recognize the helpfulness.

No one enjoys being corrected. No one enjoys being made to feel inferior. Usually we hear those words after we have said or done something that someone finds offensive or unacceptable or just plain wrong. Emerson is suggesting that we discard the "world against me" mentality, and display an openness that will allow us to embrace the advice or counsel which comes to us free of charge.

Certainly there are people out there who have an opinion about everything, who will give advice to anyone who will listen, who know it all. These are not the bearers of truth to which we are referring. We are talking about someone whose opinion you respect — someone who has earned the right to give advice. These are the people whose corrections, though they may still be painful to hear, will actually help us to grow spiritually and emotionally.

To refuse criticism is to suggest that we know far more than others — far more than our teachers, our mentors, our superiors, etc. This is hardly the case. And I believe that deep down we know this, but it is the context of this advice that causes us to resist. When advice is offered to us, labeled "criticism," then no matter how valuable it may be, we choose not to hear it.

Emerson refers to this action as a "vulgar mistake." We can choose to apply or not to apply the suggestions of others, but we mustn't be so proud that we refuse even to listen. Many of us would be offended if someone were to label us as close-minded. We like to think of ourselves as open to fresh ideas and perspectives. But are we, really? Maybe a little.

Or only if they are offered in a non-threatening way. We must rethink this position. We owe ourselves the opportunity to hear the wisdom of others.

Can you remember an English teacher in high school or college assigning a novel that you were just dreading? And when you finally got through it, do you recall that this same novel turned out to be one of your all-time favorite books? It was probably a text that you never would have picked up on your own, but you were fortunate to have had a teacher who knew that once you gave it a chance (not that you had a choice), it would turn out to be a very pleasant experience.

For me, the assigned novel was <u>Lost Horizon</u> by James Hilton. I was a sophomore in high school, and I was not looking forward to this assignment. Within a few days, however, I was hooked. *I* was Hugh Conway. *I* had been taken to Shangri-La, a Tibetan hideaway where time stood still. *I* had a meeting with the high llama. *I* was falling in love with a mysterious young woman. And *I* would never have had that experience had I not been open to the advice of others.

I have listed this Emerson quote under the "Accountability" section. I did so because when you are rigid and inflexible and close-minded, you had better be able to defend your position. You had better be able to explain why yours is the prudent approach. You had better be accountable for your decisions. But if we allow others to penetrate this facade, we become open to corrections and criticism. And we don't view them as threats, but rather as welcome bits of information. Some may be valuable. Some may not. But at least we become wise enough to pause and to process this new learning, and to determine whether it deserves to supplant previous knowledge that we were so certain of before.

ATTITUDE

"Nothing great was ever achieved without enthusiasm."

Ralph Waldo Emerson

(from "Circles," *Essays, First Series*, 1841)

Each time I read this quote, I can't help but think of a book title that expands on Emerson's advice: <u>Do What You Love, The Money Will Follow</u> by Marsha Sinetar. As the title suggests, Ms. Sinetar is encouraging us to identify a passion in our life, to commit to it, to act on it, and somehow we will find a way to make a living at it. It is an interesting and exciting premise, and who wouldn't enjoy making money doing what we love.

    Although I see similarities between these two quotations, I don't believe that Emerson is offering any monetary guarantees with his. In his reference to accomplishing something great, he indicates that enthusiasm is required—which makes perfect sense. I believe it all has to do with your definition of the word "great." One could certainly argue that a new invention or discovery that aids mankind is indeed great, and that these accomplishments could not have been achieved without enthusiasm for one's work. And it is probable that the inventor or discoverer was ultimately compensated handsomely for his/her efforts. So, perhaps Emerson *is* suggesting that financial gain may be a by-product of achieving greatness through enthusiasm, but I doubt it.

Who among us wouldn't want to be credited with having accomplished something great? We tend to connect greatness, however, with celebrity, and celebrity with wealth. Look at Blessed Mother Teresa. This was unquestionably a great woman. But a wealthy woman? Some might say that her life, as well as the lives of those she served, were full of riches. Without intending to, Mother Teresa achieved greatness. And you can be certain that she assisted the people of Calcutta with selflessness and *enthusiasm*.

Our own goals and dreams cannot be realized without enthusiasm. It's relatively easy to be enthused about reaching new, exciting heights. But let's not dismiss our daily responsibilities and obligations. There is no reason that we cannot accomplish something great each day at work or at school. If we are enthusiastic about even the most mundane chores, we can raise the bar for ourselves, and discover contentment and satisfaction in doing what simply pays the bills. If we want to see greatness in our lives, we must seek to be the best at whatever we do, not because the boss is watching or because we'll make more money. We do so because it is the only way we know how to perform these tasks.

I think this point was so poignantly made by Dr. Martin Luther King, Jr. when he said:

> "If a man is called to be a street sweeper, he should sweep streets as Michelangelo painted, or Beethoven composed music, or Shakespeare wrote poetry. He should sweep streets so well that all the hosts of heaven and earth will pause to say, here lives a great street sweeper who did his job well."

One can only assume that Dr. King had to have read Emerson at some point in his life. We come to this conclusion because he so aptly captured the gist of the author's words with a beautifully-crafted concept that illustrates a way for us to apply Emerson's principle to our daily lives.

Imagine doing everything as enthusiastically as possible. Now, I'm not naïve enough to suggest that everyone is capable of this feat. There are times when even the most positive, most upbeat individual experiences frustration, and is unable to smile in the face of setback. But all one need do when enthusiasm begins to wane, is to get right back on that horse and have another go at it. Don't stop and beat yourself up for losing your focus. Instead, rejoice in having maintained it for as long as you were able. Perhaps next time you may be able to remain in a spirited, productive state even longer. And the time after that, longer yet. If you get upset with yourself for not being perfect, you'll be miserable for most of your life. We slip sometimes. It's okay. Just don't stay down for long.

Stay optimistic. Stay enthusiastic. Stay positive. If not, as Emerson reminds us, we will never accomplish the great things in life.

> "We cannot see things that stare us in the face, until the hour arrives when the mind is ripened; then we behold them."

Ralph Waldo Emerson

(from "Spiritual Laws," *Essays, First Series*, 1865)

Have you ever noticed that we seem to deal with obstacles in different ways depending on our frame of mind? On Monday we may trip over a crack in the sidewalk and curse the city fathers for not having repaired it. Then on Tuesday we may trip over that same crack but this time we chuckle about how clumsy we are. The same crack. The same trip. But a completely different reaction. We begin each day with a certain attitude, then judge every occurrence, good or bad, based on that mindset. If something bothers us one day, shouldn't that same event bother us each time it occurs no matter what day it is? If we slough off some mishap as just a minor setback one time, wouldn't we react in a similar fashion if the same thing were to befall us later on? We not only seem to react to different things in different ways, we react to the same thing in different ways.

Emerson reminds us that "We cannot see things that stare us in the face…" If we prepare ourselves for the best possible outcome—if we see life as a road filled with challenges that will strengthen us as we overcome them— then surely we will see things in a radiant light. If we, however, see that same road as filled with potholes, we will undoubtedly be swallowed up by them. Emerson seems to be advising us that if we begin each day with unequivocal optimism, we will view problems as opportunities, and hardships as minor inconveniences. What exactly are we prepared to see each day? Expect good things to occur, and don't be surprised when they do. Expect pitfalls, and you'll get just that.

I have a herniated disc in my back. Every so often it flares up. It can be uncomfortable at times, but we all have to deal with nagging ailments. I don't enjoy it, but it's a part of aging. I also have had kidney stones a number of times. Now that is certainly a more humbling experience. I dread those. Whenever I get a pain in my side near the kidney, I assume the worst. Oh no, not another stone. But when I realize, based on the symptoms, that it is not a kidney stone attack after all, but just the herniated disc flaring up, I am thrilled. I rejoice that I only have a backache. If, however, I were to assume that the discomfort was a backache from the start, and never considered a kidney stone, I would never have been as relieved that it was only back pain. Change your mindset, and you handle adversity in a completely different way.

When we walk into a room and turn on a light, we never seem to stop and admire the fact that with the flip of a switch, our life is illuminated. We rarely appreciate that we are fortunate enough to live in an age where electricity is taken for granted. But do you remember the last long power outage you experienced? Now try to recall how relieved and delighted you were when the electricity finally returned. We tend to forget just how dependent we are on one of life's little conveniences.

Have you ever considered showing gratitude each time something seemingly simple goes right in your lives — when the alarm clock goes off at the precise time we had set it to the night before — when we turn on the hot water, and *hot water* actually comes out — when we slide our key into the ignition, and the engine turns over. Do we ever seem pleased or thankful for those occurrences? Imagine our reaction if the alarm clock started buzzing an hour too late, if only cold water came shooting out of the shower head, or if we placed the key in the ignition and heard nothing.

If you hold a door open for someone and they say nothing, we tend to react negatively. If we allow another driver to merge in front of us and they fail to wave back, we're sorry we ever extended the courtesy. But what is it that we want? If we're expecting thanks or recognition for every little thing we do, we had better prepare ourselves for disappointment. Wouldn't it be better not to expect a show of gratitude from others? That way there's no letdown. Then, when someone smiles, nods in appreciation, waves, or says thanks, it's not a gesture we are expecting, but rather an unexpected gift.

> "Our faith comes in moments; our vice is habitual."
>
> Ralph Waldo Emerson
>
> (from "The Over-Soul," *Essays, First Series*, 1841)

With these words, Emerson appears to have little faith in humanity. He seems to be saying that we are only at our best *occasionally*. And if that weren't bad enough, a moment later, he castigates us for being creatures of habit. It is as if he blames our lack of inspiration, of genius, of giftedness, on the fact that we are slaves to our daily routines. Certainly we all have a schedule that we follow each day, but we have probably never thought of it as something that gets in the way of accomplishing great things. Are we such followers of behavioral patterns that we shut out moments of reflection that might lead to greatness? If we are to believe Emerson, it just may be that if we allowed ourselves more flexibility in our daily routines, we might find our minds more open to inspiration.

When we begin to examine our daily schedule (get up, shower, eat breakfast, drive or ride to work, etc.), it isn't surprising to see that most of us are in a rut. That in itself should be reason enough for us to want to rewrite our daily ritual and to infuse into it a certain degree of newness. But at least consider the possibility that monotony may be standing in the way of our success. To escape, we must embrace change. It might mean altering our dietary habits, getting up earlier and squeezing in exercise or yoga before work, taking a different route to work, enjoying a walk at lunchtime, volunteering our time at a hospital, nursing home, library, or wherever — anything to break the routine — and it might just turn out to be a healthier regimen for both mind and body. Then, if all goes well, the muses will visit — and voilà — inspiration.

There are many of us who have identified our life's passion but haven't quite figured out how to alter our schedule in order to fit it in. A few years ago I decided that I wanted to write, that I needed to write. Writing was therapeutic for me — but only when I found the time for it. Initially, I tried to continue to do everything I was doing, and then somehow squeeze in some occasional writing time. After a couple of weeks, I knew it wasn't working. I was managing to accomplish everything — I just wasn't doing the same things as efficiently as I once had. I was getting sloppy. I was happy to have found time to be creative, but unhappy with the overall results.

And then I came across an interview with Lamar Hunt, son of billionaire, H. L. Hunt. When asked how his father had become so successful, he shared the elder Hunt's lifelong philosophy: *Identify what it is you want…then decide what you're going to give up to make it happen*. After reading that advice, I knew exactly what I needed to do. I knew that I couldn't manufacture time, and I knew that I couldn't continue doing things in a haphazard manner just so that I could "have it all." I needed to make some sacrifices. I asked myself what I was willing to give up to accomplish this goal. I soon had the answer.

I decided to give up my lunch hour. I would pack a sandwich the night before and eat at my desk while working. Then I would walk to the library in town at lunchtime each day and write. But it still wasn't enough. I also decided to give up the last hour of the evening—for me from 11:00 pm until midnight. I would forego late night TV, head to a basement office, and write. And I have successfully done so for quite some time. I've turned down a number of luncheon invitations in the past few years, and missed the monologues of late night comedians, but I am far happier getting my "fix" each day.

Of course, finding the time to write and making efficient use of it were two different things. Some days the ideas poured out so quickly I couldn't type fast enough. Other days I would just sit and stare at the monitor. I made a promise to myself that I would not waste those precious hours. I would not quit even if writer's block, illness, or exhaustion set in. I soon learned that you cannot expect inspiration to appear whenever summoned. I needed to be patient. And so, I would go about my daily routine, always aware that an idea could materialize at any moment. For me, it was while I was walking the dog or taking a shower or driving to work that I would experience a brainstorm. I learned to keep a small handheld recorder within reach at all times. And when the creative juices began to flow, I would quickly harness them.

Whether you are a woodworker, a homemaker, a tradesman, a teacher, a technician, a poet, a salesperson, an aspiring entrepreneur, or whatever, follow the advice of Emerson and Hunt. Identify the passion within. Then find the time to pursue it. "Our faith comes in moments; our vice is habitual." Alter your schedule…break some habits…jar your senses…and wait for inspiration to strike.

> "Every young man is prone to be misled by the suggestions of his own ill-founded ambition which he mistakes for the promptings of a secret genius, and thence dreams of unrivaled greatness."
>
> Ralph Waldo Emerson
>
> (from *The Journals and Miscellaneous Notebooks of Ralph Waldo Emerson*, Vol. 2, 1960-1978)

How often have you heard someone say "It's a sign?" How often have you said it yourself? Have you ever noticed that you are more receptive to "signs" when you are searching for an answer to a problem, or need help making a decision? If we are to follow what Emerson refers to above, then we should probably dismiss the happening or event that we were about to declare a "sign." When a strange occurrence takes place, is it really some "secret genius" that is trying to guide us to a specific solution, or simply a meaningless, unrelated coincidence?

For quite some time, I was big on "signs." And in most cases, I wasn't certain what they meant. For years I had been noticing a particular time on clocks, watches, timers, etc., and I was never sure what to make of it. As a matter of fact, I still see this same number from time to time. I'm referring to 11:11. For a while, I marveled at the number of times I just happened to glance at my watch or a clock, and there it was. It had to be a sign I thought. I kept telling myself it meant that something good, even great, would happen someday at 11:11. And then when nothing did, I decided that it meant something else. I became convinced that on November 11th something spectacular would happen. But as each year and each November 11th passed without fanfare, I began to wonder if I had been either misinterpreting the message—or fooling myself that the numbers had any meaning at all.

When I began to research this 11:11 phenomenon, I soon realized that I wasn't the only one who was seeing it all the time. Thousands of people claim that they see that number far more often than chance would allow for. Some folks think it is an omen of good things to come. Others feel that it signals the presence of a spirit. Self-proclaimed psychic, Uri Geller, suggests that 11:11 has mystical powers. I suppose that I wanted to believe all these things—until I read Emerson's quote.

He seems to be telling us that if good things happen in our lives, it isn't because of some sign, it is because of hard work and focus and determination. This particular Emerson quote is from one of his many essays. If we continue reading beyond the above quotation, we find:

> "Nevertheless it is not time or fate or the world that is half so much his foe as the demon indolence within him…But if a man shall diligently consider what it is which most forcibly impedes the natural greatness of his mind, he will assuredly find that slothful sensual indulgence is the real unbroken barrier, and that when he has overleaped this, God has set no bounds to his progress."

*Indolence…slothful…*you can see where Emerson is going here. He is suggesting that those individuals who look for signs or signals, and then make decisions based on those occurrences are simply lazy. Decisions cannot be made in a frivolous way. If you need guidance regarding a relationship or a new business venture or whatever, you had better not rely on what Emerson refers to as a "secret genius." Pure and simple…do your homework. Make certain that the decision in question has been researched and fleshed out in an appropriate manner. If an idea suddenly pops into your head, and you are naïve enough to believe that someone or something has actually put it there—and if you then recklessly invest your hard-earned capital, then you are a fool.

I don't believe Emerson is dismissing an occasional brainstorm that you might have, he is just indicating that it's the first step in a long process of development. Research the topic. Determine if this new venture is viable, and ultimately marketable. Is there an audience for, let's say, a new business or product? Can you build a customer base? Is there any competition out there already? These are the types of questions you must ask yourself. Just because you happened to have found a shiny, new quarter on the sidewalk, it doesn't mean you now have the answer to your problem. It means you have twenty five more cents in your pocket than you did a moment ago.

Emerson's quote at the top of this section is very simple, yet very profound. If an idea begins to take shape, and starts percolating in your brain, grasp it, embrace it, and be sure to follow it up with persevering, painstaking research. Then the only secret genius around is you.

AWARENESS

"Why need I volumes, if one word suffice?"

Ralph Waldo Emerson

(from "Blight," *Poems*, 1867)

Little interpretation is needed here. This Emerson directive is short and to the point—by design. He praises the individual who wastes not our time with verbosity, but instead communicates with succinct language. It is exceedingly clear that Emerson prefers short, substantive discourse to inane chatter. Without saying so directly, it is likely that he supports the notion that listening is a virtue. We all know someone who has an opinion about everything, and whether you are interested in hearing it or not, this individual is hardly shy about sharing it with you. I don't believe that Emerson is interested in creating a legion of followers to confront the chatterboxes of the world. His message is to remind us that less is best. It doesn't mean that a less talkative person is in any way less communicative than those who so desperately need to endlessly flap their jowls. It simply means that there is no reason to be long-winded when a short, well-crafted phrase will do. Why waste yours or anyone else's time.

You, no doubt, have attended meetings that seemed to have been arranged for no other reason than for the organizer to dominate conversation. And if that weren't bad enough, it is a time for coworkers to position themselves politically. They want their superiors to remember that they contributed to the discussion. But a savvy supervisor can easily recognize the difference between a short, substantive comment and the sterile offering of a professional blabbermouth.

If you sense a tone of cynicism regarding meetings, I have only one response—guilty as charged. I am not a fan of meetings. I'm not saying that every meeting is worthless—just most of them. And the worst are the regularly-scheduled get-togethers (weekly, monthly, quarterly, etc.). How often have you found yourself in one of these settings and realized that the only reason you were there is because it was on the calendar—not because there were critical matters that needed discussion. Another bitter pill is the open-ended meeting—the one that keeps going until each item on the agenda has been covered.

If you are a person who must arrange and chair meetings, please do your employees a favor and never let the attendees control you. Always draw up an agenda, and always share it ahead of time with co-workers who will be in attendance. Demand that they come prepared. The meeting is not a time to think. That needed to take place earlier. The meeting is a time to share thoughts. Determine the amount of time that you will allow for discussion, place it next to each agenda item, and by all means, adhere to it. Don't let overzealous participants ramble on. Discourage repetitious comments. Avoid tabling matters unless absolutely necessary. Be decisive. Your colleagues will thank you for it.

Back to those folks who must always hear themselves speak—no matter what comes out of their mouths. In my 30-plus years as a college professor, I frequently come across students who will raise their hands incessantly in order to participate in class discussion. And unfortunately, more often than not, their contribution is either incorrect or irrelevant. If the class is filled with an active group of learners who always seem prepared for lively discussion, you can usually tolerate a few tongue-waggers. But when you are faced with a room full of the living dead, and the only one waving his or her hand is the individual with an answer—not the correct one, mind you—but an answer for everything, it can make for an awfully long period.

I also have taken Emerson's advice to heart when creating exams. I encourage brevity from my students, but not for brevity's sake. I do so to force them to skim the fat. I always leave a minimal amount of space following each question on my essay exams. If you allow students to write volumes, you will most often get volumes—but then you are forced to wade through the minutia as you search for the substance. Demand economy of language. Every good writer must get to the point sooner or later. They either know the answer or they don't. Many of us have, at one time or another, BS'd our way through an exam. It is a timeless art that has been handed down to generations. But, as you might guess, it is very easy to detect. It is best not to waste anyone's time. It is for those individuals and the rest of us who like to gab for whom Emerson's words are intended, "Why need I volumes if one word suffice."

"The man in an ecstasy of fear or anger is an unconscious actor."

Ralph Waldo Emerson

(from "Art," *Society & Solitude*, 1870)

It is likely that if Emerson had discarded his pen and instead had conducted anger management classes, he no doubt would have enjoyed success. His advice is simple—so simple that it is profound. If our moments of anger are carried out within an unconscious state, as Emerson suggests, then they are no more than knee-jerk reactions…impulsive gestures…actions without thought…and therefore, contrary to right thinking. An intelligent person would never allow an emotion to cloud his or her judgment. And so, if we accept the fact that anger is a moment of unconsciousness, and if sensible individuals are always in control of their mental faculties, then feelings of anger are simply unacceptable to them. It's easy to follow Emerson's line of thinking. A display of anger is such a wasted effort that a rational human being would have to be in some sort of altered state in order to react in such a manner.

Try to imagine a world without anger. No revenge, no retaliation, no retribution, no reprisals—and think of the time you would save. If we were able to replace anger with something else—anything else—the results would be staggering. It is almost incomprehensible to think that an entire people could dismiss their anger, shrug their shoulders, and move on with their lives. It seems unnatural. Anyone can tell you that giving in to anger is a lose-lose proposition. Who can argue with that? First of all, it is a great time-waster. It gets us nowhere. If anything, it gets us further entrenched in self-loathing—since many of us are prone to feelings of guilt following an outburst. Where do we go from there? Only to greater depths.

And secondly, it can be downright dangerous. An angry reaction can trigger a physical altercation. A good example is road rage—where relatively sane people become lunatics. This is certainly one instance where discretion is not only the right thing to practice, but the smart thing. Every one of us has at one time or another been cut off by an overly aggressive driver. A typical reaction is to ride that person's bumper just to send a message. A less confrontational approach is to talk to the steering wheel, using language not usually found at a family get-together. For most of us, it stops there. But for some, the response is not only an outburst, but confrontation. And we have all read the news stories of how an incident of road rage escalated into injury and even death. Psychologists tell us that we somehow feel invulnerable behind two tons of steel. But all it takes, of course, is one kook to change all of that.

Personally, I have tried different approaches to road rage. Sometimes I will imagine a biblical figure in the passenger seat next to me, and I would certainly not want this anointed one to hear me blurt out anything foul, or heaven forbid, irreverent. But usually I just tell myself that an overreaction on my part could end up being very unhealthy. I often wonder what might happen when one reckless driver crosses paths with someone of the same ilk. Now that would be a lethal combination, and one of which I would want no part.

For a clear-headed, well-balanced human being to act out in a fit of anger is completely out of character, out of sorts, out of touch…and out the time. As the father of three daughters, I have enjoyed—*enjoyed* is probably the wrong word here—my share of drama. Girls express their emotions more openly than do boys. It didn't take me long to learn that. So when one of my daughters would become angry or frustrated, and the problem in question had no simple solution, I would immediately try to explain to her that anger or disappointment was self-defeating. They needed to redirect their frustrations, and to channel them into positive energy. For every moment that they lamented over a situation that was unalterable, they wasted precious time. Imagine, I would tell them, the things you could accomplish if you were to use that time in a productive manner.

I realize that it's very easy to suggest this approach to a problem when you're not the one in a huff. And no one would argue that it is difficult, if not impossible, to turn off one's emotion and replace it with another—but there's no reason not to try. This particular Emerson quote may be one of the most difficult to put into practice—even though we know it makes perfect sense. But we can't surrender. At the very least, we need to stop, take a breath, count to ten, or employ whatever delaying mechanism works for us when an anger-producing situation presents itself. And we just may be able to buy ourselves enough time to react in a logical manner and diffuse some of the fury within. It's certainly worth a try.

"The first wealth is health."

Ralph Waldo Emerson

(from "Power," *The Conduct of Life*, 1860)

I think that the older we get the more we realize that good health is one of the most precious gifts one can enjoy. Let me further say that if Aladdin's genie were hovering over me right now, I can safely say that perfect health would be my first wish — and if I were given just one — it would be my only wish. Oftentimes we don't realize how valuable a healthy body is until we're more mature. But unfortunately by that time, we have ingested any number of undesirable substances that have done untold damage to our bodies, and we have not participated in a serious ongoing exercise program. With that said, however, we are told by experts that it is never too late, and that exercise and healthy eating at any age promise positive results.

Much of the difficulty of making significant changes to our diet and exercise regimen is in escaping the bad habits in which we are so deeply entrenched. The literature available regarding healthy eating is abundant. The same is true for exercise. Then why does it take a wake-up call (hypertension, chest pains, elevated cholesterol levels, etc.) to set us straight. Let's face it — some of the foods that are most harmful are the best-tasting. Conversely, those foods which provide the most nourishment are the ones devoid of fats, sodium, sugar — and dare I say it — flavor. There is no easy way to put it — maintaining one's health is work — hard work sometimes. And this is nothing new. In fact, Emerson came to this realization in the nineteenth century. We knew far less about good nutrition back then, but the value of good health did not escape gifted thinkers. He found it important enough to include in his writings. And he must have taken his own advice. After all, the man died just short of his 79th birthday. No small feat considering that this was back at a time — the late 1800's — when life expectancy in the U.S. was 50-60 years of age.

The text that you are reading is not a medical or nutritional journal, and I would never suggest how one should alter his or her diet, or begin or maintain a particular exercise program. There are hundreds of books and websites and programs on the market that can do just that. You can't watch the evening news without hearing about a study that is being conducted, or the results of a research project that enlighten us on how to live healthier lives. Newscasters quote, on a seemingly endless basis, new findings published in the Journal of the American Medical Association. There are plenty of resources at our disposal. There is no excuse for not taking advantage of them.

The point that Emerson is making is that we must make healthy living a greater priority in our lives. In order to do so, we must make sacrifices. If we smoke, or live a sedentary lifestyle, no one has to tell us what changes are necessary to live a longer life. Most people will tell you that they will make smarter choices about their health when they're ready — but what will it take for them to begin this quest? Will it be the premature death of a parent? The illness of a sibling or close friend? Their own brush with death?

If you picked up this book because you feel that the wisdom of Ralph Waldo Emerson could make a difference in your life, then don't follow just some of the suggestions within. Don't just pick and choose the Emerson tenets that are convenient, and seem to fit your schedule. Embrace as many of them as possible, and put this one — "The first wealth is health" — near the top. No one can deny that if you follow this advice, you will become healthier. You'll become stronger. You'll have more energy. You'll feel better about yourself…and your future. And you will have the enthusiasm and the drive to make other difficult choices, listed on these pages, that will bring you closer to your ultimate goals in life. In fact, if the only advice you follow from this book is to improve your health, it will have paid for itself many times over. Get to work.

> "We are by nature observers, and thereby learners. That is our permanent state."
>
> Ralph Waldo Emerson
>
> (from "Love," *Essays, First Series*, 1841)

If you were to study the writings of Emerson, it wouldn't be long before you might come to the conclusion that he was not a proponent of idealism. If fact, the quote found just a few pages earlier seems to confirm that:

> "Every young man is prone to be misled by the suggestions of his own ill-founded ambition which he mistakes for the promptings of a secret genius, and thence dreams of unrivaled greatness."

Yet the quotation at the top of this section appears to rebut that. When Emerson suggests that we learn by observation, it almost minimizes earlier messages to take action, and to realize our goals, not by simply talking about how we plan to achieve them, but by going out and doing them. If we look closer, however, at this passage, I don't think he is contradicting himself as much as he is inspiring us to first be observers — then to take action. It only makes sense. If we learn through observation, then observation would have to precede action, since we would never want to undertake a task until we have fully prepared for it. Simply put: observation → learning → action.

It might be interesting to note that the above quote: "We are by nature observers, and thereby learners. That is our permanent state," actually comes from an Emerson essay entitled: "Love." But I think one can argue that by encouraging us to be more observant, and therefore to open our eyes to learning, we find here advice that can be applied in a myriad of situations, not just in a discussion of relationships. Observation suggests concentration, and concentration suggests quietude. And before you know it, we're back to: "Why need I volumes, if one word suffice?"

Remember our discussion about meetings, and how some individuals need to dominate conversation. These people place little value on the opinions of others. When they open their mouths, they say very little, but the endless flow of verbiage from their lips can fool some into thinking that they are actually contributing to the exchange. Don't make that mistake. These same individuals, once someone has wrestled the floor away from them, fail to listen to their co-workers. Instead they wait for an opening to win back the dominant position. They are not listening. They are not *observing*. They are not learning. They are only speaking. But don't expect them to act. They are unprepared for action.

Emerson seems to applaud men or women of action. But he reminds us (with the featured quotation) that action preceded by poor planning is doomed to fail. Whether you are sitting in a meeting, stuck in traffic, waiting at an airline gate, on a nature hike — wherever — be an observer. You will be surprised at how much knowledge can be gained. And, if nothing else, you will be allowing yourself an opportunity to do nothing but observe the world we live in. You'll be free to witness events you never knew existed. You will learn more about human nature by simply becoming aware of the actions of others. And by taking the time to observe someone or something, you might even find the experience interesting, entertaining, informative, or even amusing.

I recall walking back from class one late spring day and being stopped by another faculty member. We began to engage in a lighthearted discussion. A couple of minutes into the conversation, I found myself somewhat distracted. Adjacent to the sidewalk was a flower bed filled with gorgeous, botanical wonders. I spotted a bumblebee perched on one particular flower. A moment later, it rose into the air, floated momentarily, then landed on its next host. I watched as it gracefully moved from flower to flower. It was entrancing. The bee was on a mission, and wasn't particularly bothered by having an audience. Occasionally I smiled and nodded and offered an appropriate "uh huh" to my colleague, but I couldn't take my eyes off of my little friend. I knew that I was watching something that had first been taught to me in grammar school, but I didn't recall ever having taken the time to observe this amazing moment in nature. The experience wasn't life-altering, but rather a brief, pleasant respite for which I was glad to have made time.

Take a moment to stop and observe. If it does nothing more than offer repose from your frenetic-filled existence, it will have been well worth the investment.

BEAUTY

> "The secret of ugliness consists not in irregularity, but in being uninteresting."
>
> Ralph Waldo Emerson
>
> (from "Beauty," *The Conduct of Life*, 1860)

Beauty. Literature is filled with references to it. Greek mythology is rich with stories of this elusive trait. Fairy tales refer to it endlessly. The quest for beauty…the battles over beauty…the curse of beauty. From as far back as we can recall, and right up to the present day, beauty plays a role in each of our lives. We may be longing for it. We may be trying to hold securely onto it. We may be willing to spend untold sums of money to acquire it. We may resent those who possess it. Whatever our reason, each of us would be lying if we indicated that beauty, at some point in our lives, was unimportant. Beauty is a natural human desire.

But beauty, unlike life, liberty and the pursuit of happiness, is not an inalienable right. It is a gift of nature. Those who possess it are usually aware of that fact. Those who do not are equally aware. It is impossible to know why some of us are blessed with beauty, while others are not. I am, at best, an average-looking person. I'm okay with that. I've made it work. But there were certainly a few times in my younger days when I would have liked to have snapped my fingers and have become an Adonis. I think I was a sixth-grader when I first realized that there was power in beauty. I also realized that I was not one of those people who would be wielding that power. And so I needed a backup plan.

As a youngster, without ever having read the Emerson quotation above, I think I soon figured out that beauty was not a requirement for popularity. It certainly helped but there had to be other ways to be liked, to be accepted, to be respected by your peers. For me it was humor. I wouldn't call myself the class clown—more like the class comic. I used humor to entertain my classmates. It successfully kept me in the circles I desired. For others it may be the creative arts. You may not possess beauty but if you are a talented musician, actor, painter, writer, etc., it just may allow you to enjoy a popularity that rivals those whose lone resource is beauty. And what about its fleeting nature. TV's Judge Judy Sheindlin reminds us of that fact in her book <u>Beauty Fades, Dumb is Forever</u>.

If you choose to read more of Emerson's essay on beauty, you will come across an even stronger passage than the one above. It further suggests that beauty itself is overrated:

> "Those who have ruled human destinies like planets were not handsome men. If a man can raise a small city to be a great kingdom, can make bread cheap, can irrigate deserts, can join oceans by canals, can subdue steam, can organize a victory, can lead the opinions of mankind, can enlarge knowledge, tis no matter whether his nose is parallel to his spine…whether he has a nose at all…whether his legs are amputated; his deformities will be reckoned to come ornamental. This is the triumph of expression, degrading beauty, charming us with a power so fine and friendly and intoxicating, that it makes admired persons insipid, and the thought of passing our lives with them insupportable."

Beauty in and of itself is fine. It's a start, but you had better develop the necessary skills to survive in this world. How many young, attractive girls dream of becoming supermodels, and how many actually make it? Beauty alone won't cut it. And Emerson is quick to point this out. He somehow makes us believe that in the long run, there will unquestionably be an even playing field. A pretty face will take you just so far. But sooner or later you'll have to stand on your own merit. It is best to worry not about the beauty that has escaped you. Instead, embrace your individuality, and refine your skills and talents. Perfect them. Or better yet, when all is said and done, and we're standing in front of the pearly gates, rest assured that God won't be judging us on how many beauty pageants we've won. He's only interested in the beauty within—a beauty that never fades.

> "Though we travel the world over to find the beautiful, we must carry it with us, or we find it not."
>
> Ralph Waldo Emerson
>
> (from "Art," *Essays, First Series*, 1841)

What exactly is Emerson saying here? Is he actually talking about traveling the world? Or is he using that phrase in a figurative manner? It appears to have more to do with the mindset that you must possess beauty before you seek out your true passions in life. His reference to "the beautiful," is not necessarily an outwardly beautiful person or thing, but rather that of which we are desirous. And he's not simply referring to a trinket that we may want, but something far more important.

We all have dreams and goals. And some of us have embarked upon the journey to fulfill those dreams. Some have enjoyed success. Others have not. What Emerson seems to be saying here is that before you begin the journey, you must truly understand where it is that you want to be. Whatever we are searching for must first somehow become a part of us before the search can begin. We first must identify what we want to accomplish, then when we are certain, we must take a personal inventory. Do we have the desire, the temperament, the patience, the commitment — to realize this goal? If not, we may be spinning our wheels.

Let's say that your goal is write an Oscar-winning screenplay. There are, no doubt, many writers who have traveled down this highway. And many who have never completed the journey. Are you prepared to make the necessary sacrifices for success? You can't simply sit down at a keyboard and begin writing. Have you attended screenwriting conferences for a true understanding of the field? Have you read various articles on scriptwriting websites and journals for a sense of what the market will bear? Have you watched dozens and dozens and dozens of films, not as a viewer, but as an analyst of dramatic structure? Have you read screenwriting textbooks, or listened to audio programs to help refine your skills? Have you enrolled in extension courses at a nearby college or university to fully comprehend this craft? Have you read an untold number of professional screenplays? You can't begin the journey until your bags are packed — packed with knowledge necessary to realize this dream. You have to start thinking like a screenwriter in order to become one.

When Emerson says that we can't find the beautiful until we are willing to carry it with us, he is telling us that in order to reach the destination we desire, we must have a clear road map, and be willing to follow it no matter what obstacles we may encounter. Otherwise, "…we find it not." From giving up smoking, to losing weight, to starting a small business, to reducing your stress level—you name it, you can't just go cold turkey. You're setting yourself up for failure. If I want to quit smoking or begin an exercise program, I can't just throw away the cigarette pack or join a health club, I have to be committed. I have to want it for all the right reasons. I have to start thinking like a healthy person. If I try to reach this goal with any other mindset, I am doomed.

If you have a friend, relative, co-worker, or someone you care about, and you are trying to convince that person to change his or her life in some way, you know what happens when you preach to them about how happy they will be when they finally take your advice. These folks will only embark on the journey when they are good and ready, and all your prodding is meaningless. If anything, they may become more resistant. If you love these people—if you care about them—don't preach, just try to educate them with a soft-sell approach. Allow them to choose the time and place. When their own personal light bulb goes on, then and only then will they be positioned for success.

I've worked with college-age students for the past thirty years. Many anguish about finding a major. Some will seek out career paths based on current shortages (e.g., health care professionals), or how much money they will make. But you can't choose a career path based on the market. You may indeed have an easier time of landing a job if there are shortages, but we haven't addressed the most important factor when wrestling with this question—happiness. Oftentimes, when students are at a crossroads, I ask them to envision their lives five years from now. I ask then to consider this scenario: The alarm on the side of your bed starts ringing. You flail your arms wildly trying to turn it off. You sit up in a bed and rub your eyes. Now I want you to imagine yourself going to Job A or Job B. Forget about the money. Bottom line: which occupation, industry, etc., will make you happier? Which one would you do for nothing? Following a moment of reflection, they are usually able to come up with an answer.

And the process begins. Once they begin thinking like those in their chosen profession, the path is clear of debris. They envision themselves living the life they have imagined. What a powerful way to begin your own personal odyssey.

"Beauty without grace is the hook without the bait."

Ralph Waldo Emerson

(from "Beauty," *The Conduct of Life*, 1860)

You don't have to be an experienced fisherman to know what will happen if you throw a hook without bait into a fishing pond. You'll come up empty. This is the metaphor that Emerson has chosen to describe a person of beauty who lacks the necessary polish, refinement, or education. Beauty alone may turn a few heads, but once an unrefined creature opens his or her mouth, an intelligent person soon sees only unattractiveness.

The world of advertising wants you to believe that if you employ every strategy to enhance your outward appearance, you will live a happier, more fulfilled life. If you purchase every product that promises softer skin, fewer wrinkles, whiter teeth, fresher breath—even no visible panty lines—you will ultimately transform yourself from wallflower to the life of the party. But what the advertisers leave out is that beauty in and of itself is hollow. To reach the social heights that many people desire, they would be well served to concentrate on developing the beauty within. Outwardly beautiful people of little substance will soon be exposed for the frauds they are. Whereas, those who culture their inner beauty will be welcomed guests at any table.

It is relatively easy to apply this Emerson principle to other life lessons. Our references above have more to do with physical beauty. But what about the beauty of accomplishment? Let's examine the professional athlete. No one would argue that a ninth-inning homerun, a touchdown in overtime, or a buzzer-beater is a thing of beauty to any fan. But success on the field, on the court, on the ice, etc., is no guarantee that the individual involved will demonstrate grace with each performance. And I'm not talking about the type of grace we attribute to an Olympian on the balance beam. I'm referring to the way an athlete interacts with teammates, coaches, opponents, officials, fans, etc.

When a player goes jaw to jaw with a manager in the dugout, he is hardly demonstrating grace. When a football player scores a touchdown, and then resorts to any number of attention-getting celebratory routines, he is hardly exhibiting grace. Oftentimes you will hear coaches, who have grown tired of the celebration antics of some players, remind them that when they reach the end zone, they should "act like they've been there before." Any other response suggests that you never expected to have accomplished that goal, that you weren't talented enough or skilled enough. Yet we are forced to watch incessant, sometimes choreographed, dance routines following a score.

The type of celebration that I personally find abhorrent is when, let's say, a defensive lineman successfully sacks a quarterback, and then begins strutting around and thumping his chest. The only problem is the fact that his team is losing by 30 points. I have never understood how a player celebrates an individual performance with his team down. It makes absolutely no sense. It is, in a word, classless.

We have opportunities every day to show a little class. Some of them are trite, overused expressions, but those among us who can master them provide the perfect example of grace in action—avoiding gossip, being non-judgmental, taking the high road, turning the other cheek, never burning bridges. When we think of a person who practices these virtues, we think of someone who we wish we were more like. When an individual resists the urge to fly off the handle and shoot his mouth off, but instead thinks through and delivers an intelligent, well-crafted, unemotional response, we see a living, breathing example of grace under fire. Are we capable of such composure?

In closing, let me apologize for the umpteen clichés in the previous paragraph, but it is the easiest way to illustrate how we can apply what just might soon become a wonderful mantra to our daily lives—*Beauty without grace is the hook without the bait.*

"Not in nature but in man is all the beauty and worth he sees."

Ralph Waldo Emerson

(from "Spiritual Laws," *Essays, First Series*, 1865)

If you are a city dweller, and you spend untold hours commuting each week, you may long for vacations that take you miles away from your current environs. You most likely yearn for open space, natural settings, any location as long as it's as far away from the human race as possible. And that all sounds fairly normal but Emerson, in the quotation above, seems to take exception with that line of thinking. He's suggesting that although the beauty of nature may be unquestionably breathtaking, there is a greater beauty that can be found within us and in our relationships with others. If you're a family person and someone who treasures friendships, you might just agree.

If you were told that you had only months to live, how might you spend that time? Would you plan a trip to the mountains or would you want to spend as many hours as possible with loved ones? Getting away for a weekend, taking a vacation, or doing some sightseeing in natural settings can be relaxing and enjoyable. But have you ever thought what makes that experience so enjoyable. More often than not, it's not where you visit, it's with whom you are visiting. The time spent with friends and family is the best of times. If you've ever experienced an emergency or found yourself homebound with an illness or injury, you know just how important family and friends can be. Besides offering you moral support, these are the people who stop by to visit, who bring meals for you or your family, or just call to see how you're doing.

There is beauty in nature but the true beauty is in mankind. Studies have been conducted to determine cancer patient survival rates with people who go through chemo and radiation alone, and those who do so with a support network of friends. Every cancer and every individual case is different, but reports have shown that those patients with a legion of supportive friends live longer than those who battle the disease on their own. Those interpersonal relationships provide stimulation and offer the survivor a reason to keep going.

Where would you rather be—sitting on the beach or in the delivery room witnessing the birth of your child? It's a no brainer. Some of the best moments of your life are those times having to do with special relationships. The beauty of holding someone's hand for the first time, that first embrace, your first kiss, when you asked someone or were asked by someone for his/her hand in marriage—these are the moments of beauty in life. And you may have been in a picturesque setting when any of these events occurred, but the most important thing was who you were with at the time. If you change locations, you still have a memorable moment, but if you remove that loved one, or replace him or her with someone else, the moment is lost. It's about people and relationships.

When my parents retired to Florida several years ago, it was hard to see them go, but we knew that we always had an ideal vacation spot. They relocated to the Clearwater area. Whenever we did manage to haul the entire family to grandma's and grandpa's for a few days, one of the highlights was going with my dad to the fishing pier in Redington Beach. It was quite an undertaking. We would load the car with kids, and load the trunk with rods and reels and bait buckets and tackle boxes and pillows to sit on and sunscreen and the most important item—a satchel of goodies packed by grandma. The drive to the pier was only a few minutes. It actually took us longer to unload the car than it did to drive over. You could sense an anticipatory buzz from our girls in the back seat. They were ready for the unknown. They knew one thing—they wanted to catch a fish. They knew one other thing—they didn't want to bait the hook themselves. Fortunately that's where grandpa came in.

When we finally found a spot on the pier in the shade, each granddaughter waited patiently for grandpa to bait her hook with fresh shrimp. When we were all set, I remember just sitting back with the gulf breeze in my face and thinking that things didn't get much better than this. I stared up at the deep blue sky, the soft, puffy clouds, the white sands on the shoreline, the gentle waves beneath us, the endless horizon, and the sailboats floating aimlessly in the greenish-blue waters. I wondered what it might be like to actually live down here and have access to all of this each day. I was beginning to understand the lure of retiring to Florida's west coast.

After a few minutes, I noticed that my dad was missing. I looked around and spotted him about thirty yards away. He was laughing and talking with a group of other retired fishermen who he undoubtedly had gotten to know the past few months. They seemed to be enjoying one another's company. Every few minutes he would drift back to see how we were doing and if we needed any help. When he was sure that there was still bait on each hook, he disappeared again. And again, we found him with the others down the pier. At first, I couldn't understand why he wasn't sitting with us with a pole in his hand and patiently waiting for a big score.

And then I realized that my dad wasn't here for the soft breeze or the puffy clouds or the warm gulf mist or the white sands or the blue skies. Those didn't really matter. He was here for the friendships that he had made, and for the fellowship that one enjoys with people in your same age group, and those with similar interests. And as he had done all his life, my dad taught me a valuable lesson that day.

In his volumes of work, Emerson has written a great deal about the beauty and majesty of nature. But he has devoted significantly more time to explaining and analyzing the human spirit. When we think about where we might find the most beautiful locales on this planet, we may consider exotic locations, but when we really stop and think about the true beauty, we soon realize that it's not thousands of miles away. It may very well be in the next room or sitting on the couch or across the dinner table or on the back porch swing. Never stop appreciating the beauty of nature, but never lose sight of the beauty of mankind.

CHARACTER

"Character is higher than intellect... A great soul will be strong to live as well as think."

Ralph Waldo Emerson

(from "The American Scholar," an oration delivered before
The Phi Beta Kappa Society, at Cambridge, August 31, 1837)

When Ralph Waldo Emerson delivered this speech, he was addressing an academic community. He wanted this very learned body to recognize that a high degree of intellect is all well and good, but if you must choose between intellect and character, you had best choose the latter. Intelligence does not guarantee that its host will be a compassionate, caring, ethical person. But an individual of character is certainly able to claim these traits. So with whom would you rather be associated, someone with a high I.Q., or a person of high moral fiber? And what type of individual would you choose to become — one of intellect, or one of character? Ideally, a combination of both would be the perfect solution. But we must be realistic. A learned man or woman who is also a model of virtue is a rare commodity.

If you were about to choose a financial advisor, would you rather work with a highly intelligent broker who understood all the nuances of the marketplace, or one who was somewhat less street smart, but whose integrity was beyond reproach, and whom you trusted implicitly? It's a tough call. As much as we want a sizable return on our investments, we like to think that those with whom we have entrusted our hard-earned savings are making ethical decisions. Which of the two brokers would be more likely to invest our capital in environmental-friendly ventures? Which is more likely to steer us away from risky transactions? Which one will treat our money like his own? I think you know the answer to these questions.

Now let's consider spouses or partners. If the person of your dreams possessed either brilliance or virtuous conduct, which would be more important to you? If you choose someone whose strength is intellectualism, that would no doubt translate into a successful career, and ultimately a certain degree of wealth. On the other hand, if your potential mate is of high character, you can count on loyalty and trustworthiness. Which seems more important? Is it becoming more clear?

What if you were standing in front of the pearly gates, and St. Peter pulled out his clipboard and began adding up your credits and debits. What traits do you think he would find most admirable? Do you suppose that advanced degrees and successful investments would be more important than the number of volunteer projects in which you participated? Would published memoirs be more impressive than the amount of tolerance and compassion you showed toward others? Which of these do you think will resonate with heaven's gatekeeper?

Now don't misunderstand what Emerson is saying or what I am suggesting. As a member of the educational community for more than thirty years, I am a strong advocate of learning. I would love to see each of my students reach a level of intellectualism. But more than that, I would hope that I had instilled in them, high ideals, a sense of ethics, and a moral compass that will guide them each and every day of their lives. I want to see them soar to new heights in their chosen fields, but I also want them to be thought of as compassionate and honorable human beings.

In a perfect world, we wouldn't be discussing which trait—intellect or character—is more important, because in an ideal society, one could not exist without the other. These citizens would live to learn *and* to serve. I am reminded of one such individual each June during commencement at North Central College (Naperville, IL). Our former president, Hal Wilde, closed each graduation ceremony with a story from his childhood about an elderly neighbor. It was as if Emerson was referring to this remarkable senior when he wrote, "...a great soul will be strong to live as well as think." In President Wilde's words:

> "Many years ago when I was a student in junior high school, I used to watch a neighbor of mine, a retired man who was nearly eighty years old, go off every day early in the morning to the public library. He wouldn't return until dinnertime. I couldn't understand it. Why when my only goal in life at that time was to avoid studying and reading, to get outdoors and enjoy life...why when the only purpose of school activities in my mind was to train for a job someday...why was this man spending his days studying and reading? He'd never hold a job again. And why was he always so happy. So I asked him. And his answer is something I have never forgotten. 'Because there's so much to learn.'"

"Life wastes itself whilst we are preparing to live."

Ralph Waldo Emerson

(from "Prudence," *Essays, First Series*, 1865)

After discovering this Emerson quote some time back, I found myself thinking about all the things that I had wanted to do with my life but for one reason or another, had never accomplished. It was fun recalling the dreams of my youth, and trying to imagine how my life might have turned out had I made different decisions. It wasn't an exercise filled with regrets, mind you. But I did have a few "what if?" moments. I can honestly say though that I am comfortable with the choices I have made in my life, and, for the most part, content with the road I have travelled. I feel no malice toward the Central Intelligence Agency for having rejected my offer of assistance in 1964. We're talking about a covert government agency that simply cannot hire everyone. I can accept that. The fact that I was in sixth grade at the time, and had just seen my first Bond film, "Goldfinger," days earlier, might have had something to do with my inquiry, but had no bearing on the agency's unwillingness to bring me aboard. I have no regrets. It just was not to be.

When I first read the above quote, I immediately began to recall the Harry Chapin song, "Cat's in the Cradle," about a father who was always too busy to play with his son, only to have his grown son too busy to spend time with him years later. It all comes back to choices. When someone is trying to convince you to find the time—to make the time—to do something, they'll frequently remind you of the story of the man on his death bed who never wishes he had spent more time at the office. We know this story but it doesn't seem to make any difference. We still put off and reschedule opportunities to spend more time with our families. We just can't help ourselves.

Many of us are familiar with the Harry Chapin song, and some of us might even remember the lyrics. We may have paused and reflected when we heard:

> My son turned ten just the other day.
> He said, "Thanks for the ball, Dad, come on let's play.
> Can you teach me to throw?"
> I said "Not today, I got a lot to do."

> He said, "That's okay."
> And he walked away but his smile never dimmed
> And said, "I'm gonna be like him, yeah,
> You know I'm gonna be like him."

When we hear these words, for a moment—just a moment—we pledge not to allow this to happen to us. But in time, we're right back where we started. And this advice is coming from someone who has missed opportunities himself. I know there were chances to spend some quality time with my kids that I let slip away. I always rationalized that I had to be occupying my time with productive activities that would someday provide a better life for my girls—even though they might not have understood it at the time. When I look back now, I realize that the perfect opportunity to provide this "better life" was staring me in the face when one of them would ask me to join them in some silly or frivolous activity.

I did do something right however. A few years ago when the girls were younger, I recognized that they were growing up too quickly, and that I was losing some irretrievable moments. I decided that each day I would set aside a certain amount of time to spend exclusively with one of the girls, and rotate that special time from day to day. They could choose what we would do. It could be reading to them or with them—playing a computer game—engaging in some sport—or just talking. It was their call. I would set the timer on the microwave and we were off. Then at some point, I recall, it ended. I don't remember when or why, but it ended. I'm sorry I didn't see it through a little longer, but I sense that as they were maturing, our time together began to compete with increasing homework demands and an ever-active social calendar. But to this day, they recall with fond memories what they affectionately refer to as "Dad Time."

"Life wastes itself whilst we are preparing to live." What dreams did you have when you were growing up? If they revolve around a career as a professional athlete, and you are somewhat past your prime, it may be time to put that notion to rest. But if that dream can somehow still be fulfilled, you owe it to yourself to at least investigate it. And if people call you silly or tell you you're acting like a child, use that as motivation to embark on your quest. People who scoff at the dreams of others usually do so because they lack the drive, determination and passion required to do so themselves. They want to keep you in their camp—the underachievers. It's time to stop talking about what you may do someday, and begin to bring it to fruition. Make a promise to yourself right now that each day—religiously—you will take a step toward making a personal dream come true. Don't let a day pass without doing something—

anything—that gets you just a little closer to the promise you made to yourself years ago. Don't waste anymore of your life "preparing to live"—it's time right now to start living.

> "Use what language we will, we can never say anything but what we are."
>
> Ralph Waldo Emerson
>
> (from "Experience," *Essays, Second Series*, 1876)

Have you ever noticed how some people are always trying to say the right thing at the right time, but before you know it, they've managed to put their foot in their mouths and show their true colors? I don't mind telling you — the above quote is a little bit scary. Is not Emerson saying that your inner thoughts and beliefs cannot be camouflaged no matter what you say or do — and that people will ultimately see right through you? No matter how good an actor you may be, your intentions are broadcast loud and clear. Each of us likes to think that we are a good judge of character — that we can smell a rat from across the room. But what happens when others are judging *us* — and what if these others are also good judges of character? Then what? Then — good or bad — we are exposed. If it's good, we have nothing to fear. But if we have serious character flaws, a perceptive person will easily be able to discern them. It wouldn't be so bad if this person were a stranger, but if he or she is a job interviewer, or someone with whom we hope to become romantically involved, then each shortcoming becomes an ugly, swollen boil.

If you pride yourself on your ability to recognize whether someone is a quality individual or someone to keep at arm's length, you will no doubt avoid a great deal of heartache. But a person with those intuitive skills didn't suddenly wake up one morning with amazing insights into human nature. It took time. These skills had to be developed and cultured. And there were probably some painful moments in the process. There were, no doubt, times when you were certain that a particular individual was forthright to a fault, then learned later that you had been mistaken. Those are the times you scold yourself for being so naïve, and pledge to become less trusting.

When we were children, we wanted so badly to find heroes in our lives — so much so that we oftentimes overlooked minor flaws in their character. We wanted to believe that so-and-so was a quality person regardless of a few minor indiscretions. We paid homage to sports figures or Hollywood celebrities, and then were heartbroken when scandalous details of their personal lives were revealed. Most adults are less surprised when news of this nature surfaces. We have come to expect this from people of means.

It's difficult, however, to watch a child, who desperately wants role models in his/her life, discover the painful truth about their heroes. I recall an incident a few years back. Let me preface it by saying that ours is a family of Chicago Cub fans. The players become heroes the minute they don the Cubbie pinstripes. So it was especially painful to watch the reaction from my daughter, Christine, when on a balmy June day in 2003, Cubs slugger, Sammy Sosa, fouled off a pitch, and in doing so, broke his bat in two. She wasn't upset about the broken bat. It's what occurred when the plate umpire noticed something in the barrel, and upon examination, discovered that it had been filled with cork. Sosa was immediately ejected. "What just happened?" she asked. Before I could explain why corked bats are illegal, I found myself making a statement that I knew was hard for her to hear. "Sooner or later," I said, "our heroes will disappoint us. It's inevitable." And with those words, I'm afraid, I had taken down both Santa Claus and the Easter Bunny in one fell swoop. But think about it for a moment. How often do we read about athletes who have been issued DUI's, have been linked to steroids, or have been arrested for domestic abuse? Only a select handful of athletes and celebrities have lived exemplary lives. Perhaps Charles Barkley was right when he said that he was no role model.

The bottom line is that we cannot fool people. If we want them to think highly of us, then we had better act accordingly. Our bad habits and indiscretions will ultimately be uncovered. It's now time to put some distance between ourselves and our previous poor choices. There's just no other way around it.

"Every man in his lifetime needs to thank his faults."

Ralph Waldo Emerson

(from "Compensation," *Essays, First Series*, 1841)

A page earlier we were telling you to put some distance between yourself and your faults, but when we read this quote, it seems to indicate that Emerson actually believes there is some benefit to these same faults. If you are teaching someone how to do something, isn't it beneficial to show them not only how to perform a task, but also how not to? It follows the age-old advice that we learn from our mistakes. When both options are presented, the preferred choice is made even more clear when we compare it to an inferior approach.

Thomas Edison is probably the poster child when it comes to learning from his mistakes. He was once asked by a reporter how he felt after having failed nearly 25,000 times in his efforts to create a storage battery. His answer certainly supports the Emerson quotation above. He replied: "I don't know why you are calling it failure. Today I know 25,000 ways *not* to make a battery." Imagine going through life with this attitude — to actually see value in your faults and failures. We're not talking about enjoying your faults, or making excuses for them, but rather by recognizing the fact that the more you know about yourself and your own personal miscues, the better prepared you are to discover the correct approach.

As a writer, I can't tell you how many times I have queried an agent or publisher regarding a new manuscript, and how many times it was rejected. More often than not, the disappointing news was contained in the body of an impersonal e-mail. But sometimes the individual took the time to jot down reasons for passing on the project. And although each one was difficult to read, I can honestly say that when I took their comments to heart, and revised the manuscript, I soon realized that I was the better for it, and significantly closer to getting it published.

In classes that I teach, when I am assigning a new project, I always share an example of the finished product that had been submitted by students in previous classes (in an anonymous fashion, of course). It's much easier for students to grasp an idea of how to accomplish something when they understand what is acceptable and what is not. It simply makes things more clear, and selfishly saves me from having to weed through inferior projects.

If you were to ask the coach of any sports team if there is any value in losing, he or she might tell you that a painful loss can be the perfect remedy for a team that has underestimated its opponent. The taste of losing can be bitter, and many successful teams draw strength from a poorly-executed performance. They are angry with themselves for having underachieved, and embarrassed with their efforts. The experience is so unpleasant that players oftentimes become inspired to do whatever it takes to avoid a repeat performance.

At some point in our lives, no matter how prudent we may be in our words and actions, we will trip up and fail. No one is expected to be perfect. It was the 18th century English writer, Alexander Pope who said "to err is human…" It's normal to slip up occasionally. Everyone goofs once in a while, and some folks more often than others. The key is not how to avoid failure—it's going to happen no matter how well we have prepared for it. The key is how we handle failure. Do we let it immobilize us, or do we use it as a springboard back to those winning ways? Those people who have set extremely high standards for themselves simply cannot tolerate failure. Rather than accepting the fact that we are imperfect and sometimes display faults, they beat themselves up. They are unable to forgive an inadequate performance.

Emerson recognized that out of weakness comes strength. He's not suggesting that we celebrate or embrace failure, but rather that we accept it as a human foible, and immediately look for the life's lesson that is revealed to us. As painful or as embarrassing as mistakes may be, look for that teaching moment. Not only will you be better able to forgive yourself, but you will be well on your way to avoiding a similar stumble in the future.

CONFIDENCE

"We acquire the strength we have overcome."

Ralph Waldo Emerson

(from "Considerations by the Way," *The Conduct of Life*, 1860)

I've placed this Emerson quote in the *Confidence* section, but I could have just as easily inserted it under the category, *Overcoming Fear*. But then we would have launched this discussion from a position of weakness. The quote above has no element of fear or weakness associated with it. The words represent victory—a victory we can enjoy by facing a problem head on, and in a relentless fashion, battling our way to the winner's circle.

Most of us, at one time or another, have prayed for the necessary strength to overcome a particular problem. And then when we finally confronted it, we somehow found the wherewithal to attack, and to ultimately vanquish it. It was then we realized that the strength was there all along. Had it not been, we would not have been able to solve the problem ourselves. Re-read the quote above and realize that we don't need to build up a reservoir of strength before we can face adversity—we gain that strength while in battle. If we wait for forces to take hold before we confront our fears, we will probably never engage the enemy. We would be accepting defeat without ever having known if we possessed the necessary means to succeed. The next time you face an obstacle, and can't seem to find the grit to mount an attack, don't wait for the strength to find you. The moment you decide to take charge and to begin your assault— that is the moment that an indomitable spirit will be bestowed upon you. You will have earned it with a courageous decision to move forward in the face of peril.

When I think about acquiring the strength to stand up for ourselves, I think about the writings of L. Frank Baum, and more specifically, The Wizard of Oz. We all know the story of Dorothy and friends and of their journey to the land of Oz. And when we think about the Scarecrow, the Tin Man and the Cowardly Lion, we recall that each of them desired a gift that, in their minds, could only be found in this magical kingdom. As the story unfolds, we realize that the brains, heart, and courage that they sought weren't actually given to them by the Wizard. These gifts were already taking shape inside of them during their journey. Each soon realized that what they desired, they had actually received long before they reached their destination.

And so it is with us—the moxie or chutzpah that we crave is deep within us, and just needs to be summoned, to be called to the surface. How often does a child who is struggling in school suddenly improve when he or she is introduced to a mentor, a tutor or an exceptional teacher? And what about athletes who show flashes of greatness but more often than not wallow in the shadows of others? Just watch what happens when they are teamed up with an extraordinary coach or manager who is able to draw out their natural abilities. And we usually find ourselves saying "We always knew you had it in you." Indeed they did.

In a simple statement, Emerson reminds us that we already possess the ability to succeed. But we have to stop procrastinating and feeling overmatched and sorry for ourselves. Once we make the decision to better our lives, the strength becomes visible. But identifying what it is that we want is only the first step. We need to seriously begin planning a strategy. And then acting upon it. We've spent a lot of time already talking about the differences between doers and talkers, and deciding what it is we need to give up to reach our dreams. At a certain point, the time for talk is over.

It's time to begin. Time to set sail. We can't wish away our problems. We can learn to cope with them, or better yet, overcome them. The journey begins. And as the ancient Chinese proverb reminds us, "The journey is the reward."

"If I have lost confidence in myself, I have the universe against me."

Ralph Waldo Emerson

(from "Journal U," November 12, 1843)

Confidence is defined as *a feeling of assurance; the state or quality of being certain*. It sounds so simple—simple enough for anyone to practice. Yet, how often can we say that we have really felt that way? Certainly not as often as we would like.

We are often reminded in life that *over*confidence will be our downfall—on the soccer or little league field when we were young—in the classroom before an exam or oral presentation—during the job hunt as we sit across from a prospective employer. In each of these cases, we are encouraged to appear confident, but to avoid overconfidence. The line between the two frequently blurs. And so we are often less confident than we need be, so as not to display the cockiness that overconfidence breeds. It would be nice to know exactly where one ends and the other begins. To determine that, all one need do is apply a little common sense—which just so happens to be the name of the essay where this Emerson quote appears.

In 1974, following graduation from Northern Illinois University in DeKalb, Illinois, I was fortunate enough to have landed an interview at WGN-Radio for a writer/producer position. I was thrilled. WGN was, and still is, one of the most successful radio stations in the country. After having sent out nearly 150 resumes, and having been invited to only a handful of interviews, I wasn't about to waste this opportunity. Before the interview, I knew this was where I wanted to be. As a lifelong Cub fan, I was ecstatic about the prospect of working for the longtime Voice of the Cubs.

The interview went fairly well. I wanted to seem confident but not cocky. When I emerged from the office of Dick Jones, the program manager, I felt pretty good about how things had gone, but I knew I was a long way from nailing the position. Mr. Jones had given me some homework. I had three writing assignments (two station promos and scripting a musical show). I cranked out them out in a few days, personally delivered them to the station, and waited…and waited…and waited.

The interview had taken place in mid-May. It was now mid-June and I still hadn't heard anything. With each day that passed, I assumed that my chances were dwindling. I made it a point of calling the station each

Friday and asking if a decision had been made. I was worried about coming off as a pest but I wanted this position so badly that I just had to know if I was still in the mix.

During that time, I remember talking to a friend of a friend, a stock broker in Chicago. I told him that I was worried about becoming a pest with my weekly phone calls to the program manager's office. He told me that the fact that I was worried about it meant that I hadn't become one. It was just what I wanted to hear. My confidence was back. If he had said that my phone calls had been a mistake, I would probably have believed him, and would have stopped. It's funny how another person's opinion can either boost or drain your confidence. But when you're 22 years old, you tend to defer to your elders in the business world.

Well, as you might guess, I continued making the calls, and continued to hear that a decision still had not been made. During the last week of June, I received a call from the WGN brass asking me to return for a second interview. It was still within my grasp. When I arrived at the program manager's office, Dick Jones told me that they had decided to take a chance on me. Granted, it wasn't the most exciting way to word a job offer, but all I remember was how thrilled I was to hear those words. When I asked him how he had come to the decision, he told me that he liked my writing style. But more importantly, he said that I seemed more interested in the job than any of the other candidates, and that no one had checked in as often as I had.

Confidence had won me that job. If I had not believed in myself and had simply waited for them to get back to me, I doubt very much if I would have been sitting in that chair that day. I felt qualified for the position. And to Mr. Jones, the phone calls were not considered the badgering from some pest, but rather the confidence and drive of a young man who not only wanted the position, but just may be the right choice.

Emerson's words, "If I have lost confidence in myself, I have the universe against me," are a reminder of just how critical it is for us to not only feel confident, but to carry ourselves in a confident manner.

> "Don't be too timid and squeamish about your actions. All life is an experiment. The more experiments you make the better."
>
> Ralph Waldo Emerson
>
> (from "Journal N," November 11, 1842)

We are all conformists to some degree. We want to fit in. We want to be part of the group. We want to be members of the club. It is doubtful if Emerson would concur with that line of thinking. Just look at the quote above. Does that sound like a man who would encourage us not to make waves, not to stick our necks out, not to express ourselves? What I love about this quotation is that Emerson seems to be giving us permission to be non-conformists…to do our own thing…to be individuals…and not to worry if others disapprove.

As the father of three daughters, I can tell you that fashion has been an integral part of our family culture. These girls, as they were growing up, were very much aware of the latest trends and styles. I, on the other hand, am oblivious to fashion. To me, clothes are a necessary evil. The main functions of clothing should be to cover up and to keep warm. So when I would see my daughters pore over fashion magazines, catalogs and websites, I would roll my eyes — not because I disapproved, but because I just didn't get it.

I could never quite buy how particular designers could dictate the fashion trends of society. Whatever colors or skirt lengths they decided were in…were in. It seemed odd that the visions of a few could influence the masses. Occasionally I would try to share my perspective on this topic, but I made no headway. And I don't suppose I gained any credibility regarding fashion sense when I would reach into a closet and pull out my favorite jacket, now some thirty years old.

Occasionally we are asked to name one person, living or dead, with whom we would like to meet and converse. The more Emerson that I read, the more I would like to speak to him. I can imagine asking him about this fashion business, and I can imagine him encouraging me to dismiss fashion trends, if that's what I choose…but not to condemn those who think differently — on that topic or any other. Emerson seems to be challenging us to take chances and to experiment with life — and the more the better. Engaging only in those activities that others will find age-appropriate should not be a concern. If we feel as though we have missed out on an opportunity from our youth, but somehow sense that people would think us foolish or silly to chase after it, imagine what Emerson might say. I think you already know.

I'll admit it. I'll come clean. A few years ago I was listening to a classic rock station on the radio. "Layla" by Derek and the Dominos was playing. I have always loved the opening guitar riff from that song. I've attempted to play it on an acoustical guitar, a birthday gift from my wife and daughters years earlier. But it never quite sounded like the recorded version. For that, I surmised, one would need an electric guitar. Now that would be fun. But who was I kidding? At age 50, those days were long gone. Or were they? And suddenly without knowing it, I was following the words of Emerson, "The more experiments you make the better."

I snuck off to the computer in my home office, tucked away in the basement. I began searching for a conservatively-priced guitar. Before I realized what I had done, I clicked "purchase." An electric guitar and amplifier were on their way. I said nothing until the UPS driver rang the front doorbell a few days later. The size of the package soon got the family's attention. My wife caught a glimpse of the return address and smiled. She wasn't quite sure what it was but she had a pretty good guess. As I tore open the box and unveiled my prize, one of my daughters said "Is that for *you*?"

It was...and I wasn't about to apologize for what others may have viewed as an impetuous purchase. I waited that night until the others had gone to bed. I scurried downstairs and hooked everything up. Before strumming my first note, I decided it best to settle for headphones instead of the amp. The first note was magical. And as I picked away until the wee hours of the morning, I imagined screaming crowds and deafening jams and long-haired roadies. And although I still didn't sound much like Eric Clapton, that was okay. I was a little closer to where I wanted to be than the day before.

I had experimented...and there were more experiments to come.

"Insist on yourself; never imitate."

Ralph Waldo Emerson

(from "Self-Reliance," *Essays, First Series*, 1865)

Whether we want to admit to it or not, most of us, at one time or another, have been influenced by others — for good, and for not so good reasons. When we were young, peer pressure consumed many of us. We wanted to fit in so badly that we said the things we thought would be well received by others. We wanted to be accepted in the worst way. And in doing so, we lost our individuality. It was as if our own opinions didn't matter. We lacked the confidence to be different. The last thing we wanted was to be ostracized. And so we didn't rock the boat much.

We knew, however, when we grew up that things would be different. Then we'd walk with our heads held high. We'd make independent decisions, and we'd scoff at others who questioned our motives. With age comes maturity — and with maturity comes confidence. We'd no longer be followers — we'd be leaders. Right? Well, I think we'd like to have answered "yes" to that question, but it may not have always been the case. Many of us still make decisions to please others, to be accepted, to join the party, even if we don't completely buy what others may think.

I recall an acquaintance from college who lived on my floor when I was a freshman. I couldn't help but notice him. There wasn't anything special about him really — it was just that he seemed to get along with everyone. When you go away to school, it is critical to make fast friends — or so you think. This guy seemed to know so many people, and virtually everyone had a smile for him. I decided one day to ask him how he had been able to make friends with all these folks. I'll never forget his answer. "I just agree with everybody," he said. And that was it. He never offered an opinion or an original thought. He would just agree with whatever anyone else said.

If your goal in life is to avoid confrontation, then this is probably good advice. But then again, if some of the same people with whom this fellow spoke had started to compare notes, they might have smelled a rat. If we take another look at the quote at the top of this section, it's virtually impossible to imagine Emerson buying into this way of thinking. It's completely contrary to what he writes about in many of his essays. Emerson believed in original thought. He believed in the courage to express original ideas. And sometimes it does take courage. It's not easy to take a side, especially an unpopular one. But if you've thought through your position, and you are totally committed to it, then it would be unnatural, even hypocritical for you to back down and not share that opinion with others.

"Never imitate." If people actually followed that suggestion, Madison Avenue would become a back alley. Some of the most successful advertising agencies in the country, in the world for that matter, call Madison Avenue home. And when they convince a client to utilize the talents of a celebrity spokesperson, they do so because they know that a prominent figure will command a certain respect, and will be more likely to influence the masses than will a non-celebrity pitchman. Advertising is advertising is advertising. It doesn't matter who claims to be a proponent of a particular brand of toothpaste or sneaker. These are paid spokespersons. They have a financial interest in hawking a specific product. Most intelligent people already know this but it's the young people, those looking for heroes in their lives, who are most affected by this type of advertising.

And I'm not suggesting for a minute that I was an individual thinker at the ripe old age of 12. After seeing James Bond in "Goldfinger, I knew that someday I would drive an Aston Martin. Nothing else would do. And I'm afraid I didn't wise up too quickly either. In my twenties, I was shopping for a suit for a family wedding when I spotted a checkered number that I was certain was similar to the one that Sean Connery had worn while a guest at Goldfinger's ranch. This was some time before you could purchase tapes and DVD's of your favorite films or check facts on the Internet, and so I had no way of knowing if my memory was correct. It wasn't. As you might guess, I didn't end up wearing that suit too often, and I doubt seriously if even Sean Connery could have looked dapper in those threads.

Now I try to follow the advice I should have heeded that day in the fitting room: "Insist on yourself; never imitate."

CONVICTION

"The ancestor of every action is a thought…To think is to act."

Ralph Waldo Emerson

(from "Spiritual Laws," *Essays, First Series*, 1865)

More often than we probably like to admit, we all remember our parents uttering those dreaded words: "What were you thinking?!" If we had been honest, we might have said that we really hadn't thought a great deal about it…we just did it. But, of course, that would not have gone over well. An impulsive youth will act without thinking. It is a part of growing up. We have all done it.

But as we mature, and as we tire of digging ourselves out of holes, we soon learn that it does pay to think before we speak or act. Emerson seems to be putting a great deal of emphasis not only on our actions but on the thoughts that precede them. Wartime generals would undoubtedly agree. To mount an assault without a strategy is irresponsible. You owe it to your troops to formulate a battle plan to outsmart your enemies and to minimize casualties.

Corporate executives are in some ways no different than field generals. They don't move forward without a business plan. Professional sports teams hire scouts to determine the strengths and weaknesses of upcoming opponents. Those learning a trade must apprentice, and physicians must intern before they can practice. We could name any number of professions that operate in a similar manner. Thinking, planning and research precede action.

Emerson's advice, however, does not just apply to vocations. This is sound advice for any of us in any situation. From *what to have for lunch* to *what stocks to buy*, it is easy to see that planning and foresight are key. Thinking for ten seconds longer before we act might produce completely different results. When someone gets into trouble, we often hear, "He made poor choices." A choice can be either well thought out or it can be rash. We determine the outcome of our actions by our thought process hours, minutes, or seconds before the action.

There are also individuals who methodically think through each move, but whose intentions are less than honorable. In murder trials, the penalty for taking a life is greater if the individual acted with premeditation. Here is a case where thought preceded action…but for all the wrong reasons.

Computer hackers who unleash viruses have no doubt put a great deal of thought into their actions. So it is important to note that allocating more time to our thoughts will only produce superior results if we have the best intentions.

Thinking before speaking is a basic requirement for those who intend on becoming contributing members of society. And it is even more important when we share our words with groups of people. All effective public speakers repeat the mantra: "Know your audience." An ill-planned comment or witticism to the wrong demographic can spell doom for any speaker. Over the years I have found myself answering reporters' questions for a variety of reasons. I have learned never to blurt out a response to a question but rather to respond in a deliberate manner, always thinking how these comments will look in print. And the same goes for e-mails. People can't read the tone of your message in a faceless e-mail. They don't see the half smile, the wink, the rolling of the eyes. They see the literal words that you have written, and they choose how they will interpret them. Plan what you intend to write. And, by all means, proof your work—if not for typos, then for a phrase that could be misinterpreted.

If you spend more time in thought, you are more likely to get it right. And less likely to have to manage the mess you may have left for yourself. But allocating additional time does not mean procrastinating. This practice can backfire when you give yourself permission to delay an action because you want to rethink all of your options. Most of us know when it's time to move from thought to action. We can recognize the signs of complacency and our inability to pull the trigger. Learn to brainstorm in an efficient manner, and take action when you are convinced you won't look back and second guess yourself.

Don't underestimate the power of thought and preparedness. Remember, "To think is to act."

"We gain the strength of the temptation we resist."

Ralph Waldo Emerson

(from "Compensation," *Essays, First Series*, 1865)

Wouldn't life be grand if we never had to make difficult decisions? If we were never tempted to do wrong? It's almost impossible to imagine a world where temptations do not exist. It would be a perfect world. But would it really be so perfect? If there were no lows—no enticements or seductions—how could we recognize and appreciate the highs? The times when we must make tough decisions are the moments that help us build character. A world with no peaks or valleys would provide us with a pretty mundane existence. Now I am not suggesting that there is necessarily anything good about temptations, but since we know that as humans we will experience our share of them, doesn't it make sense to prepare for the frustrations that life has planned for us if we fail to choose wisely?

We're all familiar with the tired expression, "We learn from our mistakes." Following an indiscretion, we oftentimes hear these words. They usually come from people who want to appear sympathetic but who actually may feel that a little comeuppance will do us some good. Emerson is offering much more to those who avoid making mistakes when temptation is present. Rather than learning from the errors of our ways, he is suggesting that there is a great deal more than just learning available to us if we have the strength to resist temptation altogether. We have not only defeated the temptress but we have gained a greater strength—one that will enable us to overcome temptation again and again and again. And each time we manage to do so, our strength increases. What a marvelous motivation for staying true to our convictions and acting in a responsible and prudent manner.

There is no getting around it—life is filled with temptation. It may be as innocent as avoiding that second piece of cake. It might, however, be as serious as alcohol or drug addiction. With this particular quotation, Emerson is not offering advice on how to beat an addiction, but rather he is sharing with us the benefit we will receive if we have the strength to resist. It is ultimately up to us to seek out whatever professional assistance is necessary in order to correct self-defeating habits. But once we do so, then we can plug in Emerson's advice which reminds us that each time we stand up to a challenge, we are the better for it…the stronger for it. And every subsequent bout of temptation will be that much easier to handle. It's how people beat addictions—with continued resistance which leads to personal victory.

So then, do we wish for temptation to befall us so we'll have an opportunity to grow stronger? Not really. Temptation will find us whether we want it to or not, and usually does so at our weakest moment...which is why it is generally so difficult to resist. We just have to keep telling ourselves that in the presence of enticement, we need to remember that we have a chance to turn a negative into a positive. In the time that I spent as a writer/producer at WGN-Radio in Chicago, I had the good fortune of working with Orion Samuelson, longtime Agricultural Services Director at the station. I was lucky enough to have produced some of his farm programs, but even luckier to have known this man. When I began at WGN, at the age of 22, I was scared to death. It was Orion who became a surrogate father to me. I joined some of the other young producers who referred to him as "Dad." It was Orion who was the rock, the coolest cucumber when problems would arise. Whenever I would barge into his office with a crisis, he would sit back and smile. "It's not a problem, John. It's an opportunity." It was as if he seemed to welcome these *opportunities*. And it didn't take me long to realize that with each problem we faced, we soon became a little more confident, a little more efficient, a little wiser, and a little better able to handle the next obstacle in our paths. I can thank Orion for teaching me how to handle adversity.

And so as Emerson would suggest, the next time a problem or temptation comes upon you, don't wish it away. Embrace it. Recognize it for what it is—an opportunity to grow mentally—and to become a better, stronger, richer person than you were the day before.

"You think me the child of my circumstances: I make my circumstance."

Ralph Waldo Emerson

(from a speech delivered at the Masonic Temple in Boston, January, 1842)

When we think of *circumstance*, we think of a condition that determines an event—something over which we have no control. And so when Emerson addressed this assembly, he wanted the members to know that although they may have believed themselves to be victims of fate, their destinies were actually in their own hands. There are many similarities between this quote and an earlier one: *"Shallow men believe in luck. Strong men believe in cause and effect."* To feel that we have no control over events that take place in our lives is tantamount to throwing in the towel. Are we to believe that outcomes in our lives are based purely on predestination? Now that would be a sobering thought.

I have chosen to catalog this quote under *Conviction*. But it just as easily could have been cross-listed under *Accountability*. Emerson is suggesting that we must dismiss the notion that events—circumstances—affect our lot in life. He instead wants us to accept the fact that the decisions we make are well within our control, and that we must be accountable for our actions.

If you have ever found yourself in the unenviable position of having to explain an indiscretion on your part, you may have considered various options as you planned your defense. You could have denied that you were involved. You could have shifted the blame to someone else. You could have explained that you were a victim of circumstance. Or you could have done the noble thing, the one which we all know Emerson would have advocated—you could have admitted guilt and accepted responsibility. This final option is certainly the most difficult but it is undoubtedly the response that will define your character.

Tossing someone else under the bus or making a flat-out denial are options that a responsible individual would never consider. That leaves us with blaming our misconduct on a series of circumstances, or acknowledging our guilt. If our accuser happened to be familiar with the writings of Emerson, we would stand little chance of arguing the former. There comes a time, no matter how unpleasant, that we can no longer blame others or circumstances for our poorly-executed decisions. At some point we need to take ownership of our actions, and recognize that we do indeed control our own destinies.

If you decide someday to take a personal assessment of the highs and lows in your life, and do so as objectively as possible, you would probably have to admit that, for the most part, you got exactly what you deserved. And Emerson would certainly have concurred because, as he says, "I make my circumstance." Have you ever felt that you were the victim of injustice, and then after you had cooled down, you could see things more clearly, and were better able to understand why this outcome took place? Let's use a workplace example. Has this ever happened? Let's say that you have just learned you have been denied a promotion. You would probably struggle with feelings of anger and disappointment. You might even feel that politics may have been involved, and that you were unjustly passed over. But if you take the time to analyze the process, you will probably see why things turned out the way they did. There was no conspiracy. The other person was simply more qualified.

It is important for us to be able to accept these types of disappointments in our lives because once we stop feeling sorry for ourselves, we gain an inner strength—a strength visible to others. And when those others witness that resilience in our character, it won't be long before we become the leading candidate for another position. It may be difficult at first, especially in a scenario where a co-worker has become your supervisor, but the more of a team player that you appear to be, the more likely that you will be given serious consideration for advancement in the future.

It's hard to watch rivals pass us by. But it wouldn't be if we were to follow the advice of productivity consultant and motivational speaker, Denis Waitley. Mr. Waitley talks about something called "The Double Win"—if I help you win, then I win. I've listened to many of his audio programs over the years, and not only is he an extremely entertaining speaker, but a forceful one as well. He suggests that if we put aside petty jealousies and rivalries, and assist others in their efforts to advance, then we too will benefit from their success. It's hard to imagine following advice like this when we've been constantly reminded not to worry about the other guy, and instead to "look out for number one." Mr. Waitley builds a case for this strategy in his audio programs and books. I personally have become a disciple of this gospel, and have found it to be powerfully effective.

It's time to accept responsibility and to be accountable for our actions. It's time to stop whining and blaming someone else for our problems. Just

remember: *"You think me the child of my circumstances: I make my circumstance."*

> **"A man is relieved and gay when he has put his heart into his work and done his best; but what he has said or done otherwise shall give him no peace."**
>
> Ralph Waldo Emerson
>
> (from "Self-Reliance," *Essays, First Series*, 1865)

We can only wonder how powerful and moving it might have been to have heard Emerson nearly a century and a half ago. He was a great orator who would oftentimes read from his many books or essays. Imagine being in an audience in the mid-1800's and listening to these words. I can only guess that the productivity level of those lucky enough to have heard him speak probably skyrocketed immediately after the experience. And there is no reason why those fortunate enough to stumble upon the writings of Emerson today can't glean from his words some of the same inspiration enjoyed by those in his day.

Emerson is making two powerful statements in the quotation above. He first talks about committing yourself to hard work and of the joys available to those who do. He then quickly turns the table and seems to chastise, even pity, those who choose to ignore this line of thinking. Relief and gaiety are your rewards for a job well done. Choosing otherwise and yours is an unfulfilled experience. In the particular passage where this quotation is found (his 1865 essay on "Self-Reliance"), he further comments on those who scoff at a strong work ethic:

> "It is a deliverance which does not deliver.
> In the attempt his genius deserts him; no
> muse befriends; no invention, no hope."

No hope. Now there is a pretty strong statement. It is my guess that if you are reading this book, you are not the type of person who is *without hope*. And I don't mean that you never feel hopeless. There are times, no matter how hard we try to stay positive, that events in our life seem insurmountable. Hopelessness is an emotion that we have all felt at one time or another. Our goal is to make certain that those hopeless moments are temporary.

It is my sincere hope that those of you who are reading the works of Emerson in this text have found particular quotations that are powerful in a very personal way. I wouldn't be surprised if some of you have marked or circled or folded over specific pages with sayings you want to remember and want to be able to refer to in the future. Some others may have written down a few of the quotes or created signs and posted them in strategic places that you know you will see on a daily basis. When we identify a particular quotation that really seems to hit the mark for us personally, we never want to forget it. It only makes sense to put it in a place that will continually remind us of its powerful message.

The quote above may be one that people will want to remember. It's probably not one that you've heard before, or one that is particularly memorable. But when it comes to work, most of us need to be reminded that there is a payoff if we act accordingly. The important thing on which we must focus is that Emerson is not just saying that if we continue to work, we will enjoy its benefits, he's referring to a much more concentrated effort. He uses the phrase: "…when he has put his heart into his work…" You know as well as I that there are different degrees of work. There is the work that someone performs only when his or her boss is watching. There is the minimal effort of doing just enough so as not to draw attention to yourself. There is putting in an honest day's work. There is the above-average performance. Then there is what Emerson refers to: putting your heart into your work. To ensure this degree of effort, it is helpful to have a constant reminder.

It is easier for some to work at this highest of levels. If you own your own business, the motivation comes naturally. But for the majority of us who work for others, we don't necessarily see the direct payoff as does someone who is self-employed. We wonder sometimes if our efforts are noticed. And that's why these words from Emerson are so important. We can't be looking for that immediate payoff or gratification. We have to have faith that a sincere effort on our parts will not only be recognized, but more importantly, will cause us to experience a feeling of fulfillment like no other. Only when we expend maximum energies day in and day out will we enjoy the fruits of our labors.

COURAGE

"If we filled the day with bravery, we should not shrink from celebrating it."

Ralph Waldo Emerson

(from "The Poet," *Essays, Second Series*, 1876)

Filling a day with bravery? Now that's what you'd call quite a prodigious achievement. And if we were somehow able to do so, then Emerson suggests that we should rejoice, we should celebrate, we should revel in our accomplishments. But who among us is capable of filling a day with courageous acts? Before you think this a silly suggestion, perhaps we should identify exactly what bravery means in this instance. I would guess that most of us at one time in our lives have indeed filled a day with bravery. And some of us may be doing so on a daily basis.

We're not talking about running in front of a speeding car and snatching up a child who has wandered into the street. We're not referring to throwing ourselves onto a grenade and saving the lives of fellow soldiers. No one would argue that those feats are anything but supreme acts of courage. We're talking, however, about our daily routine—the unheralded acts of courage. We're referring to what some may call the little things. When we faithfully get up each morning and go to school or work…when we make an honest day's wages…when we volunteer our time…when we care for our children or aging parents…when we engage in a home improvement project…these are the acts of bravery to which we are referring.

Just doing the right thing each day is something to celebrate. We may not think that we have accomplished anything special, but living a virtuous life, avoiding temptation, acting in a responsible manner, providing for ourselves and our family members—these are daily acts of courage. Don't think of them as routine undertakings that we must do for little or no recognition. Think of them as significant accomplishments. Remember we have choices. We could have elected to have done things differently. We have chosen to do the prudent thing, and though we might argue that we were just doing our jobs, we should be congratulated for having toiled in a faithful and fruitful manner.

When I see a mail carrier battling the elements—below zero temperatures and blizzard conditions—my heart goes out to them. When I see construction workers who faithfully plod along in 100-degree heat, I can't help but applaud their efforts. For that matter, anyone who works out of doors or in sweat shops, and whose life is at the mercy of climatic conditions, is a hero. And this list is endless.

Those people who work a 10 to 12-hour day, and then are forced to bring work home just to keep from falling behind are filling the day with bravery. Those who work part-time jobs on top of their regular employment, and parents who are up at dawn with the first little one who awakens, and not back to bed until all homework has been checked over — are heroes as well. There are those who work double shifts or work under difficult conditions… those caught in loveless marriages…single parents trying to do it all…those who have lost loved ones who try to keep their families and themselves together…those battling serious illness…and the caretakers who assist them.

It would be futile to continue to identify those individuals who bear crosses each day. Suffice it to say that there are millions of them on this planet. And each day when they rise, they look for the guidance and inspiration to survive yet another day. And so, every once in a while, it's okay to stop and appreciate all you have accomplished. Pat yourself on the back. It's okay. You've earned it. When the opportunity presents itself, as Emerson suggests, celebrate your accomplishments. Pamper yourself a little.

It might seem that everyone, in some way or another, is a hero, but that sadly is not the case. As motivational speaker and writer, Denis Waitley, likes to say: "There are two types of people in this world — the winners and the whiners." The winners are the heroes. The whiners are the takers, the ones who feel that the world owes them a living. And we're not simply talking about the common criminal. We're referring to those who feel a sense of entitlement — those who live showy, ostentatious lives.

Where do you fit in? My guess is that you are already a hero or on the cusp of becoming one. Just remember though — there are no medals, no gold watches, no parades — for acting is a responsible manner. There is, however, the personal satisfaction of having done so. And with that satisfaction comes something very special — something unknown and unavailable to the whiners — it is that inner peace that gives you the strength to get up each morning and to continue to act in a heroic manner.

"A great part of courage is the courage of having done the thing before."

Ralph Waldo Emerson

(from "Wealth," *The Conduct of Life*, 1860)

Courage. Noun. *The state or quality of mind or spirit that enables one to face danger or fear with confidence or resolution.* Sounds about right. Most folks would accept that definition. So how do we drum up enough of that spirit to face danger with confidence? It is one of the eternal questions. Emerson's answer certainly makes sense, but it just seems too obvious. He suggests that it is easier to act in a courageous manner if, in fact, we have previously faced the same fear. Well, of course it would be easier. If we knew what to expect every time, we would be less likely to avoid taking action. The phrasing seems almost too simple, too commonplace to have been penned by the same man whose writing has been so insightful up until now. We have come to expect something more substantive from this great writer and philosopher. I mean…couldn't any of us have come up with that line?

The more I thought about this quotation, the more I realized that there had to be an additional meaning or application that I was missing. I tried to imagine various scenarios in which these words could be applied. For a while I kept coming back to the same conclusion — it certainly makes a lot of sense but it's just too apparent. There's got to be something more. I began to recall the challenges and obstacles in my own life, the ones that required courage to overcome. Before long, I understood where and how to apply these words. I had already done so without realizing it. And I was then able to see the hidden message within.

Let me explain. I began my teaching career more than three decades ago. During that time I have encountered eager, energetic, responsible, and creative college students. It's been a blessing. They have been a joy to work with. It's probably why I left commercial radio years ago and am now so deeply entrenched in higher education. But in my first year, I was introduced to a young man who I would not describe with the accolades above. Since he was a member of the campus radio station which I managed, we saw a lot of one another. And unfortunately we were on a collision course early on. This student had a problem taking direction, and with authority in general. I soon realized that my best efforts would not be enough to turn him around and win him over. And so we clashed frequently.

His purpose on this earth seemed very clear — make my life miserable. And he was good at it. In the big picture, I suppose we need people like that in our lives. Without them, how would be ever appreciate just how special the others are? Let me point out that this was not a student who simply liked to challenge his instructors in class. That is more than welcome — it is encouraged. It keeps you on your toes. This was a young man who embraced confrontation — with his professors, his classmates, or anyone else who disagreed with him. This particular individual was a senior when I arrived so I knew at least that his days were numbered. I found myself counting the weeks until graduation. I used to imagine how easy and uncomplicated my life might be without him. And so the months dragged on, but June finally arrived. I attended the commencement ceremony, watched him collect his diploma, and realized that it was over. I had survived the worst.

The summer was quiet and peaceful. But then in the fall, something strange happened. No, I'm not going to tell you that he re-enrolled. Something I should have anticipated. A new student, a virtual reincarnation of my friend, appeared. He was packaged differently but he reclaimed the role of cancer in the clubhouse. And he was a freshman. I was beside myself. I couldn't imagine daily confrontations with a new student who arrived on the scene ready to change the world…as long as he came out on top.

It was then I realized that I had made a huge mistake a year ago. I had spent my time wishing away a problem. Looking forward to the weekends. Counting the days until graduation. I had dealt with this all of this in the wrong way. Instead of imagining how pleasant life would have been without this individual around, I should simply have learned to cope with the situation. I should have realized that I was wasting valuable time — time you can't reclaim. If I had spent my time not wishing away this problem but rather developing coping mechanisms, it would have better prepared me in the event the same problem reoccurred. Which it did. Which it usually does.

And so now as I re-read the opening Emerson quote, I see what he is trying to tell us. He's not just saying it is easier to confront a problem that you have faced before. He is telling us that when we build up the courage to address our problems, and attack them head on, we must, at the same moment, prepare a strategy in the event that the problem resurfaces, and resurfaces after that. If we simply muddle through a particularly challenging moment without keeping track of our efforts, how will we ever learn from the experience? Paying attention to how we handle adversity will allow us to put a battle plan in place for the future. We should never have to expend the same amount energy to resolve a problem we have tackled before, and we should never allow it to take the same emotional toll on us again.

"Always do what you are afraid to do."

Ralph Waldo Emerson

(from "Heroism," *Essays, First Series*, 1841)

Have you noticed a pattern in the Emerson quotations that we've touched upon thus far? I'm not referring to writing style, or the depth or insightfulness of this gifted author. I'm referring to the bar — the one that Emerson is setting so high for us. For some reason, he seems to believe that we possess the power and ability to reach new heights. Why else would he challenge us with phrases like "Always do what you are afraid to do." If we made a daily habit of facing our fears or confronting our demons, we'd probably be a nervous wreck most of the time. Or would we?

It's doubtful that Emerson would suggest we do anything that would cause us harm. He is simply advocating that we should spend less time worrying about what might happen, and instead take the initiative and make something happen. Have you ever noticed that when we finally build up the nerve to do something we have been putting off, more often than not, it wasn't nearly as dreadful as we had imagined. In fact, we frequently find ourselves wondering why we had put it off so long.

When people plan for an undertaking that they have been avoiding, they will usually prepare for the worst. Not because it's likely to happen — it's just that they want to be ready for any consequences, including the most dire. But rarely if ever are the results worse than you were expecting. It's the fear that things *could be* catastrophic that often immobilizes us. I am not in any way suggesting that we shouldn't plan for the worst that could happen. It's always best to be prepared for any eventuality. But in many cases, prepping for the most unfavorable condition is not an example of great foresight, it's one of procrastination.

Some folks might tell you that they like to invest a great deal of time before facing a difficult challenge because they just want to take the necessary precautions. And these same people would probably bristle at the suggestion that they were just stalling. In your life, how often have you avoided facing your fears? And this is nothing to be ashamed of. It's part of human nature to leave the best for last — and the most difficult — for last. I don't want to tell you how many times I have put off a doctor's or dentist's appointment, or have avoided confrontations with people I knew I eventually would have to spar with.

In the quotation above, Emerson gives us a directive—an order, so to speak. But what he doesn't tell us is *why*. Are we simply to blindly follow what he is saying? How could he possibly know what fears haunt us? How can he be so sure that we possess the initiative, the drive, and the courage to confront danger? It's easy for him to suggest that we should do what we have been avoiding for so long. How can he possibly guarantee a positive outcome?

Emerson, as you might guess, knew exactly what he was talking about when he issued this challenge. He knew he didn't need to elaborate. He knew what we were about to find out. And he was confident that once we came face to face with our deepest fears, we would come to know the secret hidden within his message. We were about to experience a feeling of contentment, of satisfaction, of tranquility. And we would grow with each obstacle we fought to overcome. With each victory, we would become stronger and better able to answer the next challenge, and the one after that.

A couple of years ago, I was fortunate enough to have sold a screenplay to a producer in Los Angeles. And every good screenwriter knows that in order to keep the audience emotionally involved, you must create a hero who will face obstacle after obstacle, and each one must be ascending in difficulty. With each triumph, the protagonist gains knowledge and fortitude and is better able to handle an even more difficult challenge…and so on…and so on…and so on. If, however, the obstacles become less difficult, the audience becomes disengaged. The suspense would be gone.

And so in life, as Emerson points out, we need to do the things we are afraid to do. And if we faithfully follow this strategy, we will toughen up physically, mentally and emotionally with each successive victory, and will soon be capable of facing challenges and solving problems we have avoided for years.

"Courage is nothing else than knowledge."

Ralph Waldo Emerson

(from Plato; or the Philosopher," *Representative Men*, 1876)

On January 15, 2009, US Airways pilot, Chesley "Sully" Sullenberger crash landed an Airbus A320 with 155 people on board into the chilly Hudson River. Flight 1549, en route from New York to Charlotte, North Carolina, was airborne less than three minutes before Captain Sullenberger radioed to air traffic controllers that he had experienced a bird strike and declared an emergency. When the pilot realized that it would be impossible to return to LaGuardia or make it to any neighboring airports, he made the difficult decision to ditch the aircraft into the Hudson. Witnesses said the pilot seemed to guide the plane down into the frigid waters in what was described as a graceful, gradual, "controlled descent." The lives of all 155 passengers and crew members were saved in what then New York governor, David Paterson, referred to as the "Miracle on the Hudson."

In that moment, Sully Sullenberger became a hero. He demonstrated courage in the face of imminent danger. He and his crew were deserving of all of the accolades heaped upon them in the weeks following the near disaster. It is safe to say that if any of us had been asked to perform the same feat, we wouldn't even want to think what might have happened. On that brisk Thursday afternoon in New York City, moments after engine failure, Captain Sullenberger quickly assessed his options and knew that a water landing was his only choice. He certainly knew that the odds of a successful touchdown were not in his favor. Attempts to ditch an aircraft of that size into a body of water had proven tragic in the past. The captain knew that his life, and the lives of the other 154 passengers and crew members, were in his hands. But he also knew something else — he knew that he had been trained for water landings. And although he had never done so, he had the knowledge of how it was supposed to take place, if God forbid, it was ever necessary.

When we consider what might have happened to that US Airways jetliner, we can see how the Emerson quote above can be applied so aptly to this incredible situation. Who would argue the fact that knowledge played an integral part in the outcome of this event? Had a pilot with less training been at the controls, the result may have been far different, tragically so. On that day, at that moment, under those circumstances, there just happened to be a superbly knowledgeable individual in the cockpit. Is it a coincidence that this former air force fighter pilot and instructor with more than 40 years of flying experience, just happened to have successfully guided his aircraft to a picture-perfect water landing?

Knowledge played a key role in the success of this mission. And you would never convince the passengers of Flight 1549 of anything different. Courage and knowledge are partners, pure and simple. When we hear on the news about how a firefighter saved the life of a victim trapped in a burning building, we immediately chalk that up to courage. But don't you think that the expert training received at the academy and the sheer knowledge of what to expect under those circumstances, were just as important? We cannot stress enough the need for knowledge. And we're not just talking about lifesaving situations, we're talking about everyday life. Knowledge is priceless. The need to acquire it cannot be emphasized enough.

In the last few years, I have become a fan of King Solomon, the son of David. After having read Steven K. Scott's book, <u>The Richest Man Who Ever Lived: King Solomon's Secrets to Success, Wealth, and Happiness</u>, I have made it a point to read a chapter from the Book of Proverbs each day. Since, conveniently, there are thirty-one chapters, it is easy to remember where you left off. Considered by many to be one of the wisest individuals of all time, King Solomon, like Emerson, recognized the importance of knowledge. In Proverbs 18:15, Solomon writes, "The heart of the prudent getteth knowledge; and the ear of the wise seeketh knowledge."

    Do your best to find knowledge—and don't be surprised if courage finds you.

DILIGENCE

"The day is always his, who works in it with serenity and great aims."

Ralph Waldo Emerson

(from an oration delivered before the Phi Beta Kappa Society, Cambridge, Massachusetts, August 31, 1837)

One of my favorite television programs from the late eighties and early nineties was a popular sitcom entitled "The Wonder Years." In it Kevin Arnold, through an adult narrator, reminisces about growing up in the sixties. We follow his experiences from childhood to adolescence with his friend, Paul, his on-and-off girlfriend, Winnie, and his relatively normal family. Whenever Kevin is so inclined to have a conversation with his father—which he avoids whenever possible—he would usually start off with "So, Dad, how was work?" And his father, Jack, would invariably answer "Work's work."

With that line, the producers and staff writers of this program pretty well captured how many people view their jobs. Work to many is a necessary evil. And testament to that is the action taken by many folks who win the lottery—resignations tendered at breakneck speed. So why is it that many people sigh, roll their eyes, or make a face when asked "So, how was work?" We somehow seem to equate work with unpleasantness. I don't think it's because most people necessarily dislike what they do, it's just that they'd rather be doing something else with their time. But since only a precious few actually ever win the lottery, we'd all better settle in for the long haul.

When I think back to my early days in the labor force, I know that I would have echoed Jack Arnold's sentiment, "Work's work." But between junior and senior year in college, I had a summer job that forever changed my attitude toward work. With the help of one of my aunts who knew someone who knew someone, I soon found myself an official employee of a trucking company that delivered merchandise for Montgomery Ward in Chicago. My job was called a "helper." I would ride shotgun in the truck and assist the driver with deliveries. It was a job like any other. Long hours. A lot of lifting. But the best hourly wage I had ever made on a part-time job.

Each morning at 7:00 am I'd arrive at the break room filled with truckers. Some chatted with co-workers. Others sat in folding chairs against the wall and snoozed. Still others just milled around quietly waiting for the bell to ring that would signal the start of another work day. I couldn't help but notice that there were very few smiles. These guys just didn't look thrilled to be doing what they were doing. But I completely understood. I wasn't thrilled to be there myself, and the thought of making a career out of this line of work seemed bleak. There was, however, a small group of drivers, no more than a half dozen or so, who were unlike the others. They were laughing and joking around and seemed almost out of place. And in the middle of that group was a fellow with a round face and a broad smile. He seemed to be the one doing most of the talking. He was the one with whom they were laughing. And this went on day after day.

And so each morning, I would drag myself in, get paired up with a different driver, and somehow survive the day. Some of the guys were better than others but none really seemed that interested in me. To tell you the truth, I'm not sure they were too crazy about the fact that I'd be leaving in less than three months. It was almost as if some of them were wishing that they'd be the ones making an escape as well. After about three weeks, I had convinced myself that despite the money, this was my worst summer job ever. I couldn't wait for it to end.

And then fate dealt me a hand that changed my summer and my outlook on life. One day I found myself paired up with Pat. He was the one I mentioned a moment ago—the one in the center of the group that always seemed to be having such a good time. We hit it off instantly. He had a perpetual grin. It was contagious. We loaded up the truck in no time and were on our way. Along the route we talked non-stop. He wanted to know everything about me. He seemed genuinely interested in some of the classes I had taken, and appeared excited for me that graduation was less than a year away. We laughed and joked as we strapped appliances to our backs and carried them up flights of stairs. And he always had such a good time with the customers. Before we'd leave each residence, he'd always have them laughing.

As we were driving back to the warehouse, Pat asked me if I wanted to team up with him for the rest of the summer. I couldn't believe it. Of course I wanted to. And with that, my worst summer job became my best. The work was the same. The hours were the same. But the attitude was completely different. I had never met anyone quite like him before. Pat was like a magnet. He drew people to himself. And I was one of the lucky ones. A week or so later I got up the nerve to ask him why he seemed to enjoy the same job that so many of his co-workers seemed to dislike. What he told me I have never forgotten. He said that this was a pretty good paying job, and that he enjoyed working with people. He told me that he needed to provide for his wife and kids, and this job gave him the opportunity to do so. He told me that he could be bitching and moaning with the others, but what would that accomplish. He said that he decided a long time ago that he wanted to enjoy every moment of every day. He didn't want to wait for the nights or weekends or holidays or vacations. He wanted to make the most of each day whether he was at work or wherever. He told me that if you just try to get through the day, you're sure to miss some pretty good times that were just sitting there waiting for you to enjoy.

Pat never spoke of Ralph Waldo Emerson but he was truly living the quotation above. He was working with "serenity and great aims." And he taught me how to do the same. He will forever be one of the most influential people in my life.

"The sum of wisdom is, that the time is never lost that is devoted to work."

Ralph Waldo Emerson

(from "Success," *Society & Solitude*, 1870)

Can you imagine a job that you couldn't wait to get to? One that you would arrive at early, and stay late without even realizing it? There are some people out there who actually seem to have jobs like that. They're the ones who make comments like, "I can't believe they're actually paying me to do this." Now it's doubtful that any of us have met many people who have uttered those words, but at one time or another, we have all probably fantasized about being in a position to make comments like that, and mean it.

There are some people who actually seem to love ordinary jobs, but it all has to do with timing. For most folks, the first few months of a new job are usually a relatively pleasant experience. You're excited about the opportunity of a fresh start, and you want to make the best impression possible. Or if you learn your company will be laying off workers, and somehow you survive the cuts, you are usually so relieved that you begin to appreciate the same job that only a week before had you flustered. Or if you *were* one of the ones let go, but were ultimately called back, you would have realized in your absence that the job had actually been a better situation than you had realized. Or if you own your own business, you are certainly more likely to enjoy what you do. People who work for themselves, if the business is healthy, usually are happier than those who work for others.

But regardless of where you fit into the examples above, a healthy attitude about work and a strong work ethic allow for a genuine feeling of accomplishment. No one ever said that you had to love your job. No one ever said you even had to like it. But have you ever tried throwing your heart and soul into your job—even if you work for someone else. And I'm not talking about doing so just to impress someone. With a sincere effort comes a sense of personal pride you can't manufacture. And ethically—there are certain expectations that a worker must live up to. We owe our employers an honest day's work. The payoff of doing so is great. Remember what Emerson is saying above: "time is never lost that is devoted to work."

As a college professor I enjoy immensely what I do. I don't dread going to work each day. Most days I look forward to. But I'd be lying if I told you that I had never fantasized about doing something else. I can't tell you the number of times I've hit a grand slam in the bottom of the ninth for the Chicago Cubs…dove for a pass in the end zone as time ran out to score the winning touchdown for the Bears…or drained a three-pointer to win the NBA championship for the Bulls. I've also imagined standing at the podium in front of colleagues at the Kodak Theatre, and thanking all of the people who supported me, while clutching the Oscar for Best Original Screenplay. It's kind of fun to think like that, and healthy for that matter. Fantasizing about being an athlete or a celebrity is perfectly normal, and for most of us, it's the closest we'll ever get to those dream jobs.

What has always bothered me though is the fact that some of the people who *have* those dream jobs, don't seem to appreciate them. When I read about professional athletes who are holding out in a contract dispute, I can't help but think that they are living in a vacuum. They don't seem to appreciate the fact that if their salaries were cut in half, or by two-thirds, or quartered even, they'd still be making far more than the average Joe. And it's the average Joe purchasing tickets that enables them to enjoy their lavish lifestyles.

And don't get me started on long-term guaranteed contracts. Athletes, like the rest of us, should be compensated based on performance, not potential. Wouldn't it be refreshing to see a professional athlete return some of his or her salary at the end of a sub-par season? Don't hold your breath. These individuals are doing what so many people just dream of, and yet they can't comprehend how fortunate they are. They're getting paid for doing what many people would do for nothing.

Just because some athletes—not all mind you—choose not to take Emerson's advice, it doesn't mean we shouldn't. If an employer was confident enough in our abilities to bring us on board and to make us part of their team, we should recognize our obligation to perform…and to do so at the highest possible level. And we just need to keep telling ourselves "that the time is never lost that is devoted to work."

"Work is victory. Wherever work is done, victory is obtained."

Ralph Waldo Emerson

(from "Worship," *The Conduct of Life*, 1860)

If you're a procrastinator, then this is the Emerson quote that you want hanging in a prominent place. There's probably not a person alive who hasn't procrastinated at one time or another. But there are some of us who are professional procrastinators. It is with these folks in mind that we have chosen to feature the above quotation. If someone who puts things off on a regular basis could see a direct benefit from not doing so, then half the battle would be won. If you buy into the message that "work is victory," you will find yourself more motivated, more driven, more empowered to finish those unfinished projects. If you firmly believe that victory is indeed a by-product of hard work, there will be no stopping you. Your days of indecision will be over. Wasting time will be a thing of the past. You will become a multi-tasker if you aren't already. Imagine being more productive than you've ever been before.

So what is this victory that Emerson references? Work is not a game. You're not competing against anyone. Or are you? I suppose you might be competing against leaks, mold, grubs, weeds, or any number of chores, etc. And if you are successful, then it is surely a victory. If we waste less time and accomplish more, is that not worthy of celebration? Why of course. On top of that, there is an internal victory that others may not see. Imagine the feeling of satisfaction, of contentment, of utter joy following the completion of a particularly challenging project.

But none of those emotions will be experienced if we fail to discipline ourselves. Imagine how productive we might be if we dedicated ourselves to productivity, and if we resisted the temptations to waste time. Think about how much time you waste every day, and consider what might be accomplished if you were to fill that time with a productive effort. My youngest daughter, when she was a senior in high school, was lamenting the fact that she had three exams on the same day. She felt that she would never be prepared for all of them. She kept taking breaks from studying to remind me of this fact. She must have mentioned it at least a half dozen times. At one point I put my arm around her and said, "Think about how much more time you'd have if instead of complaining about the exams, you used that time to study." She rolled her eyes. She was looking for empathy. Instead she got a lecture.

Productivity has always been important to me—maybe even an obsession. I've always felt that our time on this earth is so short that we need to accomplish as much as possible, and to do so with the aid of a moral compass. A few years ago, on my 41st birthday, I decided to finally get serious about my writing. I had been a talker, not a doer up until that point. I used to fantasize about writing a screenplay or a novel but I never made the time to do so. It was easy to talk about it—and even easier to imagine the accolades I'd receive once it had been accomplished. But at age 41, I had an awakening. I suddenly began to think that I had waited too long—that I was too old to write something that might get purchased or published. It was depressing to think that way—but even more depressing to accept the fact that I was about to give up on my dreams. I decided at that moment to dedicate myself to writing, and to allocate a certain amount of time each day to do so. I just didn't want to be sitting in my Lazy-Boy watching The Price is Right when I was 85, and wondering what might have been. I decided to write two hours each day. I would give up my lunch hour, as well as the last hour of the night, usually 11:00 pm until midnight. And I simply would not give into the temptation of taking a day off due to tiredness, illness, etc. I knew that if I did, it would be easier and easier to do the same thing again and again and again. And so I faithfully followed this personal mandate—without any guarantees of success.

And even with this self discipline and determination, it still took me thirteen years to sell a screenplay, and three more years to sign a contract with a major publisher for a three-book mystery series. And there were plenty of times along the way that I questioned my own abilities. I wondered if I had been fooling myself for all those years. What if I had no talent at all? What if I was just a hack? Had I wasted all of those hours? But I must tell you that even with all those reservations, whenever I would conclude an hour of writing, I would always be on a high. I didn't know where it would lead but I felt good about the accomplishment—good about having invested another hour in my dream. It was work, and even if it had led nowhere, it was still a victory.

> **"Do your work and I shall know you. Do your work and you shall reinforce yourself."**
>
> Ralph Waldo Emerson
>
> (from "Self-Reliance," *Essays, First Series*, 1847)

College students will oftentimes seek out internships to gain a better understanding of a particular career. But an internship can be even more valuable. If an intern performs at an exceptional level while at his or her place of employment, the student may be in for a far better outcome than simply a high grade, the individual may very well have impressed someone enough to be able to use that person as a reference on a resume. And I have seen many an internship turn into a job offer when the student graduates. What employers seem to like about internships is not only the prospect of cheap labor, but it gives them an opportunity to really get to know the student. It's more or less a three-month job interview.

I try to impress upon my students how important it is to treat an internship like a real job. It's not just a class that you might occasionally skip. It is the closest thing yet to a real-world experience in your chosen field. If you don't take this opportunity seriously, you will be making a grave error. But if you are punctual, respectful, cooperative, work well independently, welcome constructive criticism, and work harder than you ever have before, I guarantee that your efforts will be noticed and rewarded. Emerson is saying this very thing when he writes: "Do your work and I shall know you. Do your work and you shall reinforce yourself."

These carefully chosen words are not just applicable for interns, they are of value for anyone in any setting. People take note of our performance and our efforts. They are quick to make judgments about us based on what they observe. We, therefore, need to send out the correct signals. We should never work our hardest only when we know we are being watched, and then decelerate when we're no longer under surveillance. We are setting ourselves up for failure. If you do your best at all times, you have nothing to worry about. Whenever a superior would happen to notice your effort, you would be at optimal performance. No false pretenses. Nothing to hide.

I have always tried to give my students advice that I think will benefit them in the classroom and in life. I tell them never to give someone exactly what they ask for — always give them more. And why? Because no one else will — and you'll be setting yourself apart from all the others. If an instructor asks students for a 5 to 7-page paper, it is virtually guaranteed that the vast majority will submit five pages — or more likely, four and a half. And if a minimum of five sources are required, most papers will have five bibliographic entries. I advise my students never to give an instructor or supervisor or anyone else for that matter the absolute minimum — always give them more. And don't do so just to stand out, do so because the learning experience will be enhanced.

If a boss asks you to submit a proposal with four or five ideas for whatever, don't return with just four or five. Don't send the message that you are a person who will only do what you absolutely have to. I had a student a few years back who, following graduation, interviewed for a job as a commercial copywriter at a medium-market television station in the area. He called me as soon as the interview was over. "So, how'd it go?" I asked. The young man told me that he thought things had gone fairly well, but he was a little nervous about the assignment he had been given. The interviewer had handed him two newspaper ads (one for a restaurant and one for an electronics store in the area). He asked him to convert each from a print ad to a television spot. The young man asked me if I had any suggestions. I told him that he would have to supply the creative juices, but I did give him two pieces of advice. I told him to call each location and to ask them how they would want their businesses featured if they were ever to buy television time. I also told him to write, not one commercial for each business, but to write two.

A week or so later at the follow-up interview, the new grad presented his ideas. Before the interview concluded, he had been offered the job. When the young man asked the interviewer what it was about his writing samples that had caught this gentleman's eye, the TV exec told him that not only were they wonderfully creative, but that he was the only candidate who had submitted more than one ad for each business.

I can't impress upon you just how important it is to strive for your personal best with each and every performance, to demonstrate a willingness to excel, and to honor a commitment to reject any effort that is just good enough. Never ever settle for good enough. And never give anyone what they ask for — always give them more.

FRIENDSHIP

> "It is one of the blessings of old friends that you can afford to be stupid with them."
>
> Ralph Waldo Emerson
>
> (from "Self-Reliance," *Essays, First Series*, 1847)

I think that anyone who has close friends would applaud this Emerson quotation. What I personally like best about it is the fact that it seems to give us permission to be silly in front of certain friends — not all mind you, but you know the ones that Emerson is referring to. These are the people to whom you can tell anything. These are the folks who will not judge you when you confess an indiscretion. They offer encouragement not criticism. And, other than immediate family, they are the first ones with whom you share your successes.

A few pages back I told you about a man name Pat, a driver with a trucking firm that delivered merchandise for Montgomery Ward. I shared with you how my time with this wonderful soul turned my worst summer into my best. He was so positive, so uplifting, and just so much fun to be around. When he asked me to be his regular partner that summer, I was thrilled. As you can imagine, we became fast friends. Within a few weeks, he became someone with whom I could share my innermost feelings. And he just didn't pretend to be interested, he was genuinely interested.

And when I recall my time with Pat, I can't help but think about how much I laughed during those hot, sticky summer months in Chicago that year. When you spend ten hours a day holed up in the cab of a delivery truck with one other person, you had better become friends. The alternative would have become relatively unpleasant. It was a joy spending so much time with someone who so loved life. Pat could find something positive in any situation. He even managed to turn back-breaking moments — lifting refrigerators and ranges and sleeper couches up several flights of stairs — into athletic contests. And then there were the games.

Pat loved games. My favorite had to do with acquiring free food. Now you have to understand that both of us had pretty good appetites. And stopping for a quick lunch at a neighborhood diner never really filled the bill. An hour later we were hungry again. So Pat came up with a game whereby we would attempt to have food offered to us by customers — but the rule was that you couldn't ask for it. You could make comments about food but could never directly request any. It didn't take long to figure out how to master this competition. If we walked through a kitchen and spotted a bowl of fruit on the table, an offhand "Now that is the shiniest apple I think I've ever seen" was quickly followed by "Well, would you guys like one?"

Our best meal took place one afternoon when we were delivering an easy chair to a second floor apartment. As soon as we walked through the door, we looked at each other and smiled. The fragrance was enticing. After we set the chair in a corner of the living room and removed the protective plastic covering, I looked up at the customer, a middle-aged woman wearing an apron and said, "Boy, something sure smells good." She smiled. We had seen that smile before. And moments later, we found ourselves sitting at the kitchen table with placemats, table settings, glasses of lemonade, and hot, steamy bowls of chop suey. And then, of course, there was the time we had to deliver a new freezer to an ice cream parlor. I don't even have to tell you what happened. I do, however, remember feeling somewhat sick after we left there.

Whenever our stomachs were full, we enjoyed another pastime called "The Frenchman." In this game, Pat would pretend to be a newly-arrived immigrant from France. When we entered someone's home, he would begin to spew a litany of unintelligible French gibberish. I, of course, was his interpreter. Everything that came out of his mouth was nonsense, so I really had to think on my feet, especially when customers would ask, and they always did, "What did he just say?" They always seemed to find it fascinating that an authentic Frenchman had graced their home.

But one afternoon when we were parked in front of someone's house, and Pat was in the back of the truck looking for a piece of merchandise, we met our match. Pat spotted a woman walking up to the truck and decided to break into his famous French tongue. And he decided to lay it on really thick. He became a crazed Frenchman, flailing his arms and babbling uncontrollably. It was priceless. I couldn't help but notice the smile on the woman's face when she approached the truck. The conversation went something like this:

> "Is he French?" she asked.
> "Yes," I said.
> "Do you know what he's saying?" she said.
> "Sometimes," I answered. "But when he gets crazy like this, I just can't make it out."

She grinned. "Don't go anywhere. Let me get my husband. He speaks French."

"Oh, that's not necessary," I said, knowing that we were about to get busted.

"It's no problem. I'll be right back," she replied.

After the woman was gone I relayed to Pat that her French-speaking husband was on his way out. We needed to think fast. And I'm not particularly proud to say that we took the coward's way out. No, we didn't tell them the truth. Instead, we made up a story that Pat was so angry now that he refused to speak to anyone—including a fellow countryman. No matter how hard her husband tried to coax him to open up, Pat remained tight lipped. And once inside the house, you can bet we didn't try to solicit any tasty morsels from those folks. We were content to lick our wounds.

When we got back in the truck, we laughed and laughed about the close call. If we were to continue this silliness, we decided that we needed a more effective escape route. And we retold that story countless times in the next couple of months.

As Emerson suggests, just get "stupid" with a friend sometimes. It's great fun, it creates memories, and it can be great therapy for what ails you.

> "A friend is a person with whom I may be sincere. Before him I may think aloud."
>
> Ralph Waldo Emerson
>
> (from "Friendship," *Essays, First Series*, 1865)

Studies have shown that a person who is more sociable is happier. A person who is more outgoing is more likely to survive longer with a debilitating illness than a person who is more introverted. A person with a lot of friends generally lives longer. These are facts that can't be ignored. Emerson has written a great deal about the importance of close friendships. There just doesn't appear to be any downside to developing a tight, close-knit grouping of friends.

In 1992 researchers at the Australian Longitudinal Study of Aging embarked on a 10-year research project to measure the benefits of friendship. They published their findings in the 2005 issue of the journal of epidemiology and community health. Researchers studied nearly 1500 people past age 70 and discovered that individuals with strong networks of close friends lived longer than those with very few close friends. The study also found that those people with strong friendships who experienced profound changes in their lives (the death of a spouse or family member, or when close friends moved away) enjoyed beneficial effects that prolonged their lives.

One of the most surprising findings of this study revealed that close contact with children and relatives seemed to have little impact on the risk of death. But a strong network of friends significantly reduced the risk. Also those older adults with a strong support network of friends were 22% less likely to die during the study than those with the weakest network of close friendships. One explanation might be that friends seem to exert a healthy influence on risky behaviors such as smoking and drinking, as well as having an effect on a person's mood and self-esteem.

The facts seem undeniable — we will live more complete, more fulfilling, and longer lives with a support network of friends. But having friends and maintaining friendships are two completely different things. There's a certain amount of work involved. If you're not willing to extend yourself and create opportunities to keep a friendship healthy and alive, then you lose some of the benefits described above. And I for one need to be taking some advice from Emerson and the Australian study.

I have one very close friend who lives 2000 miles away. We communicate via e-mail at least once a week. But we only see one another once a year when we meet up for a weekend in Las Vegas. Our friendship goes back to fourth grade. He knows things about me that my wife doesn't know. Something that makes our friendship so strong is the fact that we were inseparable during our adolescent years, the formative years. All of the questions and uncertainties surrounding puberty we shared. During that time you experience some of the most important, emotional, and character-building moments of your life. And you usually remember with whom you shared them.

Other than this person whom I consider my best friend, I don't have a lot of other close relationships. I have dozens of acquaintances, but very few who might be called best friends. I have two siblings, and my wife has ten, so we have a number of close family ties. I did have a very close friend, one from college, who died of complications from AIDS a few years back. I still miss him. I suppose what I am trying to say is that you should do as I say, not as I do—or rather what Emerson says. This is an area where I need to improve. I've known that for years. I need to do a better job of picking up the phone, or cranking out an e-mail, if for no other reason than just to say hi.

The reasons to do so could not be any clearer. The Australian study says it all. The benefits of rekindling friendships, as well as maintaining friendships, are obvious. The times we spend with friends are not only pleasant experiences, but they are mentally and emotionally uplifting, and good for our overall health. If you're anything like me, make it a point this week to pick up the phone or just send a quick e-mail to someone whose friendship you would miss if that person were suddenly gone. In his opening statement, Emerson virtually guarantees that the experience will be something we wish we would have done weeks, months, or even years ago.

"The only way to have a friend is to be one."

Ralph Waldo Emerson

(from "Friendship," *Essays, First Series*, 1865)

A couple of years ago, I was approached by a couple of my students who asked me to consider joining Facebook. I declined. I have always felt that you need to maintain a level of professionalism when dealing with students, and joining a social networking site, for me, just didn't seem appropriate. I am not condemning those instructors who do, it's just that I believe the relationship between a teacher and a student is a fragile one, and if you cross a certain line, you risk muddying things up. Students need mentors and role models, but it is very difficult and very dangerous to be both a teacher and a buddy. There needs to be a safe distance. It's not that you can't be a sounding board for young people who just need to dump on someone occasionally, it's just that you need to remember your role.

When I asked these same students *why* they wanted me to join Facebook, they said "So, we could be your friends." Look closely at Emerson's words above. It takes more than someone "friending" you on Facebook to create a friendship. These sites too loosely throw around the term "friend." If you were to glance over someone's shoulder while they were visiting one of these sites, and you happened to see that this individual had 132 friends, would you really believe that there are 132 other people with whom this person would share his or her deepest, darkest secrets? It's highly doubtful. It might make more sense for social networking sites to refer to these so-called friends as "acquaintances." Emerson does not make light of friendship. And neither should we.

"The only way to have a friend is to be one." And it's so much more than being "friended" on the Internet. Friendship is work—hard work at times. As you get older and take on more responsibilities, there are distractions in your life that now are competing with the time you may have previously spent with friends. With career commitments and family responsibilities, even keeping up with friends through an occasional phone call is an effort. And if you count on just happening to remember to contact someone when you have time, you soon find that more and more time passes between calls. The only way it seems to maintain those important friendships in your life is almost to treat them like chores on your "To Do" list. Now don't get me wrong, I don't mean to minimize the significance of close friends, but work and family obligations and any number of things may frequently trump them unless you make a concerted effort to keep the friendship alive and well.

And how do you know if the friendship needs a restorative shot in the arm? Well, it's easy—you simply find the time to do it. Regardless of your hectic schedule, you make the necessary time to refuel the relationship. I'm not going to suggest that at the end of this section you pick up the phone or sit at the computer and crank out an e-mail to a friend who has been on your mind lately. There's no need to make such a suggestion because if it truly is important to you—truly important—you won't have to be reminded to do so. If, however, you keep meaning to reconnect with someone but never seem to find the time to do so, then for whatever reason, this friendship is not quite as important to you as you might have thought.

One mistake that people tend to make in an effort to stay current with friends is when they wait for the other person to contact them because it's *their* turn. Close friends don't have to take turns. If a friendship is important enough to you, it matters not who called last, who e-mailed last, or who invited you over last. And if you're keeping track of these stats, then re-think your commitment to this friendship. It may not be as genuine as you think.

When in doubt, simply take Emerson's advice: be a true friend to someone and give them the same attention that you would want to receive. If you do so, you'll never again have to be reminded to call or write. It will all happen naturally.

"A friend may well be reckoned the masterpiece of nature."

Ralph Waldo Emerson

(from "Friendship," *Essays, First Series*, 1865)

In 1946 RKO Radio Pictures released the Frank Capra holiday classic, *It's a Wonderful Life*. In the film's final scene, we find George Bailey holding a copy of Mark Twain's, *Tom Sawyer*, and reading a note from his guardian angel, Clarence Oddbody. It is a hand-written note with a message that captures the essence of this film: "Dear George, Remember no man is a failure who has friends. Thanks for the wings, Love, Clarence." The American Film Institute chose this film as the #1 most inspirational movie of all time. It's hard to argue with that decision.

This movie once and for all answered the question: How do you measure the value of friendship? If you believe the lessons learned from the film's main character, it is easy to see that true friendship conquers all. But are friends more loyal than our own flesh and blood? Or is it still safe to say that blood is thicker than water? Solomon has his own take on this subject. In Proverbs 18:24, he writes: "A man that hath friends must shew himself friendly; and there is a friend that sticketh closer than a brother."

Like George Bailey, some of us never learn the meaning of friends until we have suffered through an injury or a personal setback. Then you will truly discover who your friends are. Another way to identify true friendship is when you experience just the opposite—success. Notice the reaction of coworkers, acquaintances, and those whom you believe to be your friends when you have been recognized for a particular honor. A few years back as I've mentioned earlier, I was fortunate enough to have sold a screenplay. I was excited about sharing the news with relatives and friends. In some cases their reactions surprised me. There were some people who seemed more excited about it than I was. It was a joy to share the details with them. Then there was a group—people who I considered friends—who appeared happy for me, but in a reserved manner. It was almost as if you could hear them saying: "The lucky stiff. Why should this happen to him?"

This was an eye-opening experience for me. I was a little disappointed in the reactions from the latter group, but it afforded me some valuable insights. I finally learned who my true friends were. As corny and as trite as it sounds, a true friend is someone who is there in good times and in bad. And although it may not seem that way, I believe that it is easier to judge a person's character based on how the individual reacts to the successes in your life, than to your failures. It isn't difficult to tell when someone is genuinely happy for you, or when they're paying you lip service. The ability to detect true human emotions is instinctive. We are all able to determine the difference between genuineness and duplicity.

If you have friends who seem so happy for you when you succeed, you had better hold tightly onto them. They are the real McCoys. I have a former student of mine, now a successful attorney in town, who has followed my writing career. When I see him, he always asks how things are going. If I happen to have good news to share with him, he lights up. It's almost as if *he* is the one who has accomplished this feat. I think it's safe to say that he exhibits more emotion about any good fortune that I've enjoyed than I do. He makes it possible for me also to feel good about the accomplishment and not be self-conscious when talking about it. I have discovered that people like this are quite rare.

Whenever I am with this individual and I see just how sincere he is, it makes me think about and assess how I react to the successes of others. I know for a fact that I can do a better job. I like to think I'm improving but there is still work to do. In the last few years I have made it a point to send a congratulatory note to colleagues who have been recognized for particular achievements. I remembered how it felt to receive notes like that, and I wanted others to enjoy the same pleasure. And you would be surprised at how many of those folks take the time to thank you for your thoughts.

So, the next time you have a moment, take the time to identify your true friends. Work tirelessly at keeping these friendships alive and healthy. And recognize these people for what they are—"masterpieces of nature."

HUMILITY

> "Every man I meet is my master in some point, and in that I learn of him."
>
> Ralph Waldo Emerson
>
> (from "Greatness," *Letters and Social Aims*, 1875)

I have always believed that virtually everyone is an expert at something. Most of us do something better than the rest of us. I am always happy to defer to a specialist—and there are millions of them out there. The sooner we recognize this, as did Emerson, the sooner we may live our lives with one of the greatest of all gifts—humility. Imagine if everyone believed that each citizen of the world was placed on this earth to contribute in some meaningful way. If there were communities where everyone valued the expertise of his or her fellow man, it just might be the perfect society. If we live by this Emerson principle, and respect one another's skills and talents, most of the arrogance, pride and haughtiness in our world would disappear. If it were only that easy.

If I am experiencing computer problems, I gladly defer to an IT specialist. If sparks shoot out of an outlet, I'm immediately on the horn to an electrician. If a toilet won't flush, I quickly seek out a plumber. These examples are relatively clear. A lot of folks would do the same. But there are other individuals out there whose skills are not as clearly defined. And it may very well be that they too are masters of some domain. We can't assume that just because a person is not wearing a uniform associated with some trade, that he or she is not a specialist of some kind.

We need to believe that everyone possesses a talent of some nature. The talents of some are quite obvious. The talents of others may not have been discovered yet. As I stated above, I believe that virtually everyone is some kind of expert. I hedged with the word "virtually." There are some individuals unfortunately who choose not to develop these skills. But it's not because they lack the talent. They just lack the initiative. Every so often on the news we are warned about the latest computer virus—one capable of infecting our e-mail address books, destroying our hard drives, or worse. And I can't help but think of the amazingly talented, but misguided individuals responsible for unleashing such havoc. Had the energies of these people been harnessed and redirected, there's no telling how much good they might have done in the legitimate computer industry.

Then there's the story of Frank Abagnale Jr., who, before the age of 19, managed to swindle millions of dollars from Pan Am and Lufthansa while impersonating a commercial pilot. He also played a doctor, an assistant attorney general, and a history professor. Before he was caught, Frank had passed more than $4,000,000 in bad checks in 26 countries. There is no question that Frank Abagnale Jr. possessed a unique gift—even if that gift was called larceny. It wasn't until he was captured that he put his expertise to good use. As part of a work release program, Frank became an indentured servant of the FBI, assisting them, albeit reluctantly, in their forgery department to help identify fraud and scam artists. In 2002, DreamWorks released the film, "Catch Me if You Can," starring Leonardo DiCaprio and Tom Hanks. It was based on Abagnale's autobiography of the same name.

But this is not what Emerson had in mind when he wrote: "Every man I meet is my master…" He knew that we all have the ability to use our God-given talents to create positive outcomes. Emerson wasn't referring to those who choose to use their talents to line their own pockets with ill-gotten gain. The "masters" he speaks of are the everyday heroes—those individuals who play fair—those individuals of high moral fiber—those individuals who recognize that they have an obligation to leave this planet in better condition than they found it.

These are the masters of whom Emerson speaks. They might be postal carriers, auto mechanics, firefighters, retail workers, carpenters, teachers, beauticians, etc. We interact with many of these folks every day, and we should recognize their unique skills, and treat them with the respect they have earned. Consider this—the next time your paths cross, just automatically assume that your fellow man is gifted, talented, and knows a little more about a particular subject than do you. Give that person the benefit of the doubt. That way of thinking allows us to practice one of the greatest of all virtues—humility.

"Every hero becomes a bore at last."

Ralph Waldo Emerson

(from "Uses of Great Men," *Representative Men*, 1876)

When was the last time you referred to yourself in the third person? Hopefully you've never done so. It is one of my pet peeves. It's like fingernails on a chalkboard. I feel an immediate disconnect whenever I hear it. You rarely if ever hear private citizens refer to themselves in this manner. More often than not, it usually comes from a person who is new to the celebrity game. It's almost an out-of-body experience. These newly-anointed celebs no longer see themselves from within. It's as if they're on a stage or on a playing field, and they are watching themselves perform. The practice is at best unattractive.

Many professional athletes have a nasty habit of using the third person when they talk about themselves. If they could only realize how it sounds to others, they might abandon it forever. This type of personal reference is a perfect example of what Emerson means when he says, "Every hero becomes a bore at last." And who's to blame? We needn't look far. We, the public, bear responsibility for nurturing this ugly practice. If we continue to pay outrageous prices for ballpark and stadium and concert admissions, we have only ourselves to blame. Besides lucrative television and radio contracts, team owners rely on the profits from admissions to offset the costs of player salaries. As long as we keep filling the stadiums and continue paying obscene amounts of money to attend sporting and entertainment events, the vicious cycle will drag on.

And what about celebrities who use their popularity to set a personal agenda? It almost gives them an unfair advantage. Should talk show hosts and actors be permitted to endorse political candidates publicly? Their celebrity status alone guarantees them an audience, but what makes *them* more informed than the rest of us? Nothing really. They have gained prominence not because of their insightful political banter, but rather for any other number of reasons. When stars use their own popularity to influence the public on matters totally unrelated to their individual specialties, that is when we must tune them out, and instead make personal decisions—informed decisions—based on our own research.

Or how about celebrities who suddenly become authorities on topics they have no business delving into. Should we follow the advice of a former sitcom star who preaches her own gospel on healthy eating and lifestyle changes? No one would argue that many Americans could do a far better job when it comes to wellness. But wouldn't it make more sense to follow the advice of licensed nutritionists and physicians before embarking on an unproven program developed by an amateur? It takes more than being merely interested in a particular topic to be able to offer sound medical opinions. And what about screen stars who have become, without training, authorities on postpartum depression, or prophets for a trendy religious organization? Now that's scary *and* boring.

The question I would like to pose to Emerson is why — why do our heroes ultimately turn into bores? Why do they become jaded? We might want to blame *fortune and fame* for having spoiled the lot? But it isn't necessarily the lot. There are a number of celebrities who manage to avoid the paparazzi and the tabloids. Are they just the lucky ones whose indiscretions haven't yet been caught on tape? Are they the ones whose lives are too uninteresting to chronicle? Or is it something more basic? Perhaps they are simply the individuals with character — individuals who value their own privacy and that of their families — individuals who don't seek unnecessary attention. Those are the heroes who have avoided morphing into bores.

One such hero is the late Paul Newman, who stepped out of his comfort zone on the big screen, and we're all better off for it. In 1982 he founded "Newman's Own," a line of products consisting of tomato sauces, salad dressings, popcorn and more. That same year he created Newman's Own Foundation, an organization that has given more than $250 million to various charities to date. The foundation continues Paul Newman's commitment to donate all of its profits to charity. And if that weren't noble enough, Newman created the Hole in the Wall Camps in 1988 — the world's largest family of camps for children with serious medical conditions. Thus far more than 100,000 kids have attended these camps, and they have all done so free of charge.

With this quotation, Emerson has issued a spoiler alert. He's divulging the surprise ending — many of our heroes, even well-intentioned ones, will eventually start believing their own press clippings, and will ultimately run off at the mouth. In no time, they will have been transformed into bores. It is important to understand the effect that power, popularity and wealth can have on a person. They can become as mind-altering as alcohol and drugs. They can fool individuals into believing that they alone, not the experts, have the answers. It is critical for us to pay close attention to this potential metamorphosis and to be able to discern when the hero disappears and the bore emerges. It is then time to pay less attention.

"A great man is always willing to be little."

Ralph Waldo Emerson

(from "Compensation," *Essays, First Series*, 1865)

When I was researching this book, I came upon hundreds of Emerson quotations—one more insightful than the next. When I stumbled upon this one from his 1865 "Compensation" essay, I knew immediately that I had to include it. For me, it is one of the most powerful statements within this text. If put into practice, it is the type of advice that can be life altering. It helps remind us that whatever our lot in life, in whatever social class we reside, we cannot forget that humility is a requirement for a prudent, virtuous life, and must be practiced on a daily basis. You can't be humble only when it's convenient.

If we examine the excerpt that contains the above reference, we can see Emerson's passion for humility:

> A great man is always willing to be little. Whilst he sits on the cushion of advantages, he goes to sleep. When he is pushed, tormented, defeated, he has a chance to learn something; he has been put on his wits, on his manhood; he has gained facts; learns his ignorance; is cured of the insanity of conceit; has got moderation and real skill. The wise man throws himself on the side of his assailants. It is more his interest than it is theirs to find his weak point. The wound cicatrizes and falls off from him like a dead skin, and when they would triumph, lo! he has passed on invulnerable.

Emerson seems to be suggesting that in order to be considered a great man or woman, we must dismiss conceit and embrace humility. Oftentimes when people climb the ladder of success, they tend to forget from where they came. We need to remember the age-old advice: Be kind to the people you meet on the way up; they're the same ones you meet on the way down. Unfortunately, not everyone seems to follow this wise counsel. It is important for us to realize that when we practice humility, we shouldn't expect a pat on the back for having done so. It's not something we do to impress someone, it is, in no uncertain terms, a prerequisite for greatness.

There are times when our corporate and political leaders need to be reminded that "a great man is always willing to be little." One such leader who needed a reminder was Lawrence Rawls, CEO of Exxon. In 1989 the oil tanker *Exxon Valdez* hit a reef in Prince William Sound, splitting open and releasing eleven million gallons of crude. The spill contaminated 1,300 miles of coastline, killing more than 250,000 sea birds, nearly 3000 sea otters, 300 harbor seals, 22 killer whales and 250 bald eagles. Instead of rushing to the scene to inspect the damage, Mr. Rawls sent an underling in his place. He did manage to break away and visit the site some three weeks later. The spill turned into a public relations nightmare for Exxon, and was exacerbated by the unresponsiveness of its leader.

Russian President, Vladimir Putin, made a similarly regretful decision a decade later. In 2000 the Russian nuclear submarine, Kursk, lost radio contact with its command base while taking part in training exercises in the Barents Sea. Initially the government told the public that the Kursk had collided with another NATO submarine, but that all of the 118 crew members were safe. It was later learned that one of the torpedoes aboard the sub had exploded, causing the ill-fated Kursk to sink to the bottom of the sea bed, some 108 meters deep. President Putin learned of the disaster while vacationing at a southern Russia resort. Instead of traveling to the Arctic to oversee rescue efforts, he elected to remain on vacation for nearly a week before visiting the Kursk's home base where he was greeted by an angry crowd. When rescuers finally reached the crippled sub, they discovered that all 118 crew members had been killed in the explosion.

Conversely, one year later, in the aftermath of 9/11, New York mayor Rudy Giuliani did what Exxon's Rawls and Russia's Putin elected not to do. Within minutes of the terrorist attacks on the Twin Towers, he was on the scene at Ground Zero making executive decisions and fielding reporters' questions. In the days that followed, he was present at dozens of funerals for the victims.

Great men must be willing to be little. In fact, all men and women must be willing to be little. They must be willing to get their hands dirty, and must never feel that any chore is beneath them. And that willingness is the true test of greatness.

"It is a capital blunder...when another man recites his charities."

Ralph Waldo Emerson

(from "Heroism," *Essays, First Series*, 1841)

Whenever my students are preparing for interviews for internships or jobs, they frequently stop in the office for a few pointers. I recite to them a litany of do's and don'ts. I tell them to dress appropriately, to arrive early, to sit upright, to maintain eye contact, to always remain positive, to never criticize any previous employer or place of employment, and when asked "why you want this job," don't tell them it's because you need a job, or that this one pays better than your last job, or that it's closer to your home, or that the hours are better, or any other number of inane reasons. You want this job because you want *this* job. And before these students leave the office, I add the most important piece of advice: "And one more thing — always remember — humility is a virtue."

I want my students to appear confident, to have faith in their own abilities, to be proud of what they have accomplished — but never to appear presumptuous or overconfident. It is an ugly trait and one sure to leave a sour taste in the mouths of recruiters. When I have to listen to someone who makes it a point to "recite his charities," I am immediately turned off. And I always think of the parable found in the book of St. Luke. I find myself wanting to suggest to these individuals that they pick up a copy of the New Testament, turn to Luke, Chapter 18, and read about the perils of pretentiousness. But I never actually do so. I just hope that someday they will figure it out.

The passage found in Luke 18:9-14 is a parable that many are familiar with:

> He (Jesus) also told this parable to some who trusted in themselves that they were righteous and regarded others with contempt: "Two men went up to the temple to pray, one a Pharisee and the other a tax collector. The Pharisee, standing by himself, was praying thus: 'God, I thank you that I am not like other people — thieves, rogues, adulterers, or even like this tax collector. I fast twice a week; I give a tenth of all my income.'

> "But the tax collector, standing far off, would not even look up to heaven, but was beating his breast and saying, 'God, be merciful to me, a sinner!' "I tell you this man went down to his home justified rather than the other; for all who exalt themselves will be humbled, but all who humble themselves will be exalted."

It is hardly a coincidence that some of Emerson's writings are in line with biblical teachings. Ralph Waldo Emerson was the son of a Unitarian minister, and he himself attended divinity school at Harvard. It's hard to believe that he wasn't deeply influenced by biblical passages, especially this one. Emerson's quote, "It is a capital blunder…when another man recites his charities," is so beautifully captured in the "The Parable of the Pharisee and the Tax Collector."

We've all known people who make it a point to remind us what they have accomplished. It may be somewhat interesting at first but it's not long before they have crossed the line to egotistical bore. We know what we would prefer not to hear. It should be a reminder to us when we begin reciting our own charities or doting on the accomplishments of our children that others, like us, would probably choose to be spared the details. Now I'm not referring to relatives or best friends. Who wouldn't want to share good news with parents and siblings, and the closest of friends. I'm referring to neighbors and coworkers and people who we'd label as acquaintances rather than friends.

If you're the kind of person who likes to share with others the names of organizations you support, you need to ask yourself an important question. Are you giving out of the goodness of your heart, or are you hoping to be recognized for your gift? When you receive a charity's list of donors, do you quickly scour it in search of your name? I think we have to ask ourselves why we give—is it truly to help others, or is it for recognition? If you can say that you would just as gladly give anonymously to these worthy institutions, then you will have answered the question.

INGENUITY

> "Explore, and explore. Be neither chided nor flattered out of your position of perpetual inquiry."
>
> Ralph Waldo Emerson
>
> (from an oration delivered before the Literary Societies at Dartmouth College, July 24, 1838)

If you're a parent or you've ever spent much time around small children, you know that little ones can be quite inquisitive. Some kids will ask you a question and be perfectly satisfied with your answer. Others, however, may pose the same question but appear less than satisfied with your response. These are the ones for whom the phrase "curiouser and curiouser" may be applied. Following each of your well-phrased answers, these children reply "But why?" over and over and over again. And after a while, your answers and your patience begin to run out. You know full well that you would never want to suppress the curiosity of a child, but at times it seems that no matter what you say, the youngster will never be satisfied with your response. It's somewhat frustrating…but it's also encouraging. This is a child who will no doubt possess a more analytical mind, and who among us wouldn't want that for our own son or daughter. And so as irksome as the "why, why, why" can be, you know that in the end, a child with a deep desire to know how things work, or why things happen the way they do, is a young person who, when he or she is older, will be no stranger to ingenuity.

When Emerson tells us to "Explore and explore," he is encouraging us to do the same as our young inquisitive friends. He wants us never to be complacent—never to settle—never to simply accept something purely on faith if we have any reservations about it. And once we have researched a subject and have confidence in our findings, he wants us to be steadfast in our beliefs—never to allow someone to "chide" or intimidate us into altering our position—and conversely, never to allow a "flattering" or smooth-talking adversary to exert pressure that might cause us to rethink our stance.

There are two messages here—never stop wondering, never stop questioning, never stop probing for the truth. And when you believe you have discovered it, remain steadfast in your beliefs and resist the pressure to alter your views. I think it is important to point out here that maintaining your conviction is significantly different than acting in an obstinate manner. We've all met people who are brick walls; it is impossible to penetrate them. They are small-minded and intolerant.

Emerson is not suggesting severe rigidity. Rather he wants us to believe in ourselves and not to waver. But it does not mean being close-minded and disrespectful of the views of others.

"Explore and explore" can be accomplished in many ways. You must allow yourself to be open to new experiences—from trying a new food for the first time, to traveling to another part of the world. From reading a new book that you otherwise might not have read, to doing something totally out of character—attending a play, a ballet, or a lecture. It might mean taking flying or skydiving lessons, swimming with the dolphins, going on a mountain-climbing expedition, or chartering a boat for a day of deep-sea fishing. It matters little what manner of exploration you choose, but if there is something that you have wondered about for years, it may finally be time to discover the mystery and fascination behind it.

Exploration also includes fighting for causes. If there is a particular social issue about which you feel passionately, don't stand on the sidelines and let the more-dedicated souls do battle—join them, embrace them, and take up this cause as your own. In order to accept this challenge, you may have to make some painful decisions about your schedule. But allocating time for an activity that energizes you physically, mentally and spiritually, is well worth re-examining how efficiently you have been managing your time. If the desire is strong enough, you will easily find the time to *explore and explore*—and never stop asking *why*.

"Intellect annuls fate. So far as a man thinks, he is free."

Ralph Waldo Emerson

(from "Fate," *The Conduct of Life*, 1860)

If we believe that our lives are controlled by fate or destiny, then we might as well just sit back and watch. We might as well just go through the motions. If free will and freedom of choice are meaningless, and our future has been predetermined, why even try? Why would it be in our best interests to live a virtuous life? If our fate is already sealed, then why not simply enjoy our mortal lives to the fullest, and not worry about the consequences of our actions? If things are already predestined, then what's all the fuss about?

There are some people who allow fate to dictate their lives. They feel that no matter what they do, things will still turn out a certain way. Personally, it would be so depressing to think that I had no control over what happens in my life. Look at the Emerson principle above. See what he's saying. If we use our minds to the fullest, we can obliterate fate. We can and do control our own destinies. Decisions that we make and actions that we take do affect our outcomes. And the alignment of the stars is meaningless. If you were involved in an accident today, it wasn't because your horoscope said you were destined to have a bad day — you had an accident because of someone's negligence — either yours or someone else's. And your horoscope could just as easily have promised you a glorious day. As you might guess, I am not a fan of astrology. I do not read my daily horoscope. I don't even read it for entertainment purposes. I don't believe in it, and I don't want it in any way to affect any decision-making process. I don't want to know if some astrologer is predicting that today is going to be a good day or a bad day for me. I plan on doing everything in my power to make it a good day, regardless of the warnings in a silly horoscope column.

The second part of the above quote, "As long as a man thinks, he is free," further debunks the idea that fate plays a role in our lives. If we use our minds, we have the ability to escape from the restraints that hold us in place — from the shackles of complacency. Right here and now, we possess the ability to create our own self-driven path, not follow some pre-produced road map. The decisions we make today will dictate future outcomes. How could we face each day thinking anything else? When we take the time to examine some of the choices we have made in our lives, we probably all have a few regrets—indiscretions that we would love to take back. We oftentimes wonder what might have been had we chosen differently.

There is one clear difference between those of us who believe that our choices directly affect our futures, and those who believe in a predestined existence. And that difference is the chance for a do-over. Just because we may have made poor choices in the past, in no way guarantees that we will continue down the same self-destructive path. If we dismiss fate, we have the ability to embark on a new life journey, and make more prudent choices.

People who abuse their bodies with tobacco, alcohol, high-fat foods, and little to no exercise will undoubtedly pay the price when their bodies rebel against them. And is it fate that causes them to have a heart attack or stroke? Is it fate that deals them a wake-up call? Hardly. For most people, heart disease is a direct result of poor choices. But it doesn't mean that you are destined to continue the same poor nutritional habits. You have the ability to make the necessary changes in your diet, your exercise regimen, etc. You will either choose to alter this behavior or not. The key word here is *choose*—not fate.

Make a promise to yourself today to make some new choices—some better choices. Never assume that you are destined to continue making decisions that you will later regret. You *can* change. You *must* change. And if you decide to do nothing—well, that's a choice as well. Never blame any outcome on fate. Recognize that human decision-making created that result. And human decision-making can undo it.

"The revelation of thought takes men out of servitude into freedom."

Ralph Waldo Emerson

(from "Fate," *The Conduct of Life*, 1860)

The phrase "servitude into freedom" sounds a lot like "rags to riches." And when I hear the latter phrase, I immediately think of Horatio Alger Jr. Over the years whenever someone has related a tale of hard work and social mobility, it wouldn't be unusual to hear someone else say, "Oh, there's another Horatio Alger story." Alger, a 19th century author, wrote a series of juvenile novels in which the main character was frequently a downtrodden boy in an impoverished neighborhood who, by working tirelessly and by exhibiting high moral character, would ultimately rise up from the slums to earn respectability and financial reward. Alger is best known for his novel, <u>Ragged Dick</u>, about a poor bootblack (shoeshine boy) who embarks on the typical *rags to riches* journey so often associated with the author.

I find the connection between Alger and Emerson so interesting for a number of reasons. Alger was the son of a Unitarian minister, as was Emerson. Alger attended the Harvard Divinity School, as did Emerson. Alger spent only a short time in the ministry before resigning, like Emerson. But that is where the comparisons stop. Following the death of his wife, Ralph Waldo Emerson left the ministry after serving only three years. Alger's reason for leaving the church had to do with a suspected, but never proven, scandal. Rather than continuing to perpetuate this rumor, let's just say that these two men, whose lives overlapped, found common ground in the belief that individuals of lesser means can and do climb out of poverty and into success and wealth.

One such example of how intellect spurred one man's rise in stature is the story of industrialist and philanthropist, Andrew Carnegie. The Scottish-born Carnegie had little formal education but was fortunate to have grown up in a home where learning was of paramount importance. The son of a weaver, Carnegie later became one of the most successful businessmen in the world. And like the characters in Alger's novels, he began with nothing. In 1848 when he was only 13, Carnegie and his family came to America and settled in Pennsylvania. Shortly thereafter he took a job in a factory that paid him $1.20 a week. A year later he was hired as a telegraph messenger, and it wasn't long before he was promoted to telegraph operator. Two years later, he was hired by the Pennsylvania

Railroad as a telegrapher. It was during his time with the railroad that Carnegie learned a great deal about the business world. And within three years, he assumed the position of superintendent.

While working for the railroad, Carnegie began making investments — wise investments — mostly in oil. He was able to leave his post in 1865 to focus exclusively on his business investments. In less than a decade, Carnegie founded his own steel company. And not just any steel company but one that revolutionized steel production in this country. He built plants nationwide and implemented new technologies that ensured higher productivity for steel manufacturing. But Carnegie wasn't content with product production alone. Instead of relying on suppliers for the necessary raw materials, he began producing them himself, along with purchasing his own ships, railroads and coal fields. This strategy of controlling each phase of the process enabled Carnegie to become an industry leader, not to mention a very wealthy man. By 1889, the Carnegie Steel Corporation was the largest steel manufacturer in the world.

In that same year Carnegie put into place a philosophical approach regarding wealth that he had held for quite some time. From a lifetime of acquiring riches, he now decided it was time to begin redistributing it. He expressed those views in a book entitled The Gospel of Wealth, where he wrote that all personal wealth, other than what was absolutely needed to provide for one's family, should be placed in a trust fund to be given away to benefit the community. And Andrew Carnegie was certainly a man of his word. During his lifetime, Carnegie gave away over $350 million, and since his death, Carnegie foundations have continued to donate untold millions to worthy causes.

One of his particular interests was the establishment of libraries across the country to be available to the public to further self-education. The institution that I have called home for nearly 30-plus years, North Central College in Naperville, Illinois, was the recipient of a gift from the Carnegie Corporation of New York back in 1908 — a $25,000 donation to build a new library on campus.

I can't think of a better example to illustrate the Emerson quotation above than Andrew Carnegie. Unlike some moguls who inherit wealth, Carnegie was a self-made man. Through drive, insight, and an incredible work ethic, he turned his investments into millions. But more than that, Carnegie was one of the most generous benefactors in history. He not only knew how to create wealth, but knew the noblest way to rid himself of it. The Emerson quotation, "The revelation of thought takes men out of servitude into freedom," had to have been coined with someone like Andrew Carnegie in mind.

"Hitch your wagon to a star."

Ralph Waldo Emerson

(from "Civilization," *Society & Solitude*, 1870)

I would bet that when you read this Emerson quote, something clicked. You probably remember having heard it countless times but may not have credited it to this gifted author. It has been tossed around for decades. To gain a better understanding of what Emerson intended, it is important to know what he is saying as well as what he is not.

At first glance, depending on how you define the word "star," one may conclude that Emerson is suggesting that we should join the ranks of a celebrity posse. Or he might be telling us to glom onto someone of means—someone onto whom we can leech. But we know better than that. One of the things that Emerson is encouraging us to do by following this passage is to simply…aim high. I am reminded of a saying by motivational speaker and author to whom I have previously referred— Denis Waitley. I recall listening to one of Mr. Waitley's motivational tapes in which he was discussing the topic of setting goals. He said that he likes to set goals *just out of reach, but not out of sight*. I have never forgotten those words. It allows us to have dreams that are achievable. He warns us, however, in the same statement not to set the bar so high that we will forever fail in trying to reach it. It doesn't in any way mean that we should not have lofty goals. It just means that it makes more sense to set for ourselves a series of intermittent achievable goals, and then when we have realized each one, to move that bar up one more notch, and to continue doing so until we reach our ultimate goals.

You can see where this strategy makes perfect sense. With realistic goals, we give ourselves an opportunity to taste success and to celebrate that success, even if it isn't that pie-in-the-sky goal we've been fantasizing about. But in time, by rewriting our list of goals following each successful campaign, we will someday find ourselves jotting down *the* goal—now a realistic goal—that before had only been realized in our imaginations.

Emerson also seems to be telling us to surround ourselves with greatness. And that can be accomplished by associating with positive individuals. It's no secret that those people who appear to possess an overabundance of enthusiasm are also some of the most successful people we know. But don't confuse success with wealth. Certainly in some cases, these individuals have enjoyed financial success, but many others have lived their lives in a compassionate, benevolent, and modest manner. And who would argue that theirs was anything but a successful existence.

Try to identify the most positive people you know. Is there a way of bringing them into your lives? When we surround ourselves with these types of people, we can't help but bathe in the collective optimism. It's contagious. Before we know it, we find ourselves thinking more positively, and we begin to look at our problems differently. They become opportunities. When eternal optimists plan a strategy to overcome obstacles, they concentrate on the rewards of success, not on the price they will pay for failure. This approach keeps everything moving forward and helps them maintain that eternal optimism.

It is important to remember that the positive effects that are created when you surround yourself with enthusiastic people can be just as easily be snuffed out when you surround yourself with negative people. You know the kinds of individuals I'm referring to — the ones who complain and gripe and whine endlessly. These folks drag you down into the depths in which they exist. They can't find a good thing to say about anyone. They live on sarcasm and put-downs. Hang around these people long enough and soon you'll be joining their ranks. The same contagiousness that takes place in positive interactions is present in negative behavior and you'd be surprised just how quickly you can catch the bug.

Examine your friendships. Do you recognize any of the types of people to which we have referred earlier? Begin to distance yourself from negative associations. Start to rejuvenate your positive relationships. And most importantly, hitch *your* wagon to a star.

INTEGRITY

"A little integrity is better than any career."

Ralph Waldo Emerson

(from "Behavior," *The Conduct of Life*, 1860)

I think that we would all like to be able to say that as long as we maintain our integrity, we will be content. But I think sometimes that we give ourselves more credit than we deserve. We fool ourselves into thinking that we are doing a pretty good job. If someone were to ask you if you believed yourself to be a good person, I think that you would probably answer "Yes," as would the vast majority. And we probably recognize the fact that we are not perfect, that we don't always make the right decisions, and that we occasionally slip up…but more often than not, we like to think that we do the right thing. But how often do you have to *do the right thing* for it to count as *most of the time*? Sixty percent? Seventy-five percent? Ninety percent of the time?

Integrity is defined as *a steadfast adherence to a strict moral or ethical code*. Let's break it down even further. Steadfast is defined as *steady, constant, unswerving*. Therefore, we can rewrite the definition of integrity to read: *a constant adherence to a strict ethical code*. Are we still so sure about maintaining our integrity? Is there anyone alive who can say that he or she says and does the right thing at the right time—all the time? I've yet to meet that person. And I'm guessing yours would be a similar answer.

So what's the point of all this nitpicking? I'm simply saying that we are all imperfect. We make mistakes more often than we like to admit. So it makes little sense for us to pat ourselves on the back for doing the right thing. Because within time, we will undoubtedly undo it. Cursing at someone who cuts us off in a supermarket parking lot, and then holding the door for someone else as you enter the store, doesn't exactly even things out. If you want to take the credit for being a person of integrity, you need to do better than a .500 average. Technically, you would need a 1.000 batting average. And it's probably about as difficult to accomplish that as it is for a ballplayer to bat at a 1.000 clip.

If we want to boast about our integrity, or at least believe quietly that we are in that elite club, then we must be vigilant about the kinds of words we use and the actions we take. We must always think before we speak, and think through each action. We must be prudent in everything we do. It almost sounds impossible. Who thinks each time you are about to utter a word? Who stops to consider the ethical ramifications of each and every action? The answer unfortunately is — very few of us. But realistically there's not much we can do about that. Most of our actions are instinctive. Therefore if we want to believe that there is a moral compass within us that guides our actions, we had better make it a point to instill morality into our own psyche. It must become second nature.

Each time we suffer an indiscretion, we need to rethink the hurtful words or inappropriate action. We need to pretend that we've been given a Mulligan — an opportunity for a do-over. We need to imagine that the clock has been turned back a few precious seconds, presenting us with a chance to make different choices. We need to see ourselves reciting the words that we wished we had uttered the first time, or taking the appropriate action that will undoubtedly produce a more pleasant result. Try to imagine this alternative response. Don't concentrate on the mistake. Think about instead the positive feeling that you would have received had you made the right decision. Replay it in your head often enough so that when a similar situation presents itself, this new, more prudent response will be triggered.

It matters little really what we do with our lives if we do so without integrity. When he wrote, "A little integrity is better than any career," it was clear that Emerson recognized the grace and purpose of those who walk with this elusive virtue. And he was not alone in his praise for those who maintain their integrity. In Proverbs 11:3, we read, "The integrity of the upright shall guide them: but the perverseness of transgressors shall destroy them."

> "Trust men and they will be true to you; treat them greatly and they will show themselves great."
>
> Ralph Waldo Emerson
>
> (from "Prudence," *Essays, First Series*, 1865)

When I first came across this Emerson quote, I immediately thought back to a tape that I had listened to years ago. It was by author and motivational speaker, Zig Ziglar. If you haven't figured out by now, I have spent untold hours reading and listening to some of the greatest motivators of our time—Dr. Wayne Dyer, Denis Waitley, Brian Tracy, and Zig Ziglar. I have found myself drawn to these individuals and their writings for a number of reasons—the greatest of which was to get that oft-needed kick in the butt to accomplish a particular project. You can't possibly read any of these authors and not come away with a sense of rejuvenation. They have the ability to help you recharge your engines and to put an end to procrastination. No matter how motivated you may think you are, there are always setbacks in our lives that will bring us down. It is at that precise moment that you may want to pick up some inspirational reading material. I don't know about you but after burying my nose in one of the works by any of the above-named authors, I always feel more energized and better able to manage the challenges at hand.

Well, back to the Zig Ziglar reference I mentioned a moment ago. I recall listening to one of Mr. Ziglar's tapes on personal and professional development. He was talking about the impressions we make when dealing with others, and just how important they are. He spoke of a critical moment in building relationships—that initial point of contact. He encouraged his listeners to do the following: When you first speak to someone, whether it is a phone call or an in-person meeting, always make sure that the individual with whom you are interacting comes away from that meeting feeling that his or her day has somehow been brightened by your presence. These individuals should be glad that they had the opportunity to have spoken with you. In a nutshell, the time spent with you should make their day. And Ziglar wasn't just referring to influential people or potential clients who might be in a position to help further our careers—he was talking about anyone on any level—people in clerical positions, restaurant servers, maintenance workers, etc.

He wanted his listeners and readers to realize that not only is this the correct way to treat people, but it may ultimately produce positive results in the business world. If we reflect on Zig Ziglar's advice, and at the same time, plug in Emerson's words, "Trust men and they will be true to you; treat them greatly and they will show themselves great," we can see that our actions will create a windfall. Other people will so appreciate the consideration and respect that we display, that they will be moved to return a similar gesture. There is nothing really new about this approach. There are a number of biblical references encouraging us to treat people in the same way that we would want to be treated.

Master speaker, author, motivator, Dr. Wayne W. Dyer, in his book, *Real Magic: Creating Miracles in Everyday Life*, seems to address this very point. In a section titled, "Fourteen Keys for Creating A Miracle Mind-set," Key #12 reads: *Ask Nothing of Anyone and Practice Unconditional Acceptance*. Read the following passage and notice how Dr. Dyer appears to reinforce Emerson's words above:

> "This principle frees you up immensely in all areas of your life. You look upon others as gifts of which you ask nothing, while simultaneously you are engaged in your world roles. Even those who are paid to serve you, such as waitresses, clerks, salespeople, attendants, employees and the like, need to have this kind of attention from you. I have expectations and am grateful for whatever they bring into my life in exchange for the salary or fees I pay, but I am not better than they are in any way simply because I have chosen to be the payer and they have chosen to be the payee. These are chosen roles. Nothing more, nothing less. The amazing thing about developing such an attitude is that the less you expect or demand, the more that seems to come your way."

It seems apparent that many insightful thinkers agree on how we should treat others. And whether it be Emerson, Dyer, Ziglar, or any number of biblical evangelists, the message is clear—we must treat others with consideration and respect. Nothing more, nothing less.

"Nothing is at last sacred but the integrity of your own mind."

Ralph Waldo Emerson

(from "Self-Reliance," *Essays, First Series*, 1865)

It is probably safe to say that we all know the difference between right and wrong. Whether or not we practice morality in our daily lives has nothing to do with the fact that we can identify good and evil. It's a choice. And most people would probably like to think that when presented with an ethical dilemma, they would make the right decision. But what if things were blurred? What if the acceptable choice was not as obvious as we would like? Then what?

In the hundreds of communications classes that I have taught in my 30-plus years of instruction, there is one component that is repeatedly discussed—ethics, and more specifically, media ethics. I frequently remind my students that during their careers, at some point, a situation will present itself that will require serious reflection—a moral conflict that will force them to choose sides. It may be a situation with no apparent winner. When I ask them how they would maintain their integrity and make the right call, I oftentimes hear things like, "I would simply do the right thing, that's all. How difficult can that be anyway?" It is at that point that I illustrate several examples where the "just do the right thing" strategy may not produce the results you are looking for.

There is a particular website maintained by the Department of Journalism at Indiana University that I find most helpful in the teaching of ethics. You can find it at http://journalism.indiana.edu/resources/ethics. It is a database that contains a series of ethics cases along with discussion questions for each case. It was created for teachers, journalists, and consumers. I have used material from this site in my classes for years, and it never fails to produce anything but lively conversation. These cases are especially helpful for the study of ethics because there is never a specific right or wrong answer. No matter what decision you make, someone will be unhappy. You are forced to carefully weigh both sides of the controversy, and to try to make the most informed decision based on the circumstances. Each case is a wonderful critical-thinking exercise.

Here is an example of one of the cases. It is entitled "When Journalists Play God," by Brian Ojanpa. Imagine that you are this newspaper reporter. See what you would do if faced with this ethical dilemma. It begins with a phone call:

> It's a plea that's hard to refuse. The person on the phone is telling you of a local family saddled with huge medical bills and looming tragedy.
>
> The parents are unemployed, there's no insurance, and their 4-year-old daughter is stricken with a rare form of cancer. A fund drive is being planned.
>
> "We were wondering if you could do a story," the caller says.
>
> On its face, the story doesn't appear to pose a problem. It has drama, tension, human interest—all the requisites for a compelling feature and heart-rending pictures.
>
> You interview the family, run the story, and go onto other things.
>
> Then the phone rings again. A family with a similar plight has the same request. At this point, news judgment, fairness, and ethics can collide.
>
> Do you agree to do a similar story—again—knowing you may be opening the floodgates for other afflicted parties? Do you fudge on a decision by telling the caller you'll "pass this information on to the appropriate editor"? More bluntly, do you say "yes" to one stricken family and "no" to another? Should you?
>
> Providing coverage of individuals with fatal or potentially fatal diseases poses some sticky questions. The stories, while they can be journalistically justified, also cast the media in the role of private fund-raiser—a role many editors and reporters find uncomfortable. More importantly, these stories cast us in a God-playing role because we, in effect, decide who gets to benefit from the public pocketbook.

So what would you do? Tell the second family that since you had just run a similar story, you would have to take a pass on their request? Or would you agree to run the story even though your editors might balk at the repetition? When Emerson speaks of integrity, it is important to remember that it may not be as simple as just doing the right thing. It may not be as easy as plugging your problem into the "good vs. evil" equation, and producing a perfect solution. It may be far more challenging. It may take careful scrutiny and analysis on your part to divine the answer. And some people may not agree with you. It is therefore critical to give careful thought to each problem you face, to make a decision consistent with your own personal code of ethics, and to remain steadfast when challenged by naysayers.

> "The less a man thinks or knows about his virtues the better we like him."

Ralph Waldo Emerson

(from "Spiritual Laws," *Essays, First Series*, 1865)

To tell you the truth, I struggled with the classification of this Emerson quote. I couldn't decide between *humility* and *integrity*. But since we had already discussed the quote, "It is a capital blunder…when another man recites his charities," it seemed as though we had successfully addressed the tale of the man who sings his own praises. The quotation above is less about pretentious individuals who never let us forget their accomplishments, and more about those who seem unaware of the good deeds they do. These are the folks who perform a task not because there's something in it for them, but because it needs to be done.

We all know people who are very much aware of their virtues. They're easy to spot. These are the ones patting themselves on the back. It's an embarrassment to be around them. It is much more pleasant to congregate with people who are either unaware of their achievements, or who are aware of them, but never let on that they know. These are the ones who gain fame, fortune and respect not because their publicist saw to it, but because it is impossible for us not to have noticed their thoughtful or charitable acts. These are the individuals who never say, "So, what's in it for me?"

I have a favorite quote that my students are probably a little tired of hearing. I will recite it whenever I am in need of a volunteer for a particular project, and especially if their response is somewhat underwhelming. It was coined by motivational speaker and writer, Denis Waitley: "Plant a shade tree under which you know you will never sit." Whenever I use that quotation, it isn't long before the hands start going up. I remind my students, and anyone else who will listen, that the perks and advantages that they now enjoy would not have been possible had it not been for former students who volunteered their time and blazed a trail.

Imagine where we would be today had it not been for the women's suffrage movement, civil rights activists, environmental advocates, etc. We owe a great deal to these individuals who came before us and who accepted the challenge of planting that shade tree. Had they declined, the health of our society would now be in peril. There are many people out there who make it a practice to do wonderful things each and every day but you would never know it by the way they act. These are the individuals who live their lives with quiet grace. They work hard, they provide for their families, they volunteer, they contribute to charitable causes, they give blood (if they can), they enroll in CPR classes, etc. They live their lives with character and purpose, but they don't keep track of their virtues. For them it's not a competition, it's a way of life.

It's only natural to want to be recognized for having done something well. Positive feedback drives all of us. It recharges us. It's a way of finding out if people appreciate our efforts. And who wouldn't like an occasional *attaboy*. There's nothing wrong with that. It's when we perform a task for the sole reason of recognition that we have become misguided. Aren't you usually amazed when you hear about an anonymous gift that has been bestowed upon an individual or group? There's something fascinating about someone generous enough to give, and modest enough to accept no credit. How often do we hear about someone anonymously dropping a gold coin into a Salvation Army kettle? We need to do things, not for recognition, but for the simple reason that responsible individuals are always on task for the good of their families, their coworkers, and their communities.

Where do you fit in? Are you the kind of person who needs to have your accomplishments acknowledged and lauded? Do you wait for the right time to perform at your highest level—when the right someone is watching? It's now time to make a habit of performing at the highest level at all times—not because there's something in it for us—but because there's something in it for us. Did that sound a little bit like double-talk? The reward is not having someone notice what we've achieved, but rather performing a deed for the pure satisfaction of achievement.

KNOWLEDGE

"Trust the instinct to the end, though you can render no reason."

Ralph Waldo Emerson

(from "Intellect," *Essays, First Series*, 1865)

Instinct—that little voice in our heads that offers guidance. We might also call it a powerful motivation to act in a specific way. Whenever you are struggling with a decision, how often have you heard someone say, "Just trust your instincts"? It can be a little scary at times though—especially when your instincts seem to be pointing you in a direction in which you have never travelled. No one would argue that instinct is a form of knowledge—although the more we know about a certain situation, the less it seems we need to rely on our instincts.

Let's take a closer look at the passage in which this particular quotation is found:

> "All our progress is an unfolding, like the vegetable bud. You have first an instinct, then an opinion, then a knowledge, as the plant has root, bud and fruit. Trust the instinct to the end, though you can render no reason. It is vain to hurry it. By trusting it to the end, it shall ripen into truth and you shall know why you believe."

It is obvious that Emerson is a strong proponent of trusting one's instincts. Notice the process he is suggesting: instinct → opinion → knowledge → truth. He advises us that in time we will understand why we reacted in a certain way—and we will find truth. He asks us to have faith in this powerful notion that leads us to a conclusion. He is trying to convince us that following our instincts is in no way an impetuous act, and that we should trust these impulses even if we are uncertain at the time of why we are being guided in a particular direction.

Do you recall the quote found under the "Attitude" section: "Every young man is prone to be misled by the suggestions of his own ill-founded ambition which he mistakes for the promptings of a secret genius, and thence dreams of unrivaled greatness"? There is a clear difference between instinct and what Emerson refers to as *a secret genius*. It is important not to confuse them. Some people mistake *signs* for instinct. It's all well and good to feel as if you have witnessed a sign of some sort—and some folks make important or difficult decisions based on these seemingly timely signals. This can be dangerous. Emerson wants us to rely less on signs (secret geniuses) and more on the knowledge that we have gleaned from research and study.

Relying on our instincts has little to do with signs. An instinct is a gut reaction. When you are in an unfamiliar location late at night, it is your instinct that leads you away from a shortcut down a dark alley, and instead to a safer option down a well-lit street. We don't need signs in order to make a decision. When we first encounter a stranger, it is our instinct, not some sign, that either relaxes us in this person's presence, or produces a feeling of uneasiness. Those of us who consider ourselves good judges of character should probably attribute those intuitive skills not to an ability to recognize signs but rather to a heightened sense of instinct. It is important to see the difference.

It is difficult to determine how our instincts are developed. They are no doubt formed through a combination of previous experiences, of knowledge gained, and of subconscious thoughts. They take shape based on the consequences we have either experienced or ones that we anticipate. When struggling with a decision, it is advisable to trust our instincts. Following instead what we perceive to be a sign may be ill-advised. Whereas following our instincts, if we buy into Emerson's way of thinking, is a much safer choice. Don't look for something that will help you make a split-second decision, rather feel it, sense it, experience it. You may not know why you are feeling the way you do. But "Trust the instinct to the end, though you can render no reason."

"Life is our dictionary."

Ralph Waldo Emerson

(from "The American Scholar," an oration delivered before
The Phi Beta Kappa Society, at Cambridge, August 31, 1837)

When we look for *meaning*, we turn to a dictionary. If we were to ask Emerson, he might tell us that we can just as easily discover *meaning* by turning to life itself—by listening, by observing, by sensing, by tasting, by experiencing. In his speech to the Phi Beta Kappa Society, shortly after sharing the above quote, he went on to say, "I learn immediately from any speaker how much he has already lived, through the poverty or the splendor of his speech."

Just as we gain insights into the lives of others by listening and observing, so do others form opinions of us in much the same manner. We tend to see this as a one-way process. We tend to think that we are the only ones who are gathering information on those whose words and actions we witness and pay close attention. We need to remember the words of Jaques in Shakespeare's "As You Like It":

> All the world's a stage,
> And all the men and women merely players;
> They have their exits and their entrances,
> And one man in his time plays many parts,
> His acts being seven ages.

Every word that we speak…every action that we take…defines us. In most cases, people are not sitting back with legal pads and red pens taking notes, but they are certain to notice our gaffes or indiscretions. I remind my students of this frequently. As a writer I suppose it is not surprising that I am anal about spelling, punctuation and grammar. When we talk about the job search in class, for example, I am quick to point out that if someone confuses *your* and *you're* in a cover letter, or who, God forbid, utters the words *on accident* in a job interview, you can be certain that the available pool of candidates has just shrunk by one. At that point, you can only hope that the interviewer is as clueless as you. I simply have no patience for misusing language skills that most of us learned in grammar school. We can blame the system all we want but each individual must accept responsibility for his or her own ineptitude. And so if we find ourselves in a less desirable position because of these failings, it's time to look in the mirror, not point the finger.

"Life is our dictionary." We learn through observation. When I was a boy, I used to love to go to O'Hare Airport in Chicago to pick up visiting relatives. I was especially pleased when we would park the car and enter the terminal. It was the home of some of the most fascinating people in the world. While we waited at the gate (before it was prohibited), I was happy to sit for hours just watching people, and imagining who they were, the jobs they held, where they were headed, and why. It was a free geography lesson. We can learn so much by observing others. But we must never forget that we are on the same stage for other spectators to form opinions of us.

Have you ever opened someone else's refrigerator or medicine cabinet? What an education? There are those who believe that the foods on our refrigerator shelves, or the drugs and toiletries in a bathroom medicine cabinet speak volumes about who we are. Admit it—when you're waiting in line at the supermarket, don't you frequently notice the items on the conveyor belt from the order in front of you? And don't you make, perhaps unconsciously, judgments concerning that shopper's penchant for junk food, processed goods, and other less-than-healthy choices? And don't you feel validated when you place produce, fish, lean meats, and other nutritional offerings on the conveyor? Somehow, however, we never seem to notice the unhealthy items that also fill our carts.

The above Emerson quote asks us to step back, to slow down, and to open our eyes. We always seem to be in such a hurry to get somewhere, or get something done, that we rarely seem to realize we are discarding some valuable learning moments. The next time you are waiting to cross a busy street, or are standing in line in a crowded store or restaurant, or stuck in traffic, just stop, take a deep breath, and open your eyes. Notice the life around you, and drink in the moments that might have gone unnoticed had you continued your frantic trek to wherever.

> "There are as many pillows of illusion as flakes in a snowstorm; we wake from one dream into another."
>
> Ralph Waldo Emerson
>
> (from "Illusions," *The Conduct of Life*, 1860)

Illusion—a false perception of reality. Illusion is all around us. It is the stuff of magic. We are drawn to it—so much so at times that illusion can take on the appearance of reality. It is important for us to recognize that illusion is entertainment—just entertainment—and not always in the purest form. When we mistake illusion for reality, we are setting ourselves up for failure. The use of drugs or alcohol create a world void of responsibilities and social pressures. It is a world of illusion. The use of these substances leads to addiction and dependency. And that is no illusion.

Emerson seemed to recognize that there is a limitless supply of illusions in our lives. And if we surrender to these temptations, we will wander aimlessly from one self-defeating seduction to another. And there appears to be no shortage of illusions to choose from. There are as many as "flakes in a snowstorm." Read what follows this particular quote from Emerson's "Illusions" essay from *The Conduct of Life*:

> "There are as many pillows of illusion as flakes in a snowstorm. We wake from one dream into another dream. The toys to be sure are various, and are graduated in refinement to the quality of the dupe. The intellectual man requires a fine bait; the sots are easily amused. But everybody is drugged with his own frenzy, and the pageant marches at all hours, with music and banner and badge."

This gifted author and transcendentalist is trying to warn us that distractions— illusions—will cause us to drift off course if we welcome them into our lives. Any amusement that we allow to divert us from accomplishing our goals is an illusion that must be avoided. If we are forthright and focused, we may be able to steer clear of the crutches that will destroy us—drugs and alcohol. But what about those less obvious pitfalls—procrastination and sloth? Do they not also infringe on our ability to succeed?

While I was writing this book, I can't tell you how many times I felt uninspired—a clear case of writer's block. There were days when I would just stare at the computer monitor waiting for the muse to speak. And the longer that inspiration eluded me, the more likely I was to drift—to daydream—about something—about anything that would prevent me from staying on task. A few minutes later I would catch myself and return to a state where only creativity was acceptable. And even though I realized that my potential for productivity at that moment was not particularly high, I would stay fixed and force myself to write—to crank out something—and even if it was simply a paragraph, I knew that I was at least a paragraph ahead of where I was when I started.

I have often read that once you identify your passion in life, you must dedicate a certain amount of time each day in the pursuit of that dream. You must find a time and locate a space where you will focus on that goal—every day. If you are tired, or ill, or busy, you are to resist the enticement to skip a day, and you are to fight through it. Because if you do give in and take a day off, the next time the same urge surfaces, it will be that much easier to give into temptation and lose yet another precious day.

For me, the temptation is sleep. I make a habit of writing twice a day—during my lunch hour and the last hour of the evening. It is trying to stay awake that last hour that frequently proves most challenging. I'm not saying that I have never given in and retired before completing my full complement of work, but more often than not I just keep battling the desire to drift off. And fittingly, as I am finishing this particular section, I am sitting at the keyboard at the bewitching hour gulping down mouthfuls of water and bouncing in my chair in order to remain attentive and focused. One of the reasons I always fight the urge to simply shut down for the night is the overwhelming feeling of accomplishment that I experience when I am able to reach my goal and beat the demons. There's nothing like it.

> "There is no knowledge that is not power."
>
> Ralph Waldo Emerson
>
> (from "Old Age," *Society and Solitude*, 1870)

What a powerful statement. If you were trying to convince someone to stay in school, this quote would have to be part of your arsenal. We oftentimes need a reminder that knowledge is so, so powerful. If survival is the greatest human desire, where does knowledge fit in? If you consider the fact that with knowledge, your chances for survival increase dramatically, you may want to make it a lifelong goal to acquire as much knowledge as is humanly possible to give yourself the best chance for survival. We need to place the desire for knowledge atop our priority list. And this quest must continue until our final breath.

There are some people out there who get it. They understand that there is far more knowledge to be gained than hours in the day to do so. A few years ago, I read about a young man who gets it. His story was featured in a Chicago Tribune article by reporter Megan Twohey and was titled: "Linguist jumped at every opportunity." It is the tale of Tom Tasche, a student at Elk Grove High School, located in a northwest Chicago suburb. It seems that while others were chowing down burgers and fries, Tom was spending his lunch periods learning Japanese. And what's more amazing is that he did it virtually all on his own.

It is one thing to give up the precious social ritual of lunch with friends, it's quite another to spend that time in an academic pursuit. And did it pay off, you may wonder? In the Chicago Tribune's 24th Annual All-State Academic Team scholarships competition that year, Tom was "ranked highest of all 263 applicants in scoring by the Tribune's panel of judges." Then when you throw in the fact that he earned a 5 (the highest score possible) on his Japanese AP exam, his cumulative 5.0 GPA, and his 35 ACT score, you can see why, following graduation, he planned to attend Princeton University's Woodrow Wilson School of Public and International Affairs.

I share the story of Tom Tasche because I feel it is so critical to point out not just the importance of knowledge, but the importance of dedicating ourselves to the pursuit of knowledge. It is easy to say that you are in agreement with this sentiment. It is quite another to buy into a commitment to make it happen. I encourage you to never stop learning.

Never feel that a degree from high school, college, or grad school is your license to discontinue your active quest for knowledge. Many people might feel that the knowledge they acquire while on the job proves that they have not placed learning on the back burner. But I'm not talking about the material that you must learn to become efficient at work. I'm referring to the Tom Tasche model — learning for the sake of learning.

And it matters little how you accomplish it. When the books-on-tape phenomenon first appeared years ago, there were some in the academic community who denounced it. How could someone, they argued, share in the same literary experience by listening to someone read the words of Charles Dickens, rather than engrossing themselves in reading the novel itself? Well, I wouldn't argue that reading a classic may be a more fulfilling experience than having it read to you, but I think that critics here are missing the point. It is likely that many who choose books on tape (now CD's or downloads) do so because of time constraints. If they were expected to read complete novels only when they had the time to do so, they might never get around to enjoying that moment. Is it not preferable for these folks to engage in a slightly different experience rather than missing out on it altogether?

It matters little how you infuse more opportunities for leaning into your lives. It just matters that you find some way to do so. If you take Emerson's advice, you will be inviting in not just knowledge, but power as well. And it is not the power that you have wrestled away from someone, it is the power that you have earned. And there is no purer form than that which comes from knowledge.

LEAVING A LEGACY

"Be an opener of doors to those who come after you."

Ralph Waldo Emerson

(from "Success," *Society and Solitude*, 1870)

We would all like to think that in the moments prior to our death, we will be able to look back with no regrets. But let's be realistic. It is highly doubtful that there is single person out there who, if given a second chance, wouldn't have done something differently in his or her life. We make so many choices in our lifetimes that we are bound to foul up a few. No one is perfect. No one is even close to perfect. With that said, however, it's not as though we now have a clean slate. Not by a long shot. But for most of us, there is time — time to reclaim integrity — time to undo some of those indiscretions still nagging at us.

But why? Why do some of us feel a need to right these wrongs? One reason might be our old friend, *guilt*. Before we had children, my wife and I decided that we would try to discipline our children without resorting to physical punishment — no spanking. We felt that there were other more effective ways to discipline. If you ask our girls, they will tell you that they were never spanked, but that *Dad* was a master of the guilt trip. Now I am not particularly fond of that title, and I'm not so sure I deserve it, but when you explain to your kids that there will be consequences (loss of privileges) for their actions, you usually get their attention. If they still elect to break your rules, you must follow through. And for a dose of good measure, a little guilt trip (the fact that you are disappointed in them) can be equally effective.

So, we can probably agree that guilt motivates our actions. Another reason to right those wrongs could have something to do with what we perceive as our ultimate day of reckoning. When we're standing in front of those pearly gates, we will want to be able to defend our actions — not to make excuses, mind you — but to demonstrate that at some point in our lives, we saw the light and did our best to live a moral, virtuous life.

Or, there might be one more reason that people choose to do the right thing — no matter their age. These are the people we might refer to as the *givers,* not the *takers* — the *winners*, not the *whiners*. They are the ones who never ask, "So what's in it for me?" They act in a prudent manner because they accept responsibility, because they choose to be contributing members of society, and because it is simply the right thing to do. They recognize that others who came before them, with similar outlooks, helped pave the way for their success. What if the others had said, "So, what do I get out of it?" Fortunately, many did not.

We are where we are today as a society because of these kinds of selfless people. Can you call yourself an "opener of doors for those who come after you?" I think we would all like to be considered worthy enough to be part of such an elite group. It requires compassion, benevolence, and an unselfish heart. It requires focus, resolve, and a strong moral fiber. It requires people with passion and vision, dedicated to a cause, with the realization that they may never see the fruits of their labors.

One such soul is the late actor/comedian, Danny Thomas. As the story goes — early in his career as a struggling entertainer, Danny Thomas prayed to St. Jude Thaddeus, the patron saint of hopeless causes. He asked St. Jude to "help me find my way in life, and I will build you a shrine." In the years that followed, Thomas' career flourished. He enjoyed international fame. But he never forgot his pledge to St. Jude. In the early 1950's, his dream began to take shape. His plan was to erect a unique research hospital that would attempt to cure catastrophic diseases in children. In 1955, with the support of several Memphis business leaders, the St. Jude Children's Research Hospital was born. You know the rest of the story. Danny Thomas died in 1991 but the miracles at St. Jude's continue on. St. Jude's generous benefactor and founder is, without question, the embodiment of what Emerson had in mind when he wrote, "Be an opener of doors to those who come after you."

> "It is not length of life, but depth of life."
>
> Ralph Waldo Emerson
>
> (from "Immortality," *Letters and Social Aims*, 1875)

Ralph Waldo Emerson died just short of his 79th birthday — quite a feat considering life expectancy in the late 19th century. But that accomplishment seems almost unimportant to Emerson. The above quote talks about quality of life, not time served. The nightly news broadcasts frequently carry stories about young people whose lives were cut short — some of them violently. The tragedy of a young person's death is multifold. Not only does it evoke sorrow, it leaves a void that can never be filled. But even more, we wonder about the potential that has been lost. Might these individuals have become great humanitarians or remarkable medical researchers or even model parents.

We can't undo tragedies of this nature but we can learn from them. Many of us have been granted longevity. And because we've been fortunate enough to live on this planet for decades, we have been given certain responsibilities. It was St. Luke in the New Testament who captured the words of Jesus, "For unto whomsoever much is given, of him shall be much required." Whatever talents we possess, we must display those talents. It's an obligation. It's a responsibility. In the closing scene of the motion picture, "A Bronx Tale," we hear, "The saddest thing in life is wasted talent." We must not…we cannot waste our God-given talents. We have been placed on this earth for a reason. It is our job to discover precisely what that is, and then to put it into motion.

When I think of lives cut short and the loss of not only a precious life but potential as well, I am reminded of two young people — Ryan White and Samantha Smith.

Ryan White was the Indiana teenager who died of complications from AIDS at the age of 18. His was a fight against, not only a disease, but an uninformed public. Ryan was a hemophiliac who contracted the AIDS virus through a blood transfusion. He knew he was suffering from an incurable disease, but he just wanted to live the life of a normal teenager and to be accepted by classmates in his central Indiana town. In 1985 at the age of 14, Ryan White began a valiant fight to attend a public school in Kokomo, Indiana, that had earlier banned him. The school had taken drastic measures due to an uproar from parents who feared that their own children might come in contact with Ryan, and might contract the disease. For several months, Ryan was forced to receive his lessons through a telephone connection in his home. Following a court decision, however, the young man prevailed and was permitted to attend school. But his reception was anything but welcome. Many classmates taunted him with insults and obscenities. And vandals damaged his home.

In 1987, the White family moved to Cicero, Indiana, about 20 miles from Kokomo. Here at Hamilton Heights High School, Ryan was treated like just one of the other kids. It was all he had ever wanted. He took this opportunity to help his classmates understand his illness. He never wanted anyone to feel sorry for him. In April, 1990, Ryan died with his mother, his grandparents, and singer, Elton John at his side.

Then there is Samantha Smith. This 10-year-old Maine schoolgirl made headlines in 1983 when she wrote a letter to then-Soviet leader, Yuri Andropov. In the letter she expressed her worries about nuclear war. The story might have ended there had not Andropov replied. In his response, the Soviet leader told Samantha that he wanted "very much to live in peace," and was doing "everything" to avoid war. He then extended an invitation for the fifth-grader and her family to visit the Soviet Union. Samantha accepted, and soon became one of the youngest goodwill ambassadors on record. She might very well have grown up to have become a peace activist had she not died at age 13 in a 1985 plane crash with her father. The pair had been returning from a trip to England.

Regardless of how long you've been on this earth, how would you measure the "depth" of your life thus far? Have you made contributions not only in your personal and professional life, but to society? How might your obituary read? If you wish to rethink those contributions, there's still time. Remember, "It is not length of life, but depth of life." Tragically, the length of life for Ryan and Samantha was tragically shortened, but the depths of their lives, without question, was far reaching. Most of us have been given more time than these two young people. Have we used it prudently?

> "Mankind divides itself into two classes—benefactors and malefactors. The second class is vast, the first is a handful."
>
> Ralph Waldo Emerson
>
> (from "Considerations by the Way," *The Conduct of Life*, 1860)

If you take the time to read this particular essay, it is hard to come away with anything other than the fact that Emerson, at this point in his life, was down on humanity—or to be specific, the masses. We live in a democracy where the majority rules. And it can be a little disconcerting, if we are swayed by Emerson, to think that the masses may not be acting in our best interests. Read the following passage. See if you agree with Emerson.

> "Mankind divides itself into two classes,—benefactors and malefactors. The second class is vast, the first a handful. A person seldom falls sick but the bystanders are animated with a faint hope that he will die:—quantities of poor lives, of distressing invalids…
>
> "(Ben) Franklin said, "Mankind are very superficial and dastardly: they begin upon a thing, but, meeting with a difficulty, they fly from it discouraged; but they have capacities, if they would employ them."
>
> "Shall we then judge a country by the majority, or by the minority? By the minority surely. Tis pedantry to estimate nations by the census, or by square miles of land, or other than by their importance to the mind of the time.
>
> "…Masses are rude, lame, unmade, pernicious in their demands and influence, and need not to be flattered but to be schooled. I wish not to concede anything to them, but to tame, drill, divide and break them up, and draw individuals out of them.

> "The worst of charity is that the lives you are asked to preserve are not worth preserving. Masses! the calamity is the masses. I do not wish any mass at all, but honest men only, lovely, sweet, accomplished women only, and no shovel-handed, narrow-brained, gin-drinking million...at all. If government knew how, I should like to see it check, not multiply the population."

See what I mean. Emerson usually finds a way to help us focus on the positive—on the glass of water half *full*. But in this instance, he is suggesting that we take a closer look at just how we interpret the meaning of *the will of the masses*. Emerson seems to be taking us to task for allowing numbers, rather than intellect, to guide us. And perhaps he is right. If nothing else, he seems to be validating those of us who have on occasion joined the side of the underdog, the less privileged, those without a voice—the minority. Although Emerson seems to be lamenting the fact there are a fair share of ne'er-do-wells out there, he also seems to be rejoicing for the "honest men" and "accomplished women" in our society. There is still hope apparently.

When you begin a discussion of basic human nature, it is difficult not to dwell on the negative aspects. We find ourselves concentrating on those individuals who make up the lowest common denominator and it is easy to come away with a rather bleak outlook. But we have to accept the fact that throughout history, a certain percentage of the population might be described, as Emerson would call them—malefactors, or evildoers. We would like to think that these numbers are insignificant, but if we watch the nightly news or read the newspapers, we know that they do exist, and we cannot take them lightly.

We must make certain that we avoid the malefactors in life and embrace the benefactors. Even more, we should reject the actions of anyone who even slightly resembles a malefactor and set our sights on becoming true benefactors in life. Most people tend to associate benefactors with individuals of great means who make sizable charitable contributions. Simply put, a benefactor is a giver. A benefactor is someone who puts a dollar in a Salvation Army kettle at Christmastime. A malefactor spends time scheming to find ways to separate the kettle from the volunteer.

Then there are those in between. They would never think of stealing, but then again, they would never think of digging into their pockets to contribute. Benefactors, as Emerson has suggested, are in the minority. You may already be part of this group. If so, you know the feeling that comes from giving. And if you work for or represent a group on the receiving end, you know just how critical it is for more people to join this elite club. And there just so happens to be a membership drive as we speak. Don't delay. Join now.

> "Rings and other jewels are not gifts, but apologies for gifts. The only gift is a portion of thyself."

Ralph Waldo Emerson

(from "Gifts," *Essays, Second Series*, 1876)

The little things in life. We oftentimes hear people talk about *the little things* — and how in the long run, they are the moments that people most often remember, and cherish. A few years back, I took off a day off to spend time with my daughters. I had purchased tickets to a Cubs game. I don't have to tell you that the cost of taking a family to a professional sports contest these days is outrageous. And then when you add in parking, concessions and souvenirs, it makes for quite a pricey afternoon of entertainment. But if you are a "dyed-in-the-wool" fan, you find yourself justifying the expense, and somehow locating the necessary resources to make it happen.

On our way to the game, I decided to take the girls down memory lane. Our first stop was The Maurice Lenell Cookie factory in Norridge, IL, a northwest Chicago suburb. Not only were there open boxes of cookies from which to sample, but you could watch the goodies being made — from the ovens, down the conveyor, and then onto packaging. This location was significant for us. When I proposed to my wife, I hid the engagement ring in a tin of freshly-baked Maurice Lenell cookies, and so every Christmas thereafter, and on her birthday, I would buy her a four-and-a-half pound tin of cookies. It's a tradition. All in all, it was delicious first stop. The cookie factory has since closed but it will always be one of my fondest memories.

Then it was onto a pair of boyhood homes. We stopped in front of two of the houses I grew up in. I pointed out where my bedroom was and what the house looked like inside. I told them about a few of our neighbors — and the quirky stories about some of them. They especially enjoyed the stories about one particular, irascible next door neighbor — Julius. Julius didn't particularly like me. I don't think he liked anyone. He would always get upset whenever people parked in front of his house. We were very much aware of the property lines back then. And God forbid if you ever stepped on his magnificently-manicured lawn. He'd come onto his front porch and just glare at us.

I told the girls about one particular day when I was throwing the football around in the street with my brother-in-law. I decided to practice my kicking skills. When I was a teenager, I used to fancy myself a would-be professional punter. Now I'm not sure if it was a gust of wind or operator error, but I shanked the kick. I should mention that it had great hang-time but it unfortunately descended directly onto an awning over Julius' front picture window. It was at that moment I knew that any chance for détente between the two families would be impossible. Julius went from a severe dislike for me to outright hate—at least that's what he told my dad one day.

Next stop—my old grammar school. We drove around each building as I pointed out the classrooms where I had spent time during those years. I showed them where I used to play marbles on the school playground. And where I was standing when, in fourth grade, I gave Adeline Mostak a rhinestone ring that I had bought for ten cents at the local drug store. Kids seem to love stories of their parents' old flames. I conveniently left out the part where she started crying and threw it at me. I showed them where Ken Schultz broke his leg during a rather boisterous game of "I got it!" (an updated version of Tag). I explained how an ambulance drove right onto the playground to pick up Ken. I had never seen that before.

Our final stop before heading to the game was my old stomping grounds at high school. I was especially dramatic when we drove around to the back of the school where the gym was—the spot where Coach Buscarini smacked me in the rump with a whiffle bat for not having performed a push-up to his standards. I then pointed to the hallway, and a particular wall of lockers, where during senior year I got in John Troiani's face for asking a girl to homecoming—the same girl whom we both agreed *I* would ask.

It was then time to head to the ballpark. I mention these stories to help illustrate Emerson's featured quote: "Rings and other jewels are not gifts, but apologies for gifts. The only gift is a portion of thyself." My plan that day had been to treat the girls to a Cubs game with all the trimmings. The stops on the way were just scheduled to kill time—or so I thought. To this day, my kids can't tell me who the Cubs played that day, whether they won or not, or what souvenir they bought at the concession stand. But they remember every aspect of my boyhood homes, and every juicy tidbit about Julius, and Adeline, and Coach Buscarini. They still talk about how much fun they had that day—and none of their memories are about the pricey afternoon at the ballpark.

I learned a lot about giving on that particular day. I learned to appreciate the little things—and what it means to give a portion of thyself—the greatest gift of all. I encourage you to leave your own legacy. Give the gift of yourself to others. Become known as the person who gives the best gifts—not the most expensive, but the ones that are truly priceless.

LIVING IN THE NOW

"The years teach much which the days never know."

Ralph Waldo Emerson

(from "Experience," *Essays, 2nd Series*, 1876)

Over the years, on occasion, I have decided it would be in my best interest to drop five to ten pounds. One thing I have noticed is that as you age, it takes a more concerted effort to shed that weight. I have no credentials in this area so I wouldn't begin to advise someone which path to follow regarding weight loss—nor have I come across any sage advice from Emerson regarding this topic. We do know, however, that he penned the words, "The first wealth is health," and we know that he died just short of his 79th birthday, an impressive feat considering the time. So Emerson was forward-thinking enough to recognize the need to adopt a healthy lifestyle.

Whenever I've tried to lose those pounds, I've always made the mistake of weighing myself daily. I've read more than once that you are setting yourself up for disappointment if you monitor your weight each day. But that hasn't stopped me. When I take the time to read the Emerson quote at the top of this section, I realize that if we gauge our success on the accomplishments of each day, it will be difficult to see significant improvements. But if we are patient enough to assess our progress each week, or month or quarter, we will get a much more accurate reading of how well we have actually performed.

Whether in weight loss or in life, monitoring and grading ourselves every day will only wear us down. We need to accept the fact that just because we lose a few battles, it doesn't mean we're going to lose the war. I have nothing against setting the bar high but it must be within reach, and we must accept the fact that we are going to have down days every once in a while. It's not as if we are making it too easy for ourselves, we're just trying to be realistic. The important thing is to get back up on that horse as soon as you've been thrown. Then, after a week, a month, a quarter, a year, or however long, take a hard look at where you are. Assess your progress. If at that point you aren't where you want to be, *then* it's time to rethink the routine. Maybe you *were* too easy on yourself. Maybe it became *okay* to fail every so often. That's the time to rewrite your strategy and implement a new plan.

Look back at the last five years. Have you corrected problems with which you have been struggling? Are you satisfied with the progress you've made during that time? Are you at the place you were hoping to be at this point in your life? Or are you still at square one, and now five years older? If you answered "yes" to this last question, you're not alone. The years sneak up on us. Our careers and family lives consume us. When things become hectic, it's okay to lose focus for a while but it just can't become a habit.

What Emerson is suggesting is not that we pay less attention to what we have accomplished each day and only measure success by the years, he is inspiring us to maintain a passion for life, to set goals, to make schedules, to do our best to meet challenges each day—but not to beat ourselves up if we fail occasionally. As in losing weight, it is best not to continually weigh in, but rather to do so periodically. In sports, it would be foolhardy for athletes to measure their success following each day's performance, and to determine their worth based on that particular effort. A hitter may go 3 for 4 at the plate one day, and based on that performance, decide that there is no reason to make changes. But if that same hitter goes 0 for 4 the following day, he may suddenly feel a need to rethink his approach, and to seek out the hitting coach for advice. This would be an overreaction and would make little sense. Look at the overall performance—the batter went 3 for 8—that's a .375 average. Not too shabby.

While writing this book, I found the Emerson quote above particularly helpful. When you set out to locate 100 insightful quotations, to identify the specific source for each, and then to write an accompanying essay, you find yourself noting precisely how much you have achieved in each day's writing session, and then you find yourself trying to project how long the entire project will take to complete. There were times when I would crank out an essay in a day. I would then make the mistake of assuming that the entire manuscript would be complete in a little over three months. Then would come a particularly challenging piece that would take more than a week to complete, and I was worried that the project wouldn't be brought to fruition for the better part of two years.

When I look back, I realize that there were two dynamics at work: 1) I just couldn't assign a particular amount of time for the completion of each essay. It would compromise the integrity of the work. It would take as long as it takes. And 2) when I looked back to determine how much I had achieved each month or each quarter, I was satisfied with the results. I can't say that I would have been satisfied with each day's efforts however, but with the patience to wait a little longer before addressing the amount of progress made, I was happy by the pace I had maintained.

Emerson is asking us to approach life in much the same way an athlete measures progress. We don't need to hit a homerun each day. We don't even need to get a hit each and every day. But we do need to assess our efforts every so often just to ensure that we are working at the highest possible level, that we are accomplishing our short-term goals every few weeks or months, and that we never lose sight of our ultimate goals. At the point of assessment, we just need to be able to honestly say that we are a little closer to achieving our dreams.

"Write it on your heart that every day is the best day in the year."

Ralph Waldo Emerson

(from "Works and Days," *Society and Solitude*, 1870)

Many motivational speakers and writers have a name for it. It is the way in which we are supposed to live—enjoying the present, and not allowing the future to get in the way. They remind us of how often we waste precious moments…when we just try to finish up a task in order to move on to the next phase in our lives—a time that we assume will be much more pleasant than the last. We have all done it—and probably more often than we'd like to admit. In fact, there are some folks who do it all the time. Psychologists and self-help gurus have for years tried to get us to stop, take a deep breath, and witness the beauty around us. The overused cliché: "Stop and smell the roses," is trite at best, but it gets the point across. It encourages us to become more aware of our surroundings. We need to stop wishing away the present, and to take a moment to see, really see, what we are missing…and dismissing. Think about what Emerson is saying: "Write it on your heart that every day is the best day in the year."

The advice is really very simple. Stop waiting for the school bell to ring. Stop waiting for the work day to end. Stop counting off the days until the next holiday or vacation. Learn to live in the now. If we wish away much of our time, two things will occur: 1) we may not realize it but we will be throwing away some very special moments in our lives, ones we will never be able to recover; and 2) when we ultimately make it to the times or places we have been longing for, they will rarely live up to our expectations. We might even find ourselves mouthing the words of the old Peggy Lee song, "Is That All There Is?"

Whenever I am away from home on vacation and have time to reflect, I like to spend a few moments trying to formulate a new or renewed attitude. Sometimes it's very simple. Sometimes it's just a mantra. But I like to feel that this break from the daily routine has produced more than just a time to sleep in and see the sights. I like returning home with a new set of tools that will better enable me to handle the challenges of a busy and active life. On a recent trip, I remember finding myself complaining more than usual, and I don't even remember why. When I took the time to examine why I was feeling out of sorts, there were really no good reasons for acting in this manner. I took that opportunity to identify the new attitude I would not only bring home with me but would put into practice immediately. I would simply try to catch myself each time I started to complain…about anything.

If I were to buy into Emerson's belief that "…every day is the best day in the year," then I would have nothing to complain about. When you're experiencing that once-in-a-lifetime, red-letter day, it's all good. What's there to gripe about? Let me tell you that I personally hate listening to someone who whines incessantly, and I'm not referring to children, although that can be irritating as well. I'm talking about adults who live to complain. When I encounter one of them, my first reaction is to try to escape as quickly as possible. If I am somehow trapped, I start to wonder if *I* sound like that to others, and then quickly vow never to subject anyone to such an irritating display.

As much as we may try to avoid this lot, we sometimes find ourselves inadvertently joining their ranks. At some time or another, you'll hear someone complaining about something and you will suddenly feel compelled to chime in. But remember—just as optimism is infectious, so too is fatalism. If you somehow make the mistake of surrounding yourself with negative people—beware. Before long you will become one of them. You will complain for the sake of complaining. You will gripe simply to fit in. You know the people I'm referring to—the ones who never have anything good to say about anyone. And as they drag down others, they drag themselves down.

Surround yourself with cheerful, motivated, hopeful, optimistic people. And in no time at all, you will see things the way Emerson did when he wrote, "Write it on your heart that every day is the best day in the year."

> "He cannot be happy and strong until he too lives with nature in the present."
>
> Ralph Waldo Emerson
>
> (from "Self-Reliance," *Essays, First Series*, 1847)

With these words, Emerson seems to be giving us permission to renounce our past, and for that matter, our future, and to embrace the here and now. It's hard to buy into this way of thinking. But it's important to accept the fact that we cannot live on our laurels. Nor can we live on what we claim we'll accomplish in the future. Individuals with character realize that all we have is the present. There is a sports cliché reminding us that we are only as good as our last at bat. And if we stick with a baseball analogy, we might see the point that Emerson is trying to make. If a homerun hitter has struck out his last three at-bats, and then comes to the plate with the bases loaded in the bottom of the ninth, do we boo and ridicule him? No. Are we expecting him to repeat his most recent failures at the plate? No. We are hoping…praying even…that he will hit the long ball. We give him the benefit of the doubt. We are willing to forget the past. All that matters is this at-bat—the present.

Shouldn't that be the same principle for society? Who we are right now is what is most important. In court, we oftentimes see judges toss out any reference to a suspect's prior convictions. The accused must be judged on this most recent incident alone. Past, unrelated events would prejudice a jury. Now, of course, we're not referring to career criminals who must be dealt with more severely. We're talking about those who are remorseful for past mistakes and who have repaid their debt to society, but who have now managed to trip up again. It is no doubt frustrating to wear labels, and never be able to shake them.

In our current penal system when inmates are released from prison, it might be best to hand them more than a new set of clothes and a few dollars in their pockets. Why not also hand them a piece of paper with the Emerson quote at the top of this section written on it. It offers hope, and the belief that rehabilitation is possible, and that (I apologize for this tired cliché) today indeed is the first day of the rest of your life.

The prisoner reference is just one application of this principle—and an extreme one at that. Many of us can benefit from Emerson's way of thinking. He seems to be suggesting that if we dwell on the past, and in some cases, our past failures, we will never be able to see ourselves in a new role—one that finds us reaching the heights we've always dreamed of. We can reflect on past mistakes all we want but if it immobilizes us and keeps us from progressing, it's time to banish the past and concentrate on the now. Perhaps former Chicago Bears and New Orleans Saints head coach, Mike Ditka, may have had it right when he took offense at a reporter's question one day in the locker room and barked out: "Those who live in the past are cowards and losers." It's hard to argue with Mike's success, and his abilities to motivate his players.

And if we continue on with the world of sports, one can only imagine how frustrated agents might be if Emerson had been a team owner. Those who represent high-priced athletes would never have wanted to negotiate with this man. If we apply the Emerson quotation: "He cannot be happy and strong until he too lives with nature in the present," one might guess at that this owner would not have been a fan of the long-term contract. If the past and the future are meaningless, a player on an Emerson team might have to sign one-year contracts, and would have to continually prove himself each and every season. But it would never work; it just makes too much sense.

Whatever skeletons or failures or disappointments in your past haunt you, take the advice of the master. First learn from them. Then discard them. And get on with the matter at hand—living a successful, productive, meaningful life—in the present.

> "This time, like all times, is a very good one, if we but know what to do with it."
>
> Ralph Waldo Emerson
>
> (from "The American Scholar," *Nature Addresses and Lectures*, 1876)

Upon reading this quote, the first thing that came to mind were the words of character actor, Dick Elliott, who played the "Man on the Porch" in "It's a Wonderful Life." You might recall the scene where George and Mary had just left the dance where they had fallen into the pool—the one hidden under the gym floor. While walking home, George, in a football uniform, and Mary, in an oversized robe, stop in front of a home and babble away. This is where Dick Elliott comes in. He was the oversized old man on the porch:

> "Why don't you kiss her instead of talking her to death," the man says.
> "You want me to kiss her, huh?" George asks.
> "Ah, youth is wasted on the wrong people," the old man snaps.

Now it might just be me but when I read the words: "This time, like all times, is a very good one, if we but know what to do with it," I think of George Bailey, who in the opinion of the old man on the porch, wasted a golden opportunity—a moment that might have turned out differently had he known precisely "what to do with it." I have sentimental reasons for referencing the work of Dick Elliot. Not only is "It's a Wonderful Life" one of my favorite films, but another classic, "The Andy Griffith Show" is and has always been my all-time favorite sitcom. And Dick Elliot just happened to play the rotund but lovable Mayor Pike on the first two seasons of the show. So much for nostalgia. Thanks for indulging me. Now back to business.

If we were to simplify the above Emerson quote, we might do so with the words, "Timing is everything." When an opportunity presents itself, we can either recognize the moment for what it is, or we can procrastinate and let it pass. Are you the kind of person who grabs onto opportunity when you see it coming, or do you talk yourself out of it with phrases like: "I'm just not ready to commit to something like that" … "I'm not the kind of person who makes hasty decisions"…"It seems too risky"…"That's for someone else, not me"…"If this (the opportunity) happens again, then I'll be ready to make my move."

Understand that I am not suggesting you leap headfirst into the first opportunity that comes along. Nor would Emerson suggest that. Remember his quote, "Every young man is prone to be misled by the suggestions of his own ill-founded ambition which he mistakes for the promptings of a secret genius, and thence dreams of unrivaled greatness." Emerson was not a fan of impetuous behavior. He, instead, insisted on decision-making based on prudent and careful research. But, let's face it, there are moments in our lives, and you can probably recall more than one, where we might have wished we had taken a particular action instead of doing nothing. We may recall an investment opportunity that sounded a little too good to be true—but actually panned out. We may have read about new inventions or ideas, and thought back to a time when we actually considered a similar notion, but had never acted on it.

I wouldn't exactly call myself a risk taker. I have started up small businesses based on notions that a need existed in the marketplace. Some have worked better than others. But I never was confident enough in the venture to risk giving up my full-time job. I admire those individuals with the conviction and confidence to have done so. I always ran my businesses on nights and weekends. And each was based on an idea that I had considered, but had not rushed into.

This particular Emerson quote can be interpreted in different ways. One is to consider business opportunities. Another might be the prudence of speech—saying the right thing at the right time. How often have you, when engaged in conversation, wished you could have taken back something you might have said? Or wished you had added a comment to a conversation long gone? If we had only known what to do at the time.

We *could* spend the next few years reliving missed opportunities, or regretting having said, or not having said, something to someone. But what would it accomplish? We should allow the past to teach us, not to rebuke us. We should store away valued lessons, not relive humiliation. Each and every day, we are presented with opportunities to improve our lot in life. The words that we speak—the actions that we take—determine our destinies. Think before you speak—in any situation, casual or business. Think before you act—prior to every action you take. The key word here is *prior*. Recognize opportunity. Think it through. If interested, prudently investigate it. And if the time is right…"know what to do with it."

OPPORTUNITY

"Every wall is a gate."

Ralph Waldo Emerson

(from "Notes," *Natural History of Intellect*, 1893, published posthumously)

This is one of my favorite Emerson quotes because of its hopeful tone in the face of adversity. It is also one of the most misquoted of all the Emerson sayings. In his paper, *Natural History of Intellect*, the exact passage reads:

> "The man truly conversant with life
> knows, against all appearances, that there
> is a remedy for every wrong, and that
> every wall is a gate."

If you were to take the time to research these words, you would find many references to a passage that reads differently than the quote above. Many sources seem to feel that Emerson's quotation was actually, "Every wall is a door." And although that interpretation of the original may present a more visual metaphor, it is important to point out that Emerson never wrote or spoke those words. But what is more important than how often a particular phrase is misquoted, is the message it conveys. And this message conveys confidence and reassurance. One can only hope that those professionals who deal with patients suffering from depression, at some point in their treatment, might share these words, "…there is a remedy for every wrong, and…every wall is a gate." This is such an uplifting expression filled with hope.

If you are facing a wall, try repeating this phrase over and over. Soon you will see the gate, and soon it will be swinging open for you. You have to believe that you will ultimately devise an escape route, and overcome the obstacles that life will undoubtedly toss your way. You gotta believe. "Every wall is a gate"—and not just because Emerson says so—because, in our hearts, we want to believe this is true. And if you can't trust the words of one of the wisest and most respected authors and philosophers in the last 200 years, who can you believe?

If you take the time to relive some of the most trying moments in your life, you may recall that not only did you survive those challenges, but you learned ways to better survive them in the future. And what at the time seemed insurmountable—a wall—was in fact a formidable opponent to be sure, but was not unsolvable, and you are living proof of that. Whenever we face a problem, wouldn't it be great to be able to see into the future—to see that we will eventually overcome what previously seemed an impossible hurdle. We have to trust in our abilities to resolve our problems. We have to believe we are more than capable of doing so. And why not—we've been getting in and out of skirmishes since we were kids. We should be pros at this by now. But for some reason, whenever adversity raises its ugly head, we seem to forget that we've been in situations like this before…and that we have battled these demons before…and that we have prevailed *before*.

The same way that a person learns to count to ten before flying off the handle and snapping at someone—this is the same type of technique we need to employ whenever we encounter a mishap. We need to remind ourselves that not only is this problem solvable but that we've tackled similar challenges in the past with success. For some reason, it's almost as if we have to retrain ourselves—remind ourselves that we are more than capable of putting this bad boy in his place. Parents do this all the time. With your first child, you are frequently a nervous wreck—making sure they're always breathing when they sleep—panicking when they choke while eating, etc. With the birth of each new child, you find yourself more relaxed when problems occur. It's not as if you aren't as concerned as you were with your first-born, it's just that you have learned from experience that things will likely resolve themselves, or that you don't need to expend as much energy as you once did to correct the problem.

We need to learn how to react in a similar way when obstacles present themselves in other venues—at work, at play, in our social lives. We need to realize that there is a solution to every problem, and that if we focus, concentrate, and think things through, before long, no matter how complicated a situation may seem, victory is within our reach if we have but the patience and tenacity to see it through. Every wall is indeed a gate. But you have to look closely. Can you see it? Can you see the gate? Can you see it swinging open ever so slightly? In no time, you'll be passing through—standing tall—and awaiting the next wall to conquer.

"No great man ever complains of want of opportunity."

Ralph Waldo Emerson

(from "The Method of Nature," *Journal XXXII*, 1841)

There are two types of people in the world — the talkers and the doers. The "great" people that Emerson refers to above are the doers. They plan out a strategy. Conduct the necessary research. And implement their business model. They talk very little about what they hope to accomplish. They realize that the more they converse with others about their plans, the more time they waste. And they recognize that if you allow it to happen, talk can become a substitute for action. As long as you continue to talk about something, you somehow rationalize that you are making progress. Doers are aware of this procrastination trap. They may have been victims of this pattern themselves at some point in their lives. But they learned from these mistakes. Talking is not doing.

Like most people, I have succumbed to procrastination at times. I was doing exactly what Emerson's *great people* avoid. I would occasionally refer to a particular project in conversation. Somehow I felt less guilty about letting it slide if I made reference to it every so often. But eventually I had to face up to this issue and address the fact that deep down I knew exactly what I was doing. I wasn't fooling myself or anyone else. If you're putting off doing something, admit to it. Admit to the fact that disinterest or laziness or fear or whatever emotions you're experiencing, are driving your decision to do nothing.

Some time ago, I developed a mantra to help battle bouts of procrastination. Whenever I would catch myself avoiding some project that I knew needed to be accomplished, I would simply, and firmly say to myself: "Just shut the _____ up, and do it." There's nothing particularly deep about these words but they get me off my butt and cause me to just shut the ____ up and do it. I also find myself wanting to utter this phase to people who talk and talk and talk about doing something, but never seem to follow through. You would never find yourself wanting to say those words to great people — and maybe that's what makes them great. They don't need to be told to stop talking and start doing — they're too busy doing.

Emerson really nailed this one. Exceptional people never seem to complain that bad breaks did them in…that if only such and such had happened, *then* they would have hit that home run…that they were just in the wrong place at the wrong time…that so-and-so is a lucky stiff…that they actually had the same idea for some new innovation as someone else but never got around to marketing it or copyrighting it or securing a patent for it…or that if they just had been born ten years earlier, boy, would they have changed the world. Exceptional people never seem to make these excuses. These instead are the lamentations of the whiners of the world—the folks who are too lazy or unmotivated to flesh out an idea, examine its viability, study the marketplace, and dive in. I'm not just referring to business ventures. I'm talking about any activity that requires purpose and resolve—starting up an exercise regimen, planting a garden, building a tree house, taking a cooking class, learning CPR, joining a service organization. If all the talkers out there suddenly became the doers, there would be no economic crisis. People would be purchasing the necessary materials for do-it-yourself projects…they would begin to work harder and smarter and better. There would be a revitalized work ethic.

But let's face it—there will always be talkers. It's infectious. The talkers, surrounded by inactivity and indecision, and without knowing it, recruit other talkers. Who wouldn't want to just talk about all the things you intend to do, and never actually have to do them? Fortunately, however, there is another club currently seeking members. The doers—better known as the winners. The hours are longer, the dues are greater, the work is more demanding, but don't forget about the benefits. The benefits are outstanding. How do accomplishment, achievement, and self-respect sound? They're yours for the taking. See you at the next meeting.

"Let him look on opposition as opportunity."

Ralph Waldo Emerson

(from "Eloquence," *Society and Solitude*, 1870)

Most of us avoid confrontation. We keep our distance from argumentative and combative people. It is a bit confusing to read the words of Emerson when he suggests that "opposition" is an "opportunity." *Opposition* means taking sides, and unless you are dealing with extremely civilized individuals, you will soon become embroiled in argument and discord. Situations like this are usually unpleasant. So how could Emerson possibly believe that we should "look on opposition as opportunity?"

We need to examine the context of his essay. When he mentions *opposition*, he is referring to those who were courageous enough to *oppose* slavery. This now makes a bit more sense. When we stand up against injustice, defend it, and fight to eliminate it, is this not an *opportunity* for both those who oppose it, and those who have been victims of it? Indeed. There will come a time in your life, if it hasn't already occurred, when you will become so outraged by the immoral actions of others that you will choose to become an advocate of change—of justice. You will no longer remain on the sidelines and allow others to enter the fray on your behalf. You will become physically and emotionally involved to right this wrong.

One individual who clearly understood the words of Emerson was Dr. Martin Luther King, Jr. Reverend King simply got it. He spent the better part of his life in opposition to accepted norms. He envisioned a day when all human beings could live in a harmonious state. He had to have believed that the *opposition* front that he had formed was an *opportunity* for all of his followers. The above quotation is from an Emerson essay entitled, "Eloquence." It seems only fitting therefore to include the *eloquent* words of Dr. King in one of his most influential works, "Letter from a Birmingham Jail." King penned this letter after having been arrested alongside fellow activist, Ralph Abernathy, for having participated in civil rights protests—a violation of a state court order in Alabama. While in isolation in the Jefferson County Jail in Birmingham, Reverend King shared his thoughts regarding the ongoing civil rights struggle. Here is one of the more powerful excerpts from his letter:

> "Injustice anywhere is a threat to justice everywhere. We are caught in an

> inescapable network of mutuality, tied in a single garment of destiny. Whatever affects one directly, affects all indirectly. Never again can we afford to live with the narrow, provincial 'outside agitator' idea. Anyone who lives inside the United States can never be considered an outsider anywhere within its bounds."

Dr. King was not an advocate of civil disobedience. He wanted to bring about change through peaceful means. But there have been times throughout history when unjust laws have been enacted and enforced. These are the times that require action. Reverend King addressed some of these examples.

> "It was practiced superbly by the early Christians, who were willing to face hungry lions and the excruciating pain of chopping blocks rather than submit to certain unjust laws of the Roman Empire…In our own nation, the Boston Tea Party represented a massive act of civil disobedience.

> "We should never forget that everything Adolf Hitler did in Germany was 'legal'…It was 'illegal' to aid and comfort a Jew in Hitler's Germany. Even so, I am sure that, had I lived in Germany at the time, I would have aided and comforted my Jewish brothers. If today I lived in a Communist country where certain principles dear to the Christian faith are suppressed, I would openly advocate disobeying that country's antireligious laws."

I think it is important to point out that no one is suggesting that the only way to correct an injustice is to act in an illegal manner. I certainly am not advocating such action. It is rarely necessary to carry a cause to such extremes. Our First Amendment rights allow us to employ alternatives to call attention to a legal system that appears to promote the exclusion of others. We may join organizations that have been formed with the intentions of righting a particular wrong. We may contact members of local government, or our state or federal representatives. We may attend rallies that promote consciousness of a specific issue. We may march on behalf of our beliefs. We may contact the press to express our opposition to certain laws. We may contribute to causes consistent with the ideals we support.

The next time you find yourself in opposition to someone, take a close look at your adversary, and the reason you have locked horns. You may just discover that the experience you have been dreading is actually an opportunity waiting to happen. "Let him look on opposition as opportunity."

> "Don't waste yourself in rejection, nor bark against the bad, but chant the beauty of the good."
>
> Ralph Waldo Emerson
>
> (from "Success," *Society and Solitude*, 1870)

Rejection. It's not pretty. Most of us have at one time or another experienced rejection. It's something that will happen every once in a while, and there is really no way to avoid it. We just need to learn how to handle it — to cope. We can't allow it to harm us emotionally or physically, but it frequently does unfortunately. No one likes to hear that he or she is simply not good enough. The rejection might have been the result of a relationship that soured, having been passed over for a promotion, or being denied a job.

Emerson is suggesting that when rejection hits, we need to stop feeling sorry for ourselves. We need to stop bad-mouthing the company or individual or whomever delivered the bad news. We need instead to find something positive about this occurrence. When I was younger, whenever I faced rejection, I would fall into the hole of self-pity. I would begrudge the successes of others. I would bemoan the fact that the world wasn't fair. I was making all the mistakes that Emerson encourages us to avoid. It wasn't until I became a fan of some of the most influential and motivational strategists (Dr. Wayne Dyer, Denis Waitley, Brian Tracy, Zig Ziglar) that I was able to see just how destructive this pattern of behavior really was. They helped me to conquer self-pity, to stop cursing and blaming others for my misfortune, and to accept each disappointment as a character-building opportunity.

If you are a fan of the phrase, "Everything happens for a reason," you may find it somewhat easier than others to handle rejection. If you buy into the notion that certain things are supposed to happen, you can find reason for negative occurrences. Things turned out this way, you tell yourself, for some reason — and you may never know why, but it's a good thing. It probably saved you from a fate far worse. And by adhering to this approach, you are well on your way to successfully following Emerson's advice. First, you accept the outcome — albeit negative. Then you dismiss any notion of berating those who contributed to the decision that led to the rejection. And finally, the most difficult of his commands — find something positive in all of this.

I recall a painful moment of rejection when I was 22 years of age. I had just graduated from Northern Illinois University in DeKalb, IL. I was living with my parents in Chicago, and desperately searching for a job in the communications field. I needed to find something…and fast. I was getting married in three months. I beat the pavement for about six weeks. Each morning I would get up and head into downtown Chicago. I would try to follow up on letters that I had sent to newspapers, magazines, public relations firms, advertising agencies as well as radio and TV stations. We were in a recession back then—sound familiar?

I managed to secure an interview with an industrial magazine serving the telephone industry. The editor was looking to add an additional writer to his staff. The interview seemed to go fairly well. I had left with him several examples of my writing—mostly magazine articles that I had written in college. Some of the articles were straight in nature; others were somewhat frivolous—but the editor wanted to see everything. On my bus ride home, I was daydreaming about being offered the job. I wanted it—or at least I thought I did. My true love was radio, but after a few initial interviews at local stations (including the No. 1 radio station in Chicago— WGN), I hadn't been called back for any follow-ups.

A few days passed, and then a package arrived in the mail. It was from the telephone magazine folks. They were returning all of my writing samples and had included a letter. Now I realize that everyone at some time or another gets turned down for a job, but this rejection letter was devastating. Rather than just indicating that the job had been filled by another candidate, this gentleman went out of his way to tell me just how incompetent I was as a writer. I will never forget one sentence: "I found your writing murky and directionless." My heart started racing. My hands went clammy. What if he was right, I thought. Am I just a hack? Who am I trying to fool? I have no business applying for a position as a writer.

As I sat on the stairway leading to my bedroom re-reading the letter, my mother spotted me. She could tell something was wrong. I couldn't spit it out. I just handed her the letter. I was ashamed to have her read it. What would she think? Would she question all the tuition dollars that had been wasted on my education? When she looked up, she smiled and put her arm around me. Thank God for mothers. She immediately told me that this fellow didn't know what he was talking about. I appreciated the support but what if she was wrong—and what if he was right? Then she told me that this was only *one* opinion—that he may not have liked my style. But someone will, she assured me.

And do you know what? She was right. Less than a week later I was called back to WGN-Radio for a second interview, and before I left the station that day, I was offered a position as a writer-producer-director. The rejection letter from the previous week was ancient history. It had paralyzed me for a short time but now I had been able to prove, to myself at least, that I did have some writing talent. Thanks to mom, I hadn't allowed the rejection letter to kill my spirits. I had decided to put it behind me and continue the hunt with my head held high—even if I was faking it.

The next time you experience rejection, remember Emerson's three-pronged advice. Dismiss the rejection. Blame no one. And rejoice in the fact that this was supposed to happen, and that there are more, and even better opportunities just waiting out there for you.

OVERCOMING FEAR

"It is the fear of the young bird to trust its wings."

Ralph Waldo Emerson

(from "Immortality," *Letters and Social Aims*, 1875)

Fear—the great immobilizer. The emotion responsible for inaction and failure. How do we recognize fear? How do we defeat fear? Like the booster tanks of a rocket that are jettisoned into the sea, how do we expel fear from our daily lives? Well, like a cold or stomach flu, we must be prepared to face our fears on a regular basis. There is simply no guarantee that they will not resurface. Let's face it. We are human. Therefore we will experience fear from time to time. It is not a matter of eliminating fear from our lives. That's unrealistic. It's a matter of learning how to cope with fear, and how to overcome it as quickly as possible.

Emerson's statement above paints a very vivid picture—that of a young bird reluctant to test its wings. It is fear that keeps it safely entrenched in the nest. But both the young bird and its mother know that at some point, the tiny creature must leave the sanctuary and venture out on its own. The laws of nature dictate that the young will at some point test their independence, or be forced to do so by their wise and loving mothers. These mother birds are well aware that the longer their young remain nest-bound, the more danger they invite from predators.

We can probably all recall a time when we were frozen by fear—afraid to make a decision or carry out an action. For me, this immobilization occurred in my late thirties. I was teaching a number of communication classes (Mass Media & Society, Station Programming, Radio Production, Broadcast Copywriting) at North Central College in Naperville, IL, a small, private, liberal arts college about 25 miles west of Chicago. I had come to the college about ten years earlier. And with the experience that I had gained as a writer-producer-director at WGN-Radio in Chicago, I felt more than qualified to prepare these students for careers in the field of broadcasting.

I was also teaching one more course—one which was a personal favorite—but one which I didn't feel quite as qualified to teach. The class was TV/Film Screenwriting. I had a thorough knowledge of the structure and mechanics needed to teach students to write a script. But what I lacked was the experience of having done so myself. For years I had planned someday to write a feature-length screenplay but I never seemed to get around to it. I kept telling myself that procrastination was the culprit, but deep down I knew that it wouldn't take a great deal of effort to simply attack this assignment. It wasn't procrastination that prevented me from answering the call—it was fear.

I was fearful that if and/or when I finally decided to write a script, I might discover that I didn't possess the necessary skills to succeed. And if that were the case, how could I walk into a classroom and attempt to teach skills and principles that I had not mastered myself? How could I claim to know the correct way to write and market a screenplay if I had never done so successfully? And so that fear held me in place. It kept me from finding out if I was qualified or not. It lasted a few years before I did some soul-searching and made the decision to jump into the deep water.

I had to know if I possessed the skills to accomplish this task. I started slowly—a few minutes each day. Then when I felt as though I was moving in the right direction, and my confidence began to grow, I made the decision to write 30 minutes…then 60 minutes…then 90 minutes each day. Currently I write about two hours a day. I am happy to report that the investment has paid off. Not only was I able to sell a screenplay to a Hollywood producer, but I have optioned numerous scripts to production companies, and have placed in the finals in a number of screenwriting competitions. Today I can walk into that classroom and not only teach the basics of screenwriting as I had done before, but now I can share with the students some personal experiences that are so much more effective in the learning process.

Like the young bird fearful of testing its wings, we need to leave that nest as soon as possible. It has been a safe environment for us but if we look more closely, we will see it for what it is—immobilization and complacency. Venture out. Test those wings. You may surprise yourself. In no time, you'll be soaring.

> "Fear always springs from ignorance."

Ralph Waldo Emerson

(from an oration delivered before the Phi Beta Kappa Society, at Cambridge, August 31, 1837)

> "Knowledge is the antidote to fear."

Ralph Waldo Emerson

(from "Courage," *Society and Solitude*, 1870)

No, you're not seeing double. These two Emerson quotations are basically saying the same thing, but each does so in such an effective way that I didn't want to exclude either. They just naturally work in tandem. And if you notice the years referenced above, you can see that Emerson is more than consistent—a span of 33 years from oration to essay with the same insightful message.

Study the words above. Emerson is addressing a topic that is paramount in the minds of rational human beings—the element of fear. No one is immune from the clutches of fear. It grabs us. It freezes us. It immobilizes and paralyzes us. It can cause us to become weak or ill. Nothing good comes from fear. Therefore we must do everything in our power to eliminate it. But that may not be quite as easy as it sounds. We all know that no one is completely fearless.

What is important in these messages is to recognize that Emerson is in no way minimizing a person's fears. The same fears that are trivial to some may appear monumental to others. Emerson is not casually suggesting that we should just suck it up and face our fears. He is instead offering a strategy for doing so. With the realization that many of our fears stem from ignorance, we can better confront those demons with a dose of knowledge. The notion that the less we know about something, the greater our fears—makes perfect sense.

For years, the number one phobia in the U.S. has been and continues to be the fear of public speaking. Anyone who has ever delivered an oral report in school or in the workplace knows the anxieties experienced during a live presentation. We have all been there—the dry mouth, the perspiration, the nausea, the fear of freezing up or forgetting material. When we think about all those sets of eyes staring at us—penetrating us...and that audience—judging and critiquing us, it's enough to rattle anyone. But public speaking doesn't rattle *everyone*.

Have you ever noticed that the more you prepare, the more research you do, the more you rehearse—the more confident you become, and the better your performance. This has nothing to do with luck or with personality. It has everything to do with preparation. And what is preparation—it is knowledge. The more we know about a topic, the more fearless we become. If you know the material, even if you lose your place, it will be much easier to recover from a momentary lapse. The more you practice your delivery, the more you can hear yourself reciting the lines.

And what about the time that we waste in anticipation of our fears? If there is a particular challenge waiting for us in the near future, and if it is the type of experience that produces anxiety, we are likely to obsess about it for days or weeks or months before it ever happens. If that obsession causes us to feel ill or defeated or hopeless, then these thoughts are not only a great waste of our time, but they are producing an unhealthy, self-defeating state—one in which we must escape from as quickly as possible. You know yourself better than anyone else. If you know for a fact that no matter what you do, you will undoubtedly worry about an upcoming event, consider doing one of two things:

1) Assign a particular period of time (the shorter the better) for the express purpose of worrying. If the event is six weeks away, don't allow yourself to worry away valuable time. Give yourself a week—no more—to do so. If you haven't figured it out by now—life is way too short. We need to be as productive as possible with the days we have been given. When that week of worry approaches, attack it. Learn to convert your fearful moments into positive thoughts. The minute you find yourself dwelling on a future fear—real or imagined—stop immediately. Tell yourself that this particular thought will not be tolerated. And redirect it. Better yet, dismiss it. Train yourself instead to conjure up a joyful picture (a favorite fantasy, vacation image, family memory, etc.) Before long your mind will be miles away from where you began.

And if you don't think it's possible to alter your thought process, and to substitute new, positive reflections for negative fearful thoughts...think again. You do it all the time...when you're not supposed to. Think about how your mind wanders in class, in a meeting at work, at church, when you're supposed to be listening to your spouse. Sometimes you wander so far off track that it's hard to recall your original starting point. It's very doable.

Or if you still find yourself obsessing about an upcoming event and just can't shake feelings of trepidation, try another strategy. To be perfectly honest, once I get a negative thought in my head, as much as I think I can simply replace it, I still find it a challenge to do so. Therefore I employ an alternative approach.

2) Instead of substituting thoughts, which is difficult for some of us, I do the following: I engage in research — I become a research engine unto myself. I attempt to learn as much as I can about whatever it is that is causing my apprehension. And I embark on a journey of preparation — over-preparation is probably more like it — so that I will be in the best position possible for what is to come. Actually, I recently did just that.

In the world of academia, it's all about assessment of the institution, and even more so, evaluating the effectiveness of teachers. Every three or five years, depending on your rank, college faculty members must submit self-evaluations of their work. Teachers at our institution are evaluated in four major categories: 1) Demonstrated Teaching Effectiveness, 2) Evidence of Personal Growth and Scholarship, 3) Advising Contribution to Student Growth and Development, and 4) College and Community Faculty Citizenship. The evaluation itself forces us to re-examine our philosophies and techniques. It allows us to step back and analyze our methods of instruction. It helps us assess the relevance of lecture material and assigned readings and to determine if they are meeting the needs of students who will soon be entering the marketplace.

One component of this evaluation process is classroom observation. This is when a senior faculty member in your discipline or division attends one of your classes. This individual is there to determine (to name a few) just how efficient, insightful, and relevant your lectures and lesson plans are, and how you manage to generate critical thinking in the classroom. Considering the fact that I have been teaching for more than thirty years, this should be a relatively stress-free experience. But, to be honest, from the time I am furnished with the date that the observation is scheduled to take place, until it actually occurs, if I am not careful, I will obsess about it. Knowing this, I always employ the second suggestion above. I prepare and prepare and prepare. I just make certain that the lecture is tight and substantive and thought-provoking.
      Not that every lecture in front of a student audience shouldn't be tight and substantive and thought-provoking, but let's face it — it's kind of

like going out to dinner with your future in-laws for the first time. You only get one chance for a first impression—everything has to be perfect. And so you are conscious of what you wear, what you say, what you order, etc. This philosophy can be applied to other situations as well. Consider, for example, the way that college and university cafeterias position themselves. Have you ever noticed (I'll bet your college-aged kids have) that the quality of the entrees always improves on the days that prospective students are visiting campus. This is not a coincidence. Current students know that these are the days *not* to miss lunch.

When you can anticipate your fears, and when you have the time to prepare for an event that has in the past produced feelings of anxiety, a state of readiness makes all the difference. Take advantage of this prep time. Use it intelligently, judiciously, and wisely. When you stop and think about it, this advice can't be expressed any simpler: "Fear always springs from ignorance," and "Knowledge is the antidote to fear."

> "He has not learned the lesson of life who does not every day surmount a fear."
>
> Ralph Waldo Emerson
>
> (from "Courage," *Society and Solitude*, 1870)

Every day? Is Emerson serious? Does he really expect us to face and overcome our fears on a daily basis? Well, actually, yes. But it may not be quite as challenging as you might guess. Stop and think about it for a moment. Most of us are already doing it. Most of us face at least one fear each and every day but never take the time to recognize it for what it is. We don't pat ourselves on the back. We don't congratulate ourselves. We don't keep track of each accomplishment. We simply live our lives and prepare for the next challenge, without ever consciously realizing that we are doing so. Are you trying to recall what fear you may have faced today? Well, you may be searching for some monumental hardship that you know you would never have forgotten had you overcome it. And you'd be right. But you may be forgetting the little fears—the ones that seemed significantly larger in years past, but today have become part of your daily routine.

Take *merging*, for instance? You remember. When you were 15 or so and learning how to drive, you undoubtedly were forced to spend some time on an expressway—for as little time as possible as far as you were concerned. I don't know about you but I did fine once I was on the expressway and settled into a lane. I would just position myself over to the right, and no matter how slowly traffic moved in that particular lane, I was comfortable. But getting there was the problem. I hated merging. I wasn't assertive enough to create a space in the traffic flow. I always waited for someone to let me in, or prayed for a space to miraculously open up. What if no one would let me in? What if the entrance ramp suddenly ended and I hadn't successfully merged? What then? Would I end up stranded on the shoulder? Would I even live to talk about it?

Merging is one of the fears that Emerson is talking about—maybe not literally, but it is one of those little annoyances that can produce the jitters. If you drive to work each day via the expressway, then you merge on a daily basis. And whether it bothers you or not, you usually decide that a momentary challenge on the entrance ramp is well worth the time it saves. Some days it is more challenging than others but we do so for convenience purposes. There are some people out there who refuse to drive on expressways, and merging may be one of the reasons they have chosen that path. The important thing to realize is that most people were probably fearful of merging when they were young, and still may not particularly enjoy it, but they have chosen to face this fear (although they may no longer look at it like that) on an almost, for some, daily basis. It's time to give yourself a little credit.

Think of the things that you fear—and I'm not talking about being buried alive, or things that are unlikely ever to occur. I'm referring to daily activities that you either avoid or are somewhat reluctant to undertake. Examine your procrastination list—tasks that you've been putting off. Have you been avoiding these projects because they are unpleasant, because they take more effort than you are willing to expend, because you're unable to squeeze one more job into an already busy schedule (usually a lame excuse)—or because you're afraid. If fear is immobilizing you, then it is time to research what it would take for you to feel confident enough to attack it head on. Have you been putting off a visit to a physician to avoid an uncomfortable procedure or because you'd rather not face the results of certain medical tests? Have you been reluctant to enroll in graduate level program because of the rigor of a new curriculum? Have you hesitated calling someone with whom you feel a certain romantic spark for fear of rejection?

These are just the types of challenges that Emerson would encourage us to accept—and to eventually conquer—each and every day. When it came to the human spirit, Emerson understood it better than most. He knew that the decision to face a fear was the first step in surmounting that fear. Remember—"He has not learned the lesson of life who does not every day surmount a fear."

PASSION

> "The reward of a thing well done is to have done it."
>
> Ralph Waldo Emerson
>
> (from "New England and Reformers," *Essays, Second Series*, 1876)

The payoff. It seems it's all people are looking for sometimes. What's in it for me? You gotta look out for number one. You scratch my back and I'll scratch yours. It's sad to think that many people live their lives for the express purpose of getting "what they have coming." How about just doing something for the sake of having done it? But that unfortunately is not a particularly popular stance. This section examines *passion* — performing a task for the sheer love of it. Not because we expect a favor in return...not because we're receiving compensation...not because we fear the consequences...but because whenever we are engaged in this activity, we grow, we glow, and we flourish.

Have you identified your passion in life? Have you thought about what you would do if you didn't have to worry about finances? If you won the lottery tomorrow, what would you do to keep yourself busy? This Emerson quotation addresses not just our life's passion, but every other task we choose to accept. Can you imagine performing mundane chores with a passion? Mowing the lawn with verve? Washing the dishes with vigor? Doing the laundry with spunk? Chauffeuring around the kids with gusto? Think about it. If you decided to employ vivacity to each item on your To Do list, imagine the effect you would have upon others—upon yourself. You would undoubtedly put an end to your own battle with procrastination. You would begin to look forward to taking on new projects. There would no longer be unpleasant tasks hanging over your head. Instead you would view them as opportunities—opportunities to experience exhilaration. After all, who in their right minds would avoid an occasion that promised a natural high?

Have we convinced you yet to instill a little passion into your daily schedule of activities? Are you starting to get excited about making the kids' lunches, unloading the dishwasher, calling on your next client, or painting the kitchen? Not really, huh? Well, if your first reaction is an unimpassioned shoulder shrug, that's fine. Don't worry if you can't seem to work up much emotion for what you probably consider drudgery. But have you ever wondered why you consider such labors as drudgery? It might be because you have decided to label them so. If you have your bathroom remodeled, you marvel at the skill and workmanship of the tradesmen. You are impressed by their natural talents, and wish that you were that gifted. If you decide, however, to tackle the same project yourself, why then do you dread removing wallpaper or tearing up an old tile floor? If *you* have to perform the task, it's drudgery. If someone else does the work, it's a skillful operation. What if you were to approach this project with a different outlook? An impassioned outlook. If you put your heart and soul into a job, your attitude will soar, you'll take pride in your work, and you'll experience the reward that Emerson refers to when he says, "The reward of a thing well done is to have done it."

Now the hard part—maintaining that fervor. I have attempted to employ this strategy on numerous occasions—forcing the passion into various actions and endeavors. Every so often, I have tried to just will myself to act differently in certain situations. For example, I might remind myself that I really need to stop complaining about things and view life in a more upbeat fashion. I glance at my watch, and see how long I can go before a complaint of some nature surfaces. In the past, I would beat myself up each time I failed. Then I began to realize that even if I had only succeeded for a few minutes, I had indeed accomplished something. Then I would try to beat my own record. The toughest part was trying to remain conscious of the challenge I had set for myself. Before long I was on to other things, and losing focus on trying to maintain an upbeat demeanor.

I decided to employ my trusted companions—sticky notes. If you walk into my office, you will find these tiny adhesive squares all over my desk. They are constant reminders of meetings to attend, bills to pay, activities to perform, as well as motivational challenges. I might simply write down the words, "No Complaints," as a reminder of the newest goal that I have set for myself. After a couple of days I will usually move this particular note to a new location, or rewrite it on a different colored note, just so it will appear fresh and current. It unfortunately is the only way I seem to remember these objectives. Sometimes, however, I don't need reminders. Sometimes I have practiced an activity for so long, and have been so successful, that it has become part of my being—a new habit that requires no jogging of memory to perform.

The next time you are dreading a particular task, try infusing a little passion into the chore. It may be insincere at first. You may be going through the motions early on. But don't be surprised if this routine exercise becomes more and more interesting, more and more challenging, and more and more addictive (in a good way). And before you know it, you'll be rewarded with feelings of satisfaction and contentment for having performed nothing more than a simple task. Soon the exhilaration you experience will rival the feelings you have enjoyed after having achieved far loftier goals.

"What is life but what a man is thinking of all day?"

Ralph Waldo Emerson

(from "Powers and Laws of Thought," *Natural History of Intellect*, 1893, published posthumously)

When you were in high school, you might have visited your guidance counselor and you may have asked for help in choosing a major for college. And you probably took an exam of sorts that tried to ascertain your academic strengths and weaknesses. Upon completion, you were presented with a list of potential career choices based on the results. Some of the suggestions may have seemed a bit bizarre, but others got you to thinking. You may then have begun exploring particular careers and researched which colleges offered programs in those areas. You may have tried to imagine yourself taking that career path, and picturing yourself in one of those professions. Trying to identify what you're good at is certainly one way of determining a career choice, but is it the best way?

Let's examine this Emerson quote, "What is life but what a man is thinking of all day." You notice it doesn't say, "What is life but what a man is good at." If you are proficient at a particular skill, should you then pursue a career that utilizes that talent in some way? Some may argue "yes." But others who feel that an individual's passion cannot be ignored might disagree. When I was in high school, math was probably my best subject. In fact when I took placements tests at my college orientation, I placed high enough on the math exam that I met the university's math competency and therefore was not required to take a class in that area of study. That was all well and good but it meant very little to me at the time. I had no interest in a math major or those job fields where math might be applied on a daily basis. The fact that math came naturally to me was in no way a factor when I chose a career path. It wasn't a subject matter that I thought about each day. But there was another field that had caught my attention.

I remember sitting at the dinner table one Sunday afternoon when I was a senior in high school. The topic of conversation, much to my chagrin, was my choice of major in college. I hadn't yet informed my parents about what field of study I wanted to pursue. I was afraid they wouldn't approve. For the better part of dinner, I had managed to avoid committing to one particular career path. For most of the conversation, they tossed out various career choices. None of which, however, intrigued me. My dad kept referencing the major that my brother-in-law-to-be had chosen — chemical engineering. Since science was not my bag, I knew that would never happen. Before long, I knew I had to share with my folks the news that I was fairly certain wouldn't please them. "I've decided to go into broadcasting," I said.

I can't seem to recall my dad's response. Oh, heck, that's a lie. I remember his exact words. But since the statement contained an expletive, let's just say he didn't approve. And as is the case with the parent/child dynamic, the more he tried to talk me out of that field, the more I knew I wanted it. Perhaps some of the desire on my part was to prove to him that I could actually succeed in a very competitive field, but to be perfectly honest, it's what I thought about all the time. And I think Emerson might have agreed with that choice — at least from the perspective of one's passion, that is. Well, I'm happy to say that I graduated college with majors in Broadcast Communication and Journalism, and six weeks after commencement, I began my career at one of the premiere radio stations in the country, WGN. I just couldn't ignore my passion. When I left the station some six years later, it was to join the North Central College faculty where I would teach broadcast and media courses, and run the campus radio station, WONC.

What is it that occupies the majority of your thoughts? Is there some profession about which you fantasize? Is it possible to translate that into a career? Many people either ignore or suppress this desire. They write it off as foolhardy, impractical, or just plain unrealistic. Others are unaware of the hidden talent within them. They go through life wondering what their purpose is, but never really take the time to find out. Discovering your passion is not an easy task. It is not as easy as identifying what it is that you love doing, and then figuring out how to make money doing it. If it were that simple, then I would be raking in the cash each night while sleeping. I love to sleep. I look forward to going to bed each night. And when on vacation, I occasionally give into temptation and take an afternoon nap. Pure heaven.

Never stop searching for that passion. Never pooh-pooh an idea because you worry that people will label you silly if you pursue it. It is never too late to give up on your dreams. It may not be particularly easy, it may cause havoc in your life, it may force you to make some difficult decisions about time/schedule/finances, but a realistic dream is rarely impossible. Every year at graduation, I see adults in their 40's, 50's or 60's earning their bachelor's or masters' degrees. It is inspirational to watch them stroll across the stage, shake the President's hand, grab hold of their diplomas, and wave to their cheering families in the crowd. It is likely that a few years earlier, someone may have called them silly for pursuing a degree at their age. But at that moment in their lives, they are probably closer to reaching their passions than they have ever been before. And there is nothing silly about that.

> "Passion rebuilds the world for the youth. It makes all things alive and significant."
>
> Ralph Waldo Emerson
>
> (from "Love," *Essays, First Series*, 1865)

When we age, our body tires. Aches and pains linger. We lack some of the energy we enjoyed when we were young. We may try our best to maintain our youth through exercise, a healthy diet, supplements, etc., but we must accept these factors as an inevitable part of the aging process. We may be able to slow things down but we can't reverse nature's cycle. And although this may appear to be a rather bleak forecast, all is not lost. Is there a way to turn back the clock? Many have tried. Few have succeeded.

We have all heard the tales of explorer, Juan Ponce de León, who in the 16th century searched unsuccessfully for the legendary Fountain of Youth. You are bombarded each day by dozens of infomercials with savvy spokespersons who hawk the benefits of any number of creams and ointments that will enable you to stop the aging process in its tracks? And if you have the necessary means, what about the plastic surgeons who will nip and tuck you back to the days before wrinkles and age spots? It seems that vanity, whether we like to admit it or not, drives many of us. It would be difficult to find folks who haven't tried in some way to appear younger (coloring their hair, getting a new hairstyle, losing weight, dressing in more youthful attire) to name just a few.

I fell victim to the clutches of vanity about a year ago. After having sported a full facial beard for nearly thirty years, I decided it was time for it to come off. I remember standing in front of the bathroom mirror one day and staring at the gray hair that had consumed my face. "Who is that old man?" I thought. I had toyed with the idea of shaving it off ever since my 90-year-old dad once told me that he'd like to see my face without a beard before he died. But I have to be frank. My decision to undo the beard was driven more from wanting to shave about ten years off my appearance than an aging parent's request.

So where are we headed with this discussion? It's common knowledge that there is no Fountain of Youth, and that cosmetics, creams and tonics just don't work. Or if they do, the result is short-term at best. There is, however, a fix for the aging process. It doesn't have a dramatic effect on your appearance unless of course you count the perpetual smile on your face. It does guarantee a more youthful, more alive feeling than creams and ointments could never deliver. You won't find it on store shelves or online nutrition websites. It can be found within. I'm referring to passion. As Emerson points out, "It (passion) makes all things alive and significant."

We've talked in the last couple of sections about how you can live and work more efficiently, more energetically, and in a more fulfilled state, just by instilling a little passion into your life. Now comes the best news of all. When you live and work passionately, one of the by-products is a more youthful feeling. You feel better about yourself. You seem to possess new-found energy that fuels you through project after project. And if you are fortunate enough during this process to somehow identify your true passion in life, consider the results. You may experience a childlike state where you can't imagine doing anything other than immersing yourself into this new hobby, activity, or way of life.

In order to identify your life's passion, you must first begin to live in a more passionate manner. It may be forced. It may be contrived. It may be an act. But before long, it becomes part of you, and the passion is no longer something that you have to remind yourself to do but rather something that becomes habitual. Once you have entered this state, you will have positioned yourself for this life's mission to be revealed to you. You will have created an openness that will allow this passion to make itself known. But it can only happen if you first adopt a drive, an energy, a lust for life, for any and all activities in which you partake — personal or professional.

Isn't it time you reclaimed your youth? Can't you imagine yourself with the boundless energy you enjoyed as a child? Can't you hear yourself saying, "Oh, to be young again." And to actually feel some of that spirit take hold — a spirit that knows only enthusiasm and optimism. It all begins when you make the decision to do everything to the best of your ability — from brushing your teeth, to cleaning out the gutters, to parenting, to running your business. Start enjoying what Emerson is promising when he says, "Passion rebuilds the world for the youth. It makes all things alive and significant."

> "Passion adds eyes; (it) is a magnifying glass."
>
> Ralph Waldo Emerson
>
> (from "Poetry and Imagination," *Letters and Social Aims*," 1875)

When we get right down to it, most of us are authorities on something — whether we realize it or not. Have you ever taken the time for a self assessment to determine what skills lie hidden within? People with low self esteem might find difficulty with trying to uncover this talent. They have little confidence in themselves and are at a loss to identify the gifts they possess. For those of you who feel that you belong somewhere in the middle of the pack — or maybe on the lower end of the scale in terms of talent — take a close look at Emerson's advice above. He is furnishing us with a strategy for breaking free from the pack and positioning ourselves firmly on the top of the heap.

You may be tiring of the term, *passion*, and if you are, it is only because you have yet to discover its power, its magic, and its uncanny ability to enable you to see yourself for whom you really are. The more passionate we become about everything we do, the more we will discover hidden treasures about ourselves that we never knew existed. If you apply endless energy and enthusiasm to your daily chores, projects and responsibilities, you will be able to delve more deeply into your innermost feelings. You will unearth desires and sensations that you have never experienced before. You are no doubt familiar with the clichés, *live your life to the fullest* or *be the best you can be* or *make the most of each day* or *today is the first day of the rest of your life*. Well, as corny and as trite as they seem, each is an absolutely perfect strategy to enable you to achieve a more satisfying and fulfilling life. And each of these strategies is impossible to accomplish without conviction, and yes, without passion.

If your effort is just good enough to get the job done, you will have missed a golden opportunity to discover a hidden truth about yourself or about the exercise you have undertaken. Every time we extend ourselves, every time we knock ourselves out, every time we put forth a maximum effort, we place ourselves in a position for magic to occur. When you work at a level that causes some folks to accuse you of overachieving, don't for a minute pay a lick of attention to them. When people criticize an outstanding effort, they do so for one of two reasons: either they don't want you to make them look bad, or they are fearful that you will be rewarded for your efforts. Only self-loathing individuals would dare criticize a spectacular effort on one's part.

Besides ignoring the ranting of such people, you would also be well advised to ignore these people period. We have earlier discussed the benefits of surrounding ourselves with positive individuals, and purging relationships with friends or acquaintances who bitch, moan, complain, or who attempt to belittle you with criticisms of your efforts. These are the same individuals who use terms like "company man" whenever someone has the audacity to think of their employers before themselves. While optimism and hard work are contagious, be aware that weak efforts and negativism are as well. Identify the types of individuals who you aspire to be more like, and find a way to bring people of this ilk into your life. They, unlike the others, will applaud the efforts of someone who works each day with passion.

As Emerson states above, passion "is a magnifying glass." When we partner up with it, we will experience new insights and perspectives. We begin to see ourselves and our goals in a light we have never before witnessed. Personally, I like to set the bar relatively high for myself. If you stay fixed on your goals, and pour yourself into your work each and every day, you will soon not only learn how to infuse passion into each project and activity to which you commit yourself, but you will be on the road to discovering your true mission in life.

PATIENCE

"Happy is the hearing man; unhappy the speaking man."

Ralph Waldo Emerson

(from "Intellect," *Essays, First Series*, 1865)

Well, here we go again. Another Emerson reference supporting the old adage that *listening is a virtue*. If we were to enlist the services of a time machine, and we were to set the dial for 1865, just try to imagine being deposited in the midst of a formal dinner party that has been arranged to honor a central figure in American transcendentalism—author, philosopher, poet, essayist, lecturer, Ralph Waldo Emerson. It would likely be difficult for us to make his acquaintance since throngs of party-goers would undoubtedly be muscling their way to position themselves as close as possible to the guest of honor. Each would be hoping to absorb any tidbits of wisdom that might come from the lips of such a distinguished guest.

But knowing what we know of Emerson, and considering the tidbit of wisdom at the top of this page, it is unlikely that the invited guests would share in the experience they had been anticipating. It is more likely that Emerson would not only refrain from dominating the conversation, but instead would assume the role of listener. He would probably drift from one conversation to the next and digest as much of the discussion as possible. He would hold onto the weighty points of view, and dismiss the blabbering of fools. And then at the appropriate moment, he would interject a witty or insightful comment.

Emerson isn't suggesting that we never express our points of view regarding substantive issues. He doesn't want us always to remain mum just for the sake of demonstrating our superior listening habits. There are times when we must speak up. There are moments when we must share an opinion. There are instances when others look to us for advice. What he is saying is that we should listen carefully to the opinions of others, that we should process these comments, that we should refrain from rash, impulsive replies, and then once we have weighed the statements of others, we can offer a few well-constructed thoughts.

The quote above is one of my personal favorites. I happen to be a proponent of the tight-lipped philosophy. If I have nothing to say, I say nothing. I rarely text. I seldom use Twitter. I have always believed that the substance of a statement is far more important than the size of the statement. The more we speak, the more likely we are to say something we will later regret. The more we speak, the more likely we are to engage in frivolous gossip. Instead, I try to listen more effectively (although my wife might disagree), and to speak only when necessary. I find that this strategy leaves me with far more free time—far more free time with which to be productive.

For years, I have half-heartedly joked that the three most important technological inventions in modern society have been the microwave oven, the VCR, and the snow blower. These advances have simplified my life. But I need to add one more innovation to the list—Caller ID. To me the telephone is a necessary evil. I have always believed that if we could harness the time that we waste on the telephone, and utilize it in a more useful and productive way, we would likely be an even more advanced society.

You are probably familiar with the *Do Not Call List* – a government-sponsored registry of consumer phone numbers that telemarketers are prohibited from calling. It has proven to be a Godsend to consumers who had in the past been plagued by solicitors. Inspired by the *Do Not Call List*, a few years ago I created my own personal *Do Not Answer List*. This is a collection of phone numbers on a piece of paper taped to our kitchen wall next to the telephone. It contains the numbers of various friends and relatives with a reputation for long-windedness. Now, when the phone rings, I glance at the Caller ID, then the *Do Not Answer List,* and I soon discover the identities of those with whom I am choosing not to speak. It's wonderful. I did manage to get busted however a few months back when a relative who was visiting happened to spot her phone number on the list. She seemed mildly offended. Oh well, it's the price we pay for progress.

Now understand that I am in no way criticizing those who choose to spend endless hours on the phone. For some, the practice is enjoyable, and even therapeutic. For me, however, more often than not, it is wasted time. And please don't get me started on the use and abuse of cell phone technology. The cell phone may have been the best and the worst invention of all time—a blend of utter convenience and dangerous addiction. Bottom line: make the choices that are best for you, but don't forget, "Happy is the hearing man; unhappy the speaking man." All it takes is a little patience.

"Adopt the pace of nature. Her secret is patience."

Ralph Waldo Emerson

(from "Education," *Lectures and Biographical Sketches*," 1883, published posthumously)

If you have ever planted a flower or vegetable garden, you know the importance of patience. And I'm not referring to the planting of seedlings or actual flowers, I'm talking about the process that begins with tiny seeds. After we have carefully buried them beneath a few inches of soil, we find ourselves monitoring the progress of our creations on an almost daily basis. We water. We fertilize. We weed. And we wait. Before long our labors have paid off. We spot a tiny crack in the earth and realize that our efforts have paid dividends. We then nurture this new life as if it were human. We point it out to family and friends and neighbors and anyone who may inadvertently drift onto our property. And by the time our new rose or daffodil or petunia or tomato or sweet pepper plant bears fruit, we have forgotten about the early days of longing and anticipating and waiting for any sign of growth.

Such is the nature of nature. If we are patient enough to wait out the magic of plant life, we need to apply the same patient effort in our own lives. We need to trust that in time, the problems that we are experiencing, or the projects that have buried us, will right themselves. But no matter how many pep talks we receive, we find that each obstacle can seem insurmountable. And it is maddening to listen to someone telling us that *in time* we will find a solution to our problems. Or *in time*, the workload issues we are facing will, one by one become more manageable. We somehow seem to forget that we have all experienced dilemmas like these in the past, and *in time*, they did indeed pass. The stress we are feeling and the problems we are facing are nothing new. We must keep reminding ourselves that we have slain these giants before. And they were just as menacing and foreboding as they appear today. We need to adopt the mantra: been there, done that.

Emerson suggests that we "adopt the pace of nature." This is not an easy suggestion to embrace. Like the slow maturation of a seed, we must have faith that bit by bit, inch by inch, minute by minute, we will ultimately succeed. Plant life oftentimes appears painfully slow but nature can surprise us. Have you ever noticed how weeds that were seemingly non-existent one day can somehow invade our lawns at an alarming rate following a few days of heavy rain? Or how about the speed at which a hungry legion of tiny red ants can form when a piece of candy or the dripping of an ice cream cone falls to the pavement. Or the speed at which a spring thunderstorm can suddenly appear. Nature can be deliberate. It can also be instantaneous. But one thing is for certain — it moves at its own pace.

While writing this book, I was forced to exercise patience on an almost daily basis. Once I determined the theme of this manuscript, I was ready for it to be done. I wanted to share the wisdom of Emerson with others, and I wanted to do so immediately. But I realized that I first needed to identify 100 inspirational quotations from this master. Then I needed to break them down into 25 subject areas. Before I would allow myself to write a single essay, I knew that I needed to verify the source of each quote. That nearly proved to be my undoing. (More on that nightmare in the Epilogue). Finally it was time to write — time to share with readers the various ways to apply the principles of Emerson to their daily lives. After I finished the introduction and attacked the initial essay, I began to gauge precisely how long it would take me to finish 100 installments. But I soon learned that each section was completely different. Each would take an undetermined interval of time depending on the amount of necessary research, the amount of personal experience, the amount of time I could allocate to writing each day, and the amount of energy and inspiration I was experiencing at that moment.

I soon discovered that, similar to the unpredictable cycles of nature — sometimes painfully slow or other times frighteningly fast — the creative juices operate in a similar manner. And because of this uncertainty, it became difficult to set realistic deadlines. I simply had to wait for the necessary brain power to kick in, and only then was I able to crank out substantive prose. For a while I monitored my own pace (e.g., 10 down, 90 to go; 22 down, 78 to go; 49 down, 51 to go; and so on and so on and so on). There was a time when I never thought I would finish. But once I realized that the clock was actually my enemy, I stopped setting quotas and settled happily for whatever A-list material I was able to hammer out each day. I decided not to beat myself up if I had a particularly unproductive day, but rather I learned to accept my humanness and appreciate whatever I was fortunate enough to produce. It was all about patience.

> "There is a tendency in things to right themselves."
>
> Ralph Waldo Emerson
>
> (from "Considerations by the Way," *The Conduct of Life*, 1860)

My father died on Saturday, June 13, 2009. He was 92. He lived a long, full life. He spent his last eighteen months in a nursing home. He actually enjoyed it there. As my dad aged—from septuagenarian to octogenarian and onto nonagenarian—we knew that the day would come when he would leave us. On that Saturday night when my sister called to tell me of my father's death, my reaction to the news surprised me. It was much more difficult than I had imagined. It takes a lot to make me cry. I teared up more in the weeks following his death than I had in the last thirty years. I thought I was prepared for something like that. I soon learned that no matter how old a loved one is when he or she passes, it is never easy to say goodbye. The void still hurts.

Considering my dad's advanced age, we knew that the bad news could come at any time. We also knew that he was one of the lucky ones. He had beaten the life expectancy for men of his era. In the last year I had actually found myself thinking about what I might say if I had to deliver his eulogy. Then I would immediately chastise myself for ever thinking that. As far as I was concerned—the way he was going, he would probably outlive me. In my fifty-plus years, this was the most difficult thing with which I ever had to deal.

For a few weeks following his passing, little things would trigger an emotional response. I recall sitting in a dentist's office and hearing a Perry Como song over the speakers. Perry Como was born in Pennsylvania, and died in Florida. My dad was born in Pennsylvania, and died in Florida. As a child growing up, I can't tell you how often a Perry Como album played on our stereo system. And so when I heard the smooth, melodious tones of this barber-turned-singer, I immediately thought of my dad—and a tear slid down my cheek. There were other moments when I found myself thinking about him. And they usually caused me to pause, reflect, get glassy-eyed, then sigh and continue on.

I thought about the above Emerson quote whenever I found myself struggling with my dad's death. I knew that in time, things would "right themselves." And indeed they have. Now when I see something that triggers a memory, I no longer tear up. Instead I smile. The hurt is gone.

It has been replaced with lasting, unforgettable memories. At wakes and funeral services, there is always someone who encourages the bereaved family members not to grieve, but to celebrate the life of the deceased. And although it seems inappropriate to do so sometimes, I have to say that concentrating on the celebration aspect makes the loss much easier to handle. It reminds us that life is a race, and it's the lucky ones who cross the finish line and leap into the awaiting arms of God.

I have thought about this same Emerson principle when other challenges have presented themselves as well. I remind myself that although the immediate future may appear bleak, that "there is a tendency in things to right themselves." You must believe that things will eventually improve. And you must exercise patience. But it takes more than patience alone. You have an obligation to apply yourself. You have a responsibility to do everything in your power to correct a problem. Just waiting for things to work themselves out, or just praying for things to improve, is foolhardy. Let's not misinterpret Emerson's quote. He's not simply saying that if we encounter an obstacle, all we need do is sit back, be patient and wait it out. We need instead to get off our butts, to commit to facing our problems, to do the necessary research in order to devise a successful strategy, to implement that same strategy — then to be patient and wait for things to right themselves.

The often misquoted, "God helps those you help themselves," can also be applied to a discussion of this Emerson precept. Some feel that these are the words of Benjamin Franklin. Others claim it is a biblical passage (although none seems to exist). Still others argue that it can be found in one of Aesop's Fables. It matters little who the first person was who said it or who first wrote it down. What *is* important is the message it conveys: besides praying for help with a particular problem, you must first do everything in your power to bring about a resolution. Then and only then can we expect God to lend a hand.

"Teach me your mood, O patient stars!"

Ralph Waldo Emerson

(from "Nature," *Poems*, 1867)

The patience of a star? Now there's a strange thought. Well, maybe not so strange. Let's examine the life of a star. These hot, incandescent spheres of gas (mostly hydrogen) are held together by their own gravitational forces. They emit light and other forms of radiation whose ultimate source is nuclear energy. As a star consumes its hydrogen in the nuclear reactions that power it, the star must change. When all of its nuclear fuel is exhausted, the stars dies, most likely in a supernova explosion. So, what's the connection between stars and patience, and what can we learn from them?

From his writings one can see that Emerson was a great admirer of nature. He makes numerous references to the marvels of nature throughout his essays, lectures and poems. He often compares human life to various aspects of nature. In this particular example, he asks us to learn from the stars. He asks us to consider mimicking the patience of the stars. It is oftentimes confusing when we assign human qualities to inanimate objects. But when you consider our perception of stars, you can see why Emerson might view a star as patient.

Day after day, night after night, when we gaze up into the heavens, we can't help but notice the beauty and majesty of the constellations. We also are comforted by the fact that the stars are constant. They are reliable. They never let us down. They never abandon us. They are predictable. They can be trusted. They are unwavering. They seem secure with their own existence. They appear unchangeable. They know their place in the heavens. We can count on the stars. And what does it take for someone or something to remain transfixed for decades, for centuries, for light years? It's all about patience.

When we look skyward, we see the same magical points of light—when we were five, and when we are fifty. Who or what could remain so steadfast? Only the stars—the patient stars. And although we see what appears to be motionless and never-changing spheres, we know by their very definition that stars are ever-changing. So how therefore is a star, in the words of Emerson, to teach us its moods? Stars appear calm and resolute. But we know that there are constant nuclear reactions taking place within them. Are the stars then deceitful? Are they saying one thing and doing another? What can we learn from something that outwardly makes one statement, but inwardly is wildly different? A great deal actually.

We can emulate the stars. All we need do is to appear calm and composed on the exterior, while our inner spirit continues to grow and evolve. People who never seem to get ruffled, people who are cool under pressure, people who are most welcome in a time of crisis — these are the types of individuals who mimic the stars. On the surface they appear peaceful and tranquil, but we know that they never stop growing and learning and maturing. We can learn a lot from the stars. We can become the kind of person that others can rely on. We all like to think that in the event of an emergency, we would remain relaxed and unshaken. We hope that we would be able to handle pressure, while at the same time make wise decisions.

Like a star, we must consume our hydrogen — growing and changing and evolving and living life to the fullest. Like a star, we must always be there when people look to us — steady and unflappable. We must be a rock. By taking on this persona, imagine the person you would become. Very likely — the kind of person you had always hoped you would be someday. Your confidence level would soar. Your productivity would increase. And the message that would be pouring out of you would shout out to others that you are available and accessible and ready to assist someone whenever there is a need. Others will be drawn to you. And it all begins when you look skyward and say, "Teach me your mood, O patient stars!"

PERSEVERANCE

"Every artist was first an amateur."

Ralph Waldo Emerson

(from "Progress of Culture," *Letters and Social Aims*, 1875)

The minute I came across this quotation, I knew I had to feature it in this collection. Initially I had intended to include this reference under the last category—Patience. But the more I thought about it, the more I realized that in order to bring these words to fruition, one would need to employ far more than patience. Patience implies discipline, and the ability to wait things out in a calm and deliberate fashion. For an amateur to evolve into an artist, patience is but a single ingredient in the recipe for success. One of the components that must be included in this concoction is the gift of perseverance. In order to succeed, you must be relentless. You must be committed. Simply put, you must do your homework each and every day. And it must become a passion.

In my day job, I teach broadcast communication courses at a private liberal arts college outside Chicago. I also advise the campus radio station. A few years back, I recall a student whose career goal was to become an on-air radio personality. There was certainly nothing unusual about that. Many of my students hope to someday claim a career in the radio or television industry. This particular student was a likeable young man whose personality would lend nicely to an on-air career. The only problem was the fact that he had grown up in a neighborhood and a household where the refinements of the spoken word had not been given the highest priority. His verbal skills were somewhat fractured. I'm not referring to a speech impediment of any kind. He was simply rough around the edges. He was basically a *dis-dat-dese-dose* kind of guy.

I make it a point of critiquing the on-air progress of students each quarter. When I first pointed out to this young man that in order to be taken seriously in the broadcast industry, he would need to clean up his speech. Initially he seemed to take the suggestion to heart and pledged that he would try to correct this deficiency. Then quarter after quarter, as I monitored his progress, I was noticing improvement in certain areas—he was becoming quicker on his feet, and he seemed more relaxed and confident—but the original problem still existed.

With each critique I would hammer home the point that in order to alter this speech pattern, he would need to do more than simply log more and more hours on the air. He was under the assumption that the more you do something, the better you get. But he was missing the point that if you never make a concerted effort to correct a problem, hour upon hour will accomplish nothing. In fact, you will become more ingrained in this bad habit. I gave him a book on improving speaking skills. I pointed out voice exercises to perform that might help. I encouraged him to physically script himself out, and to make certain that he was pronouncing not just every word, but every syllable, and in his case, every letter.

Fast forward to his senior year. His on-air skills continued to improve. He had developed a true personality. But he was still a *dis-dat-dese-dose* kind of guy. As a teacher, you can prod and encourage and motivate and inspire until you are blue in the face, but until the student decides to accept responsibility and tackle his or her problem, there is little else you can do. With only weeks before graduation, this same young man asked me to listen to his audition tape, the one he planned to send out to prospective employers. There was nothing new here. I reminded him once again of this glaring flaw—one that had to be resolved before anyone would hire him for an on-air position. For the first time, he seemed to display a sense of urgency. He became panicked that he might not be able to improve his delivery before the job search began.

This story does not have a happy ending. This young man decided to take his chances and to send out the same tape he had asked me to critique. I wasn't surprised when he received little to no response from radio station program directors. The last I heard from him he was working in a factory. He had given up on his dream. But in reality, he had given up on his dream years earlier after having ignored advice from me and others (alumni who frequently offer to critique the work of current students). I'm not saying that if he had corrected this particular speaking style that he would have been guaranteed a career as an on-air personality. After all, the broadcast industry is extremely competitive. But at least he would have given himself a chance to succeed.

The point of this story is to remind us that we need to do more than just *wait* for our skills to improve. We can't just say that in time we are bound to make progress. We need to develop our talents…not just age them. We need not only to work hard, but to work smart. Each day, in order to get closer to our dreams, we must set aside a certain amount of time to realize these goals. Whether we are tired, or under the weather, or busy, or whatever the excuse, we must discipline ourselves to spend fifteen minutes, a half hour, an hour, or whatever time you can afford, to work toward this passion. We may only be taking baby steps initially, but those steps add up, and soon we are taking leaps, and in no time, realizing our dreams. Wines may age and improve with time, but talents need to be nurtured and fostered and exercised. Because after all, "Every artist was first an amateur."

> "Do the thing, and you shall have the power; but they who do not the thing have not the power."
>
> Ralph Waldo Emerson
>
> (from "Compensation," *Essays, First Series*, 1865)

We'll all familiar with the overused phrases, "Put your money where your mouth is," or "He talks a good game," or "There are two types of people in the world—talkers and doers." We've heard them all a million times. But do we really listen to these messages, or, due to their familiarity, do we just tune them out? These expressions may be trite and tired but they speak the truth—oh, do they speak the truth. If you are reading this Emerson text in earnest, then there is no question that you are a doer, or you are someone well on your way to becoming one.

To be perfectly honest, talkers bore me. I try to get as far away from them as possible. I find myself wanting to tell them to just "keep quiet" and *do* something for a change. We all know the talkers—the ones who trap us on the street, in the supermarket, at work, or at a party, and tell us about the big plans they have. They have accomplished less than the rest of us but since they talk big, they try to position themselves in a far superior social class. These individuals are pathetic and sad, and if we had our druthers, we would gladly avoid them and their drivel. But most of us are too polite to challenge the talkers. We smile and nod and look for an opportunity to escape their grasps.

And there's really nothing wrong with walking away. If we were to wait around long enough to put the talkers in their place, it would surely require a confrontation—and I don't know about you, but I prefer a less confrontational approach. If I see them coming, I head the other way. I would rather join a conversation of doers—those people who have concrete and realistic plans and dreams—those people with a track record of accomplishment. It's clear that Emerson is a fan of the doer, "Do the thing, and you shall have the power…" Not only will you be more productive than the talkers, you will have acquired "the power" associated with achievement.

When I think of talkers, I immediately think of the professional takers—politicians. During a campaign, candidates make an awful lot of promises to the voting public. But how do we know when the office seeker is sincere or just blowing smoke? I'm afraid that it takes a little research on our parts.

Larry Sabato, Founder and Director of the University of Virginia Center for Politics, reminds us that if a candidate runs on an environmentally-friendly platform—pledging to reduce pollution, preserve wildlife habitats, support greater recycling efforts, and the like, we can't just accept these promises at face value. We must identify the candidate's past voting record on bills supporting environmental preservation. And if the individual has never held office, has he or she at least received the endorsement of a mainstream *green* organization? Food for thought from a respected educator and political pundit. Politicians must prove to us that they are sincere in their advocacy of a particular issue. Campaign promises without the necessary proof are often just empty promises.

I'm afraid our political homework has just begun. Kathleen Hall Jamison, Professor of Communication at the University of Pennsylvania, tells us that when a candidate, in an impassioned campaign speech, says something like, "If I am elected, I will not allow our country to become weak militarily," what exactly is he or she actually saying? The inference is that this candidate's opponent holds a different opinion regarding military spending. And if we were to buy into that notion, we would be fools. It's very likely that the opponent in this particular situation also wants the country to maintain a strong military, and is willing to support legislation to accomplish just that.

As voters we have a responsibility to recognize the differences in the ranting of various political party nominees. With the use of clever semantics, one would have us believe a complete untruth about another candidate. We must be able to discern the differences between political talkers and doers—or for that matter, the differences between any talkers and doers.

When Emerson tells us, "Do the thing, and you shall have the power; but they who do not the thing have not the power," it should be crystal clear that there is no prize for talking about what we plan to do. The real prize is the fulfillment and satisfaction and enjoyment of having undertaken a project and having completed it. And it is only then that we can experience the *power* of accomplishment of which Emerson speaks.

"Every young man of good faculty and good habits can by perseverance attain to an adequate estate."

Ralph Waldo Emerson

(from "Social Aims," *Letters and Social Aims*, 1875)

It seems pretty clear that Ralph Waldo Emerson, in his various essays, poems, and lectures, created a road map for a successful existence on this Earth. The precepts contained in this book are testament to that. No one would question this sage advice. With each principle presented, I have tried to identify those quotations that offer wisdom, inspiration and motivation. When we consider the fact that most of the Emerson quotes featured in this collection have to do with creating a more ethical, more compassionate, more principled, more virtuous, more intelligent *you*, it may seem a bit out of place to include an Emerson maxim regarding financial advice. But why not? By creating a sound financial base, we are better able to provide for our families, and if we are successful enough, we are then in a position to become benefactors to needy and worthwhile organizations and individuals.

Let's take a closer look at these words. If we expand the Emerson reference, we find:

> "There is in America a general conviction in the minds of all mature men, that every young man of good faculty and good habits can by perseverance attain to an adequate estate; if he have a turn for business, and a quick eye for the opportunities which are always offering for investment, he can come to wealth, and in such good season as to enjoy as well as transmit it."

With these words, Emerson is, in a simple and direct manner, offering a recipe for financial success. There are no specifics however — no blue chips stock recommendations — no advice on how to flip real estate. Just common sense.

Not to minimize these words of wisdom, but isn't Emerson really telling us something we already know? Is he not saying that intelligent individuals who work hard and do their homework regarding their finances will accrue modest wealth? He's not making outrageous claims. He's not buying time on cable TV channels and running infomercials hawking an ingenious financial strategy guaranteed to double and triple your investment. He's simply saying that if you pay attention to reputable and wise financial advisors, and if you read books and articles on the subject, you will in time reap rewards—*adequate* rewards.

Although he is not saying it in so many words, one can glean from Emerson's tone that he is not a fan of get-rich-quick schemes. He instead appears to be a proponent of a sound, patient, and methodical approach to investing. He would probably avoid high-risk funds in favor of long-term growth. This strategy is hardly exciting. It is not the way to hit a home run in the financial markets. It is a slow, deliberate means of acquiring wealth—*adequate* wealth. I feel a need to continually highlight the word *adequate*. It is the precise way that Emerson describes what one can expect from wise, intelligent investing.

Every month or so in the news, we read about someone who chose a shrtcut to wealth—someone who fell prey to scam artists. "Cash this check for me at your bank…and we'll split the proceeds." "Just pay the taxes on your new-found lottery winnings, and keep the rest." And don't forget: "Dear Sir: I am the nephew of the deposed leader of Nigeria and I just need to find someone with a bank account so that I can transfer my untold wealth out of the country before the rebels take over our banks. And, oh, by the way, there's something in it for you."

As ridiculous as these stories sound, each day someone looking for an easy buck makes a poor choice and falls victim to these scoundrels. Consider the words of British author, Douglas Adams who wrote, "If it looks like a duck, and quacks like a duck, we have at least to consider the possibility that we have a small aquatic bird of the family anatidae on our hands." Let's face it—if something looks too good to be true, it generally is. When Emerson advises us to make deliberate, well-thought-out, fully-researched decisions regarding our savings, it makes a great deal of sense to follow this wisdom. In doing so, we eliminate risk, we eliminate heartache, we eliminate deception.

Be careful—be smart—but most of all, be patient. Never be in a hurry to accumulate wealth. Your haste may be your downfall.

> "I have failed, and you have failed, but perhaps together we shall not fail."
>
> Ralph Waldo Emerson
>
> (from "New England Reformers," *Essays, Second Series*, 1876)

I have to be honest. One of the things I enjoy about the teaching profession is the fact that you have a live audience each and every day. Although the responsibility of a college professor is to motivate and challenge and prod and question and educate — I have always made it a point to incorporate humor into my lectures. I find that it oftentimes rouses a somnolent early morning or late afternoon class. It's also a kick to see those smiling faces enjoying a well-timed quip.

I have always believed that lecture and discussion, combined with critical thinking exercises create a great master plan in the classroom. During lecture, for the most part, I avoid sharing personal opinions. I would rather share the opinions of experts in the field. Students should never confuse the opinion of an instructor with his or her role as devil's advocate. We frequently take on that role. It tends to produce more lively discussion, and forces students to defend their positions on particular topics.

When you teach you have the ability to influence young minds. I must confess that there are times I take advantage of that. A moment ago, I said that I avoid sharing personal opinions. I suppose I should have said that I almost never do so. But there is one subject area in which I am somewhat outspoken — the topic of smoking. When I walk into various campus buildings, I can't help but notice the young people a few feet from the front door puffing away before class. I find myself concerned about the damage they are doing to their bodies. I worry that since they have adopted this habit at a young age, they are destined to spend the rest of their lives as smokers. And so, during classes like Mass Media & Society or Broadcast Copywriting or Communication Law, I will launch into a history lesson regarding the tale of tobacco advertising on television and radio. This offers me a springboard for a rare opportunity to step onto the soapbox.

I first ask the students: How long have we known that there is a connection between the use of tobacco and cancer? Many will guess the seventies. Some even toss out the eighties. When I inform them that a Reader's Digest article in December, 1952, entitled "Cancer by the Carton," was the first article written in a mass circulation publication, many are surprised. They find it difficult to believe that we have known the dangers of smoking for more than half a century. We then discuss the evolution of smoking and cigarette commercials from the early days of old-time radio up until the broadcast ban in 1971. Most students are also surprised to learn that in the mid-1950's, nearly one-half of the adult population in the U.S. were smokers.

Once the foundation has been established, I will ask if there are any smokers present who will voluntarily identify themselves. There are times when nary a hand will rise. Other times, a flurry of students will respond. On one particular day, a young lady raised her hand. She appeared nervous. I tried to reassure her by stating that I love the smoker, but hate the smoke. I knew that this particular student was a senior and that she would be graduating in a few months. I then asked her to do a favor for me. I asked that she begin to slowly wean herself off of cigarettes between now and graduation. And then I indicated that I had a challenge for her on the day of commencement. Once her name is called, I asked her to walk onto that stage as a smoker, and to walk off as a non-smoker. I told her that this would be the greatest graduation gift she could receive. I just asked her to consider it. She smiled and said that she would think about it.

Fast forward about six weeks. There was a knock at my office door. This same young lady appeared. She walked in and proudly announced that she had not had a cigarette in a month, and she wanted me to know that. I was elated. I told her that if I had anything to do with it, I was glad. She said to me, "You did. After that class, I went back to my room and cried." Now this was not the answer I was expecting. I never intended for this to take an emotional toll on the student. "I didn't want to make you cry," I said. "I just wanted you to consider my proposal." She told me that the crying was a good thing. She mentioned that she had wanted to quit smoking for years. She said that friends and relatives had been after her to quit but that she just wasn't ready. She told me she really needed that challenge—that kick in the butt—to finally do something she had wanted to do but didn't have the motivation or strength to do so. To my knowledge, she is still smoke-free today.

So what does all of this have to do with the featured Emerson quotation? Well, let's take a closer look—"I have failed, and you have failed, but perhaps together we shall not fail." This young lady had failed in her attempts to quit smoking. But together, we did not fail. I was more than happy to have provided the impetus to bring about this lifestyle transformation. If I in any way can help prolong my students' lives, count me in. Each day life presents us with challenges. And sometimes we may struggle to overcome these obstacles on our own. It is at this precise moment that we need to forget our pride and seek out assistance. Trust me when I tell you that I am the type of person who likes to rely on no one but myself. I like to act as independently as possible. I have been approached by other writers who have asked me to collaborate with them on other projects. In each case, I have politely refused. But there have been other times when I have been researching a manuscript or screenplay, and I did not hesitate to ask for help when I knew that I was in no way qualified to opine on a particular topic.

The key is to be able to recognize the times in which you need to seek out the assistance of others, and then not to be too intimidated or proud to request help. And if others approach you for the same sort of guidance, be as generous with your time as you would hope someone else might be if it were you in need. Remember — you may have failed in the past in a solo effort, "but perhaps together, we shall not fail."

PURPOSE

"We aim above the mark to hit the mark."

Ralph Waldo Emerson

(from "Nature," *Essays, Second Series*, 1876)

Goal-setting. We should all be doing it. Whether we write it down and tape it to a wall, affix it to the refrigerator, or think about it each day, we need a constant reminder of what we hope to someday achieve. Many motivational speakers will tell you that we move in the direction of that which we think about most. So it only makes sense to spend a significant amount of time contemplating our goals. But don't make the mistake of just thinking about what it is you hope to accomplish. You must do something about it.

Throughout this book we have seen a number of Emerson quotations that have inspired us to discover our passions and to realize our dreams. This one is really no different. Our goal is to "hit the mark." In order to do so, we need to set the bar slightly higher. We do so because of the time it will take us to reach these heights. The effort that we produced a month ago may not be adequate enough a month from now. If you're trying to save a down payment in order to purchase a new home, you must account for inflation. Real estate, other than during a recession, will incrementally increase in value as time passes. The 20 percent down, or more, that you are trying to accumulate will need to be greater as the value of the home increases. We therefore need to "aim above the mark to hit the mark."

If you're running for political office, and you need to secure 1,000 signatures in order to be placed on the ballot, it is unlikely that you will present a list of exactly 1,000 names to the Board of Elections. More often than not, inaccuracies are found in most documents of this kind. In order to avoid disqualification, it is in your best interests to gather more than the required number of names so that in the event some signatures are eliminated, you will still reach your quota. Aiming "above the mark to hit the mark."

When we set goals for ourselves, it is often difficult to know if we have set a standard that is challenging enough. What if we set the bar slightly higher? And what if we were then able to reach that level? Had we not reset the bar, we would have been satisfied with a lesser accomplishment, without realizing what we may have achieved. We would never want to set a goal that is so out of reach that it would be virtually impossible to attain. In those cases, we set ourselves up for failure and feelings of inadequacy. So how do we know when the bar is just *above* the mark so that we will confidently *hit* the mark?

We can accomplish this by using a *floating* bar. We first need to set a series of incremental goals. When we reach each one, we nudge the bar slightly higher to the next goal level. But before doing so, we celebrate. It is important to recognize the accomplishment. If we fail to do so, we will begin to feel as though nothing is good enough, and that we will never reach our ultimate goal. This floating bar approach is especially effective when dieting. If you are trying to lose 30 pounds, you are facing a program that will last several weeks. Rather than experiencing feelings of frustration when you drop weight at a slower rate than you were hoping, you need to set goal intervals at 3 or 5-pound marks, rather than setting your sights on 30 pounds or bust. And it is also helpful to set your ultimate goal at 33 or 35 pounds even though you would be reaching your ideal weight with a 30-pound loss. If you have ever dieted before, you are well aware of the rebound factor—hitting the intended mark only to slip back to an undesirable weight a few weeks later. When we follow Emerson's advice, "…aim above the mark to hit the mark" when dieting, we build into our program a cushion that allows for minor fluctuation without feelings of frustration or failure.

The next time you identify an objective you hope to achieve, remember to set a series of incremental goals that will allow you to see and feel and enjoy the progress you have made. Then as you inch closer to your ultimate goal, you will realize that it is truly within your reach, and you will soon begin to envision yourself in the winner's circle—and it no time at all, you will taste victory.

> "I look on that man as happy, who, when there is a question of success, looks into his work for a reply, not into the market, not into opinion, not into patronage."
>
> Ralph Waldo Emerson
>
> (from "Worship," *The Conduct of Life*, 1860)

A strong work ethic." We would all like to believe that people are speaking about *us* when they use those words. It would also be especially nice to think that our supervisors might use such glowing language when describing us. But really — whether someone notices our efforts or not, it matters little. Earlier in this text we mentioned that you don't need to remind your boss what a great job you're doing. If you're working at the level you claim, he or she will notice without being told. We work hard each day because we owe an honest day's work to our employer. We work hard each day because it's the only way we know.

I especially like the Emerson quote above, but even more I like the words that immediately follow this quotation in his essay on Worship:

> "In every variety of human employment, in the mechanical and in the fine arts, in navigation, in farming, in legislating, there are, among the numbers who do their task perfunctorily, as we say, or just to pass, and as badly as they dare, — there are the working men, on whom the burden of the business falls; those who love work, and love to see it rightly done; who finish their task for its own sake; and the state and the world is happy that has the most of such finishers. The world will always do justice at last to such finishers; it cannot otherwise."

My favorite part of this citation is the final sentence: "The world will always do justice at last to such finishers; it cannot otherwise." This is in a sense a formal proclamation that in the end, if we work in an honest and relentless fashion, we will get what we deserve. It's comforting to think that way, especially when you are feeling unnoticed or underappreciated. The cynics might say: "Who is this Emerson fellow who can make such guarantees?" But by now, at the point you are in this collection of

Emerson principles, you know that this writer/philosopher was no ordinary thinker. He seemed to possess insight, perspective, and wisdom unlike others who have come before him or since—and if Emerson suggests that we will ultimately receive a payoff for our efforts, I for one would never question him. I would simply buy into his beliefs and move forward happily and with confidence.

The quotation at the top of this section is a call for self-assessment. It asks us to look within ourselves for the answers. If we are wondering why we have been fortunate enough to have achieved a level of success, or why success has been so elusive in our lives, all we need do is examine our efforts. This is what Emerson is saying when he writes that a "man...looks into his work for a reply." In our hearts we know whether or not we are deserving. We know if we have really earned that raise or promotion. We know if someone else was more entitled. We know these things, and yet we allow ourselves to wallow in self pity when we are refused what we want so dearly. There are many times in our lives when we are denied something that we desire. There are many reasons why we are not chosen to receive them. If we look hard into ourselves—if we look "into our work for a reply"—more often than not we will see the reasoning. We may not like the answers, but we do at least understand why and how these decisions were made.

The time to feel sorry for ourselves has long since passed. The time to hold grudges is behind us. The time to unleash a retaliatory strike is over. Look into your work. Examine your effort. You will soon see what others have seen, and your eyes will be opened. It is never too late to assess your performance. You are likely to discover areas needing improvement. It is now time to address them. In life, more often than not, we get what we deserve. Learn to accept responsibility for your actions. It may be time to turn a corner, and to dedicate yourself to fulfilling the promises you made to your employer when you accepted this challenge. You owe it not only to them—but to yourself.

> "A great man scarcely knows how he dines, how he dresses; but without railing or precision, his living is natural and poetic."
>
> Ralph Waldo Emerson
>
> (from "Heroism," *Essays, First Series*, 1841)

As we age, the more likely we are to pay closer attention to the obituary page in the newspaper. When I come across that section each day, I am drawn initially to the stories of people who have recently passed away, then to the death notices. I first seek out the age of the deceased, then the cause of death, then the significant aspects of the person's life. I don't consider myself maudlin or fatalistic by any means but age and cause of death will resonate with anyone who reaches middle age. It is just something to keep in mind — not because you fear death or impending doom but rather as a guide or a reminder to address health issues you may have been avoiding. And being conscious of mortality can also help you to cherish each day and inspire you to make the most of it.

The headline of an obituary is especially interesting. It encapsulates a person's life and his or her contributions to society, and it does so in a matter of a few column inches. Have you ever wondered how you will be remembered? Have you ever considered how the headline might read for your own obituary? We would obviously all like to be thought of as persons of integrity, compassion, and generosity. And I suppose we wouldn't mind if the term *great* were thrown around a few times in the article. It is doubtful that anyone ever set out to be great. It is more likely that individuals simply set out to be the best they could be in their chosen field. They didn't worry about newspaper clippings or press releases or how many times their names came up when they flattered themselves with a self-search on the Internet. People who ultimately become great are too busy passionately living their lives and fulfilling their missions.

Emerson's comment above really captures the essence of great people. They are not concerned about the exclusivity or the ambiance of restaurants at which they dine. They needn't shop at upscale retail outlets. They're not worried about being seen without make-up. They don't need to reside in a gated community. Their vehicles need to safely transport them from one location to another; the make or model is meaningless. These individuals are so focused on their own personal missions in life that they simply have no time to be bothered with maintaining their status in the community. Where they eat, how they dress, what they drive, where they live—all have little to do with who they are and how successful they can be in accomplishing their goals.

The life of a great person is, according to Emerson, "natural and poetic." Great people don't plot out every aspect of their lives. They leave room for spontaneity because they know that discovery and inspiration are triggered not always by planning and detail but by allowing your mind to drift and to consider possibilities that never would have emerged had you not sat down and willed them to be. A great person is flexible. He or she does not curse interruption or distraction but rather embraces it. The great person, although never intending to be great, realizes that accomplishments are achieved by careful planning *and* by tolerance and a lack of rigidity.

Great people don't need the approval of others in order to co-exist and to thrive. On the contrary, great people seem inspired by doubters. Some of the greatest thinkers—Galileo, Robert Fulton, Alexander Graham Bell, the Wright Brothers—were scoffed at. Had they listened to their critics, they may never have discovered the principles or invented the conveniences we now take for granted. To be great is to have the strength not only to withstand the brickbats from detractors, but to harness the criticism and to convert it into the energy necessary to fuel further exploration. A great person is not only blessed with the gift of knowledge but also with determination and relentlessness. Do we have what it takes to be great? You can acquire the knowledge, and the determination comes from within. Yours may be in the development stages, just waiting to be unleashed. It may be time to release it and taste greatness.

"All mankind love a lover."

Ralph Waldo Emerson

(from "Love," *Essays, First Series*, 1865)

If you take issue with the statement above, all you need do is stroll down the aisles of your favorite bookstore and notice just how many offerings fill the shelves under the heading of *Romance*. If nothing else does, the sheer numbers will convince you that indeed "All mankind love a lover." If you're seeking more proof, consider the thousands of love songs that have been written and performed through the ages. Soap operas have survived on a heavy dose of love (or should we say love-making) for years. And don't forget the silver screen. Not only have there been countless romantic comedies produced since the early days of film, but nearly every movie genre (thriller, action/adventure, horror, comedy, family, etc.) contains a love story of some kind. We are bombarded by stories of love but we don't seem to be tiring of them. Our appetite for love stories appears just as voracious as it has always been.

Emerson recognized that we all possess a fascination with love — whether in story form or in life. He shares the following examples from his 1865 essay on the subject:

> "The rude village boy teases the girls about the school-house door; — but to-day he comes running into the entry and meets one fair child disposing her satchel; he holds her books to help her, and instantly it seems to him as if she removed herself from him infinitely, and was a sacred precinct. Among the throng of girls he runs rudely enough, but one alone distances him; and these two little neighbors, that were so close just now, have learned to respect each other's personality.
>
> "Or who can avert his eyes from the engaging, half-artful, half-artless ways of school-girls who go into the country shops to buy a skein of silk or a sheet of paper,

>and talk half an hour about nothing with
>the broad-faced, good-natured shop-boy."

Long before contemporary romance novels, soaps and film, Emerson recgnized our love for love. He observed that whether we are participants or not, we have an inherent interest in this topic. How often are we entertained, even mesmerized, when we happen to notice or overhear flirtatious banter—at a bar, on a flight, in class, at work, just about anywhere. If two people are discussing the economy, we listen with half an ear. But when there is discourse between two potential lovers, even if it be trivial, we are all ears.

Most of us can recall our first real boyfriend or girlfriend. It's not something you easily forget. We can also recall our first moments of puppy love, and later on, true love. And we will always remember the circumstances surrounding relationships that turned sour. Heck, I can still remember the day when Cookie C. told me that she didn't like me anymore. It was August 15, 1966. It was the summer following eighth grade. It was a clear-cut case of true love. Who was I kidding?! It was merely infatuation. We had been an item for about three months. Then out of the blue, she decided she didn't like me anymore. To tell you the truth, I expected to feel worse. After all, I was the victim. But all I felt was a sense of relief. She was my first real girlfriend, and I didn't have the faintest clue what I was doing. It had been fun while it lasted. But I think I liked the sound of having a girlfriend more than the real thing. I just didn't know how to culture the relationship. I knew I needed to do more than just sit on her front porch. Oh well, I survived.

At the movies, audiences want to see the hero and heroine end up together—and they usually do. In life, we want the same for ourselves. We would like our relationships to be as exciting and vibrant as they are on the screen. But is that even possible? It's not only possible—it's very doable—if we work at it. You are certainly aware of the fact that some of your most pleasant memories have to do with relationships. Recall what it was about your significant other that first caught your eye. Is it possible to rekindle some of those magical feelings? Is it possible to breathe life into your romance? Remember the excitement you felt in the early stages of your courtship. Wouldn't it be phenomenal to feel that way all the time? If you choose, you can to bring that zing back into your lives. What do you have to lose? Everyone will be pulling for you because "all mankind love a lover." So give mankind something to love, something to talk about, something to enjoy. You have the power to grant this wish. Do so—and feel the love.

SERVICE

"Make yourself necessary to somebody."

Ralph Waldo Emerson

(from "Considerations by the Way," *The Conduct of Life*, 1860)

Here is a simple directive, but an important one. Emerson is asking us to be the type of individual whom others cannot live without. He's not suggesting that we become someone's crutch, or someone's free ticket, or to allow others to leech onto us. He is just requesting that we live the kind of life that will be recognized by others as meaningful and as substantive. It's as simple as setting a good example. By doing so, we make ourselves necessary to somebody. We become a model to be emulated. We set the tone as a winner, and hope that others will follow in our path.

But as easy as it may be to set the right example for others, we can just as easily fail in our mission to make ourselves necessary. If we cut corners, take shortcuts, look for the easy way out—we are setting another type of example. And we are just as capable of drawing followers to that end. But the types of individuals who imitate a slacker are no better than their misguided leader. These are the folks for whom the phrase, "misery loves company," may have been penned. But I have a sense that I'm preaching to the choir. The kind of person who picks up a book like this is hardly someone who makes a habit of setting an improper example. The kinds of people who pass time in the advice/motivational/self-help aisles at bookstores are those who are making an effort to better themselves. So I needn't waste my time denouncing the pitfalls of hanging out with the wrong crowd, as your mother had to have done countless times.

Making yourself necessary to somebody is really easier than you might think. If you're worried about having to live the perfect life in order to set the proper example, then worry not. Making yourself necessary to somebody is as simple as letting another driver in who's been waiting to enter a long line of traffic. It's allowing someone to go before you as you enter or leave a building. It's giving up your chair in a crowded room to someone more needy. It's offering to help someone carry groceries to their car. It is all of these things and many more. You don't have to act in a flawless manner to become someone who others admire. It's as basic as holding the door for someone else.

Allow me to digress for a moment. My favorite story about someone holding a door took place in the late 1970's. I was a young producer/director at WGN-Radio in Chicago. I remember climbing a set of stairs on my way to the main studio while trying to juggle an armful of tapes. I knew that I would have a hard time opening the door at the top of the stairs but somehow I would have to manage. I noticed two people a few steps ahead of me. I decided to pick up my pace with the hopes that one of them might hold the door for me. But alas, as they passed through, I noticed the door closing behind them. I was now on my own, or so I thought.

Less than a second later, the door swung open and one of the people who had passed through a moment earlier was now holding it for me. When I looked up to say thanks, I was in for a surprise. Holding the door and wearing a warm smile was veteran actor, Richard Chamberlain (Dr. Kildare, The Thornbirds, King Solomon's Mines). "Why, thank you…Doctor," I said. I'm not sure why I felt comfortable enough to have spoken to this gentleman in that way. I was 25, and I guess I wanted to seem clever and witty. Fortunately it worked. "Oh, you're quite welcome," he responded with a chuckle. Then he stepped aside allowing me to pass by in front of him.

When you are fortunate enough to have worked for one of the premier radio stations in the country, you are bound to have a few brushes with greatness, but this was the first and only time I remembered someone of this stature performing a polite gesture of that manner. There was something special about it. It was more than being able to tell friends and relatives that a Hollywood actor had held the door for me, this was a statement of character. We oftentimes think that when someone reaches a certain level of celebrity, he or she is somehow excused from performing the little niceties that others are expected to perform. It was refreshing to see that courtesy had not been lost on this veteran entertainer. He was undoubtedly holding doors and doing little things for others when he was a struggling actor years earlier.

From that brief encounter, I take the following: Never allow yourself to be too busy or too important to "make yourself necessary to somebody." Don't miss the opportunity when it presents itself.

> "The life of a man is a self-evolving circle, which, from a ring imperceptibly small, rushes on all sides outwards to new and larger circles, and that without end."
>
> Ralph Waldo Emerson
>
> (from "Circles," *Essays, First Series*, 1841)

In May, 1990, playwright, John Guare, watched the curtain rise in Lincoln Center for the premiere of *Six Degrees of Separation*. The story is based on con man, David Hampton, who posed as David Poitier, the son of actor, Sidney Poitier. During this scam, Hampton successfully conned prominent New Yorkers, including Jay Iselin, the President of WNET, and Osborn Elliott, Dean of the Columbia University Graduate School of Journalism. Hampton was eventually exposed, found guilty, and served 21months in prison. The play's title comes from the idea that everyone in the world is separated from everyone else by six links. So if a person is one step away from each person they know, and two steps away from each person who is known by one of the people they know, then everyone is at best six steps away from any other person on Earth.

It's an interesting theory, and one worth noting, considering this particular Emerson quotation. The same way that a pebble tossed into a brook creates a circle, and produces a series of seemingly never-ending concentric circles, so the actions of one person can touch and influence the lives of so many others. Emerson is reminding us that our actions, good or bad, don't begin and end with us alone. In many cases, these actions will have an effect on far more than the immediate audience. Therefore we have a responsibility to act in an unstained and incorruptible manner. But how many of us really consider this social obligation? How many of us ever think of the Big Picture? How many of us really ever think about what effect a single noble or impetuous act will have on our neighborhood, our community, or our society for that matter.

If we are truly separated by only six links, then one can see just how easy it would be for this news to travel well outside our immediate circle. And even if that news never made the newspapers, or was never picked up by the electronic media, or social media for that matter, there is still a human communication network out there capable of broadcasting our successes — or our indiscretions — to the masses. With this in mind, shouldn't we think more carefully before we speak or act? These days an innocent gaffe can be recorded on a cell phone camera, and in minutes end up on the Internet, and available to all the citizens of the world. With his words above,

Emerson is asking us to practice the virtue of prudence each and every day. He is imploring us to consider how the actions of a single person can affect an entire community. And if Emerson was so concerned about the dissemination of information in 1841, imagine how strongly he would urge us today to be responsible to a fault.

Although it may appear as such, it is not my intention to highlight only the negative effects that might occur unless we take this Emerson principle to heart. We certainly have the ability to influence others in a positive manner as well. And the ripples produced by those actions can be just as powerful and effective as the results produced by poor decision-making. When I think about bottling acts of kindness and distributing them in an endless chain, I think about the Warner Bros. 2000 release starring Kevin Spacey, Helen Hunt, and Haley Joel Osment entitled, "Pay it Forward." This is the story of a boy who, as part of a social studies assignment, promotes the idea of paying a favor, not back, but forward. His idea is to repay good deeds, not with payback, but with additional good deeds extended to others.

In many ways, paying it forward takes the Emerson observation of life as a "self-evolving circle," to a whole new level. It suggests that our positive actions are not only noticed by others through a natural course of communication, but that these same acts can be even more effective when those on the receiving end continue the chain of giving through new actions of their own. We can never assume that a simple act of kindness or courtesy is just that—simple. These actions multiply, influence others, and encourage them to create "new and larger circles" of giving. Let each new ripple in our own pond be produced by an act of kindness.

"Serving others is serving us."

Ralph Waldo Emerson

(from "Uses of Great Men," *Representative Men*, 1876)

Millard Fuller was an energetic, young man from Alabama who was determined to succeed in business. He attended Auburn and the University of Alabama Law School. While still in college, Fuller and a fellow classmate started their own marketing firm. For this young entrepreneur, success in the business world was a foregone conclusion. And at the age of 29, Millard Fuller was a millionaire. His future was bright. He seemed unstoppable. But as his business grew, his health and marriage deteriorated. Fuller decided to re-evaluate his life and the direction it was taking. He soon reconciled with his wife, and renewed his commitment to Christianity.

Not long after, the Fullers made a decision that few others in their position would likely consider. They decided to sell their belongings, distribute all of their hard-earned money to the poor and underprivileged, and begin a search for a new direction in their lives. They found this challenge in a Christian community in Georgia where they joined others looking for practical ways to live by and apply the teachings of Christ. There they initiated a ministry in housing where they built modest homes and made them available to low income families.

In 1973, the Fullers, along with their four children, traveled to Africa to test out their housing model. They set up shop in Zaire (now the Democratic Republic of the Congo), and in no time, the project became a success. This convinced the Fullers that this particular housing model had the potential for expansion, and ultimately could be applied anywhere in the world. In 1976, the family returned to the U.S., and along with a group of supporters, they created a new organization: Habitat for Humanity International.

This non-profit ecumenical Christian housing ministry seeks to eliminate poverty housing and homelessness. Today volunteers for Habitat for Humanity International have built or repaired over 800,000 houses around the world, and have provided homes for more than 1.5 million people. Former U.S. President Jimmy Carter and his wife, Rosalynn, are two of Habitat's most famous volunteers. The Carters have been faithful supporters of this project since 1984. In a White House ceremony in 1996, President Clinton presented Millard Fuller with the Presidential Medal of Freedom, the nation's highest civilian honor. The award recognizes individuals who have made major contributions to the country and to their own communities. At the presentation ceremony President Clinton said, "I don't think it's an exaggeration to say that Millard Fuller has literally revolutionized the concept of philanthropy."

Most of us will never come close to the accomplishments of this generous benefactor, but we really don't need to. We are not measured by the amount of our contribution but rather by the sincerity of our commitment. And who benefits from our decision to give to others? The less fortunate certainly. But don't underestimate the gift we return to ourselves. There is no greater feeling than that which comes from helping others. A single charitable act will not only lift the spirits of those on the receiving end, but will do wonders for our spirits as well. Service is a win-win. There's no doubt about it. You give and you get. Those who dedicate time to service each week or month or whenever are blessed with riches that cannot be measured in dollars. What you bring home following an experience of volunteerism is a sense of peace and compassion and a better understanding for those who live in an environment not quite as blessed as our own.

From volunteering your time at the local nursing home, library, hospital, animal shelter, etc., to helping construct a new home for people who have never had the good fortune of living in a residence they can call their own, service opportunities are more than abundant. And don't forget the payback—an exhilaration that cannot be matched by any other experience. If you don't believe me, just try it. There are so many reasons to serve, not to mention the therapeutic benefits of helping others. One way to kick the blues is to seek out a volunteer opportunity. The quickest way to stop feeling sorry for yourself and to appreciate your lot in life is to thrust yourself into an environment with poor, needy, underprivileged, and uneducated individuals.

If you haven't actively volunteered in the past, it may be time to give it serious consideration. And remember that "serving others is serving us." No one walks away from a volunteer experience feeling worse than when they entered into it. Think of service as providing a free therapy session…but without the couch.

"Men achieve a certain greatness unawares, when working to another aim."

Ralph Waldo Emerson

(from "Considerations by the Way," *The Conduct of Life*, 1860)

Have you ever noticed how certain mundane tasks that you may have been avoiding can somehow be made more tolerable once you redirect your thoughts away from these tasks and onto a more pleasurable mindset? I am not a huge fan of yard work but it needs to be done. I find this chore much less burdensome as long as I can plug in a set of earphones tuned to a favorite radio station or mp3 player. And have you ever tried jumping onto an elliptical or treadmill or exercise bike without a distraction of some sort? You know as well as I do that by watching a particular program while exercising takes most of the pain away from the task at hand. While engrossed in the lives and loves of TV or movie characters, you can travel untold miles while at the same time burning those dreaded calories. It is doubtful that Emerson had this application of the above principle in mind when he offered it to his readers in 1860, but it is safe to say that one can interpret this quotation in various ways.

One such interpretation stems from a set of beliefs held by a number of motivational speakers and writers. Some life coaches will tell you that we naturally move in the direction of that which we think about most. It seems to make sense. But remember that there is significant difference between thinking and doing. If you just think about something without putting those thoughts into action, you may end up thinking about nothing. The rationale is that the longer you contemplate accomplishing a particular thing, the more you prepare yourself, the more you train yourself, the more likely you will eventually act upon it.

Then there is the advice that parallels the Emerson quote above: the more you desire something, the less likely it is you will acquire it. On the surface, we seem to have two completely contradictory statements, but there is a difference. The latter statement has more to do with obsessive behavior than does the former. If you desire something to such a degree that you ignore obligations and responsibilities, then you will find yourself moving backwards. It is one thing to dedicate yourself to realizing a particular dream. It is quite another to dismiss everything and everyone in pursuit of it. For quite some time I have wanted to sell a screenplay and have a book published, but those desires did not relieve me of my responsibilities as a full-time college professor, as a father, as a husband, as a volleyball and soccer coach for my kids, and a host of other obligations to which I was committed.

There were times when I wanted to accomplish these goals so badly that I did place those desires ahead of my commitments. And oddly enough, those were the times that I was least productive in my writing. It wasn't until I decided to dedicate certain periods each day to writing that I truly felt I had achieved harmony in my life. I was no longer obsessing about how few pages I had cranked out the day before, or despondent about not having heard back from a producer, publisher, or agent. I finally accepted the fact that I had other responsibilities — more important responsibilities in my life that needed attention. There were people out there — my kids, my students — who were counting on me. And it mattered little to them if I were a published author. I needed to accept the fact that if I were to accomplish these goals, the process of getting there could not and would not detract from my duties as father, husband, and teacher.

If you are being haunted by unfulfilled goals, and obsessing about it, now may be the time to let go. I'm not talking about giving up. I am just suggesting that you release your grip somewhat. Identify what obligations cannot be neglected. Build time in your daily routine to address them. Then look for concrete blocks of time for activities leading to the fulfillment of your dreams. I can only wish for you the same thing that has happened for me in the last few years. When I finally felt that I had created a balance in my life, a strange thing occurred. Whenever I would engage in non-writing activities, I found my mind open and clear, and ideas began to pop into my head — the same ones that had eluded me when my priorities had been misaligned.

Don't abandon your dreams. Seek balance and harmony in your life. And you just may discover that you *can* have it all.

WISDOM

"We are wiser than we know."

Ralph Waldo Emerson

(from "The Over-Soul," *Essays, First Series*, 1865)

Now that is quite a statement…especially coming from Emerson. Are you surprised to hear it though? Or have you known it all along? If we are indeed "wiser than we know," then why do we so often defer to others? Why do we so dearly need the approval of others? Why do we succumb to peer pressure so often? Those are the actions of the unwise, the uneducated, the imprudent. Most of us would balk if someone used those words to describe us. But those words describe people who lack the ability to make their own decisions…who have little to no confidence in their choices…who always tend to blindly follow another. If you are oftentimes indecisive, uncertain, iffy, then you need to re-read the above quote, and learn to trust yourself.

If your parents tell you that you have a beautiful baby, you no doubt enjoy hearing those comments, but you realize that your folks just may be a bit biased. They're grandparents. That's their job. But when Emerson isn't afraid to stick his neck out to remind us that "we are wiser than we know," then we had darn well better take those words to heart. With his reputation for insight, we can be fairly confident that he knows just a little about human nature. So, does that make you feel any better about yourself? Do you think that the next time you face a difficult decision, you will draw from your own well of knowledge? Am I asking you to believe something just because someone says it? Well, yes, considering the source.

Why do you suppose Emerson has so much confidence in us? Think for a minute about how we gain wisdom. Much of our wisdom comes from trial and error, and we begin accumulating it at a very young age. When we were toddlers, we learned rather quickly what would happen if we touched a hot stove, pulled the dog's tail, or took a toy away from a playmate. Following those unpleasant results, we began storing this data in our own wisdom vault. From that moment on, it is doubtful that we were likely ever to make those poor decisions again. That is wisdom.

If you paid attention to the people around you when you were growing up, you undoubtedly learned right from wrong, along with the consequences that you are likely to suffer if you engage in inappropriate behavior. All of that information is knowledge. Most people learn something new every day. Just stop and think about everything you know, and how you might apply that knowledge the next time you face a difficult decision. If we were forced to make our own choices, and were unable to seek the opinions of others, it is likely that we would still make the right decisions. And that is why Emerson has the confidence in us to have made such a bold statement.

Now, just because we know how to choose correctly doesn't mean that we always do so. When we speed on the expressway, we know what the consequences will be if we are caught. And since we have established the fact that "we are wiser than we know," why wouldn't we drive the speed limit? Wouldn't a wise person automatically act in that manner? You would think. But being wise and acting wisely are two different things entirely.

It is important to remember the following from this discussion:

1) Since we are actually wiser than we know, we need to trust ourselves more. We need to draw from that wisdom well whenever necessary to make prudent choices. Heck, we've most likely been there before. We know the consequences. We need to forget about what others may think. We are intelligent enough to make an informed decision. If we meet resistance, we need to be able to defend our choices even if things become rather unpleasant. That's life, and that's what responsible people do.

2) If we really want to demonstrate the fact that Emerson was right all along and that we are indeed wiser than we know, then we need to *make* the correct choice. There's a big difference between knowing what to do, and having the guts to do it. If we possess wisdom, but we fail to exercise it, then it was never ours at all.

> "The invariable mark of wisdom is to see the miraculous in the common."
>
> Ralph Waldo Emerson
>
> (from "Prospects," *Nature Addresses and Lectures*, 1876)

It's time to take a deep breath. In through the nose…hold it…out through the mouth. When life's hectic pace causes our blood to boil, it is important to slow things down — not just to maintain our sanity but for our overall physical well-being. So why do we allow ourselves to compete at such a frenetic pace? Why do we feel the need to run around frantically and to multitask whenever possible? When we do manage to stop momentarily and evaluate our situation, we remind ourselves that our pace will eventually lead to health problems someday. And so in response, we slow down for a while, then before you know it, we have resumed our frenzied schedule.

Is the pace we maintain something that is out of our control? Has it been determined for us? Or have we chosen this course? One might argue that the pace we maintain is chosen for us. Think about the expectations of your boss five years ago. Now think about his or her expectations today. If you are expected to produce more than you have in the past, you are not alone. This is one of the American worker's growing complaints. When the economy suffers, and layoffs follow, if we are fortunate enough to have survived the cuts, we may still be affected by an increased workload.

Now combine that with the desire to be the complete parent — wanting for our children every experience that we enjoyed as youngsters, and every experience we were denied. In order to deliver this pledge, we overextend ourselves both physically and financially, which adds to our hectic pace. It is difficult to advise people on how to create balance and serenity in their lives when they feel an obligation to their families and their employers. And so rather than suggesting that individuals take a personal self-assessment and identify those activities that can either be scaled back or eliminated (which is the best advice), we instead take a closer look at the Emerson precept above which can assist those of us who can't seem to slow down.

When we examine the featured quote, we can't help but feel that Emerson is wanting us to develop a greater appreciation for the simple things in life. He is challenging us to investigate the common, the unadorned things around us, and to discover the beauty and the miracles within. If you, like me, are a fan of the works of Emerson, then you know how often he wrote about nature. He was a true fan of nature. He was impressed by it, entertained by it, awed by it. He felt that there was much to be learned by studying and observing nature. He also found connections between man and nature, and would frequently advise us to learn from it. Whether it be strolling through a field of daisies and soaking up the magic around us, or watching an ant carry a crumb many times its weight to an undisclosed location to share with its colony, these are the kinds of activities that return a huge payoff.

Each day when the sun sets and darkness blankets the Earth, a magical light show takes place in the heavens. If you're a stargazer like me, then you know the beauty of the night sky. On clear nights in the country when there seems to be a million points of light, it is difficult to take your eyes off of this incredible show. I think of stargazing when I read this Emerson quote. For some, however, the planets and constellations are nothing more than commonplace. "They're up there…so what?! What's the big deal?" Oh, but it is a big deal. Though they are carefully positioned in the skies whether we notice them or not, the brilliance of those heavenly bodies is breathtaking. I will never forget the first time I set up a telescope on my driveway. It was a perfect night. I could see Jupiter and Saturn with the naked eye. But that wasn't good enough. Since it was a relatively inexpensive unit, I struggled keeping the telescope steady. But after several minutes, I was starting to get the hang of it. And then, I saw it…Jupiter…before my eyes. I could even see its moons. I just stared for minutes. It was chilly out but I didn't care. When I had had my fill, I redirected the telescope to Saturn. And as with my first look at Jupiter, I was suddenly star struck. There it was…Saturn…and I could see its rings. I remember thinking just how incredible this sight was. I will never forget those images. At that moment, nothing else seemed to matter. There were no wars, no tax hikes, no high gas prices…just miracles.

There is so much beauty out there…hidden within the common. It is a wise person who realizes that there is a magic show tucked away and waiting to be discovered…and re-discovered time and time again. So, stop for a moment, take a deep breath and find the miraculous within the common. You may not know what you're looking for at first…but when you find it…you'll know.

> "Before we acquire great power we must acquire wisdom to use it well."
>
> Ralph Waldo Emerson
>
> (from "Demonology," *Lectures and Biographical Sketches*, published posthumously, 1883)

This quotation gives us perspective about Emerson, the man. It sheds light on the type of personality he may have had. We know that he was a brilliant and successful writer, poet, philosopher, minister, and Transcendentalist. But what about *coach*? There's little to suggest that Emerson was an avid sportsman. But from this quote, it is fairly clear that if he had indeed spent some time on the sidelines, he would have insisted that his players invest hours and hours of practice before stepping onto the field. Before you can acquire the power, you must acquire the wisdom. It's all about preparation. Former NFL coach, Vince Lombardi, is credited with a similar refrain: "Practice does not make perfect. Only perfect practice makes perfect."

We are all in such a hurry to prove ourselves. We want to get out there and test our wings. We tire quickly of the little kids' table. We want to sit with the adults. Why the need to rack up hours with a learner's permit? We're ready to get behind the wheel right now. So why this impatience? Why do we want to forego practice and get to the bigs? Is it because practicing is so boring, so tedious, so unexciting. Or is it because we want to play with the big boys...right now? Most kids who are forced by their parents to take music lessons will tell you what they hate the most— practice. But without practice and preparation, life might be a tad risky? Would you really want to be on the same road with a first-time driver...who's flying solo. And speaking of flying, would you want to be on the same plane with a flight crew that had never flown before or hadn't even sat in front of a simulator? This all takes us back to the famous Carnegie Hall joke: a boy walks up to a New Yorker and asks, "Pardon me sir, how do I get to Carnegie Hall?" The man smiles and replies, "Practice, practice, practice."

When it comes to practice, there appears to be a double standard. *We might not need the required number of hours to be certified to do something*...but don't expect us to hire someone who hasn't done his or her homework. We insist that plumbers, carpenters, electricians, etc., be members of their respective unions because it guarantees that the individual has invested at least the minimum number of hours that the trade requires. But do we hold ourselves up to the same standards? We need to demand the same level of expertise from ourselves that we do from others. We're just plain too easy on ourselves sometimes. We don't seem to recognize that at times *we* are the ones who are under-qualified. It's as if we're wearing blinders.

Every so often in the news we read about a politician who has suffered an indiscretion—inappropriate behavior with a page, intern or campaign worker—or who has allowed him or herself to accept funds under the table. The general reaction from the public is outrage. People are appalled by this behavior. Many call for the ouster of the office-holder. Initiatives for recall elections are discussed. We have no patience with corrupt politicians. Although the indiscretions may have had little to do with their decision-making abilities, we see the actions as character flaws, and we feel betrayed. These individuals have acquired great power as Emerson points out, but have not acquired the necessary wisdom with which to use it.

Our history books are filled with stories of dictators who have wrestled power away from legitimate governments and have installed themselves as supreme rulers. If these misguided individuals manage to maintain military support, they might remain in power for years. These leaders repeatedly violate the human rights of their citizens, and many commit crimes against humanity. These tyrants have acquired the power, but where is the wisdom that is required to wield it effectively and morally? The only way to unseat these despots is through a counter-revolution, economic sanctions, or outside military intervention. And you know how unpopular the final option can be.

When Emerson suggests that we must acquire wisdom before we can assume power, he is warning us that before we can accept major responsibilities, we must have acquired the necessary training and preparation to perform these tasks. We cannot cut corners to make the process easier for ourselves. We must raise the bar, and keep it there, so that those who rise to the position in question have earned the right to be there. This is not an easy task. We must therefore be vigilant to make certain that only the most deserving capture the prize.

"If you are wise you will dread a prosperity which only loads you with more (debt)."

Ralph Waldo Emerson

(from "Compensation," *Essays, First Series*, 1865)

When I first stumbled upon this Emerson quotation, I found it listed on a website with other quotes from the master himself. But it didn't appear as it does above. The word in parentheses, *debt*, was not present. I've added that. The quote ended with the word *more*. Read the quotation again, but this time leave off the word *debt*. It now has a completely different meaning—one which seems to suggest that *excess* is our enemy. And that almost sounds like something Emerson might say. But that's not what he is saying. This is one of the problems you encounter when you take something out of context. Not that excess can't get us into all kinds of trouble, but the villain here, according to Emerson, is debt.

Here is the text that precedes this quotation from Emerson's essay on *Compensation*:

> "A wise man will extend this lesson to all parts of life, and know that it is the part of prudence to face every claimant and pay every just demand on your time, your talents, or your heart. Always pay; for first or last you must pay your entire debt. Persons and events may stand for a time between you and justice, but it is only a postponement. You must pay at last your own debt. If you are wise you will dread a prosperity which only loads you with more."

You now see what I mean. Emerson clearly wants to encourage us to resist borrowing and to pay off our debts at all costs. There is an interesting use of the word *prosperity* in this citation. Emerson uses it almost facetiously. It is hardly a reference to prosperity as we know it but rather a false prosperity.

A few pages back we analyzed the quotation, "We are wiser than we know." And we came to the conclusion that we are indeed wiser than we give ourselves credit for. We almost don't even need to be told that we will dread an existence that allows us to fall into the depths of debt. We know that. We hear about it on every newscast or talk show that features a segment on fiscal responsibility. We read about it at least once a week in newspaper columns or radio and television talk shows dealing with wise investing. We are certainly intelligent enough to know that debt spells doom, but with all that knowledge, and with all that wisdom, and with all those articles and news reports, we still manage to fall prey to the credit crunch.

It all probably started innocently enough. We were issued our first credit cards, and likewise consumers, we faithfully paid off the entire balance each month. Then an emergency blindsided us, and for the first time we paid off only a portion of the balance. But we vowed to return to our fiscally responsible habit of carrying zero debt. And then we got married, started a family, needed to furnish a living space, suffered an illness, had an accident, lost our jobs…you name it. And before long, we found ourselves paying the monthly minimum. It was the beginning of the prosperity, or rather the false prosperity of which Emerson refers to above. As long as we were able to fit that minimum payment into our monthly budget, we felt as though our heads were still above water…but the debt continued to mount. One credit card turned into multiple cards…with balances on each. We probably then sought relief by consolidating our debt into a home equity loan. What could be better—a lower monthly payment and a tax advantage. We were solvent again—or so we thought. But then the nasty cycle started all over but this time we faced a monthly home equity payment (not counting a mortgage and/or a car payment or two) along with new credit card payments.

I am not a financial guru. There are plenty of those out there—or those who at least claim to be. I am not in a position to tell you how to climb out from under the mountain of debt. There are low-cost, and even free credit counseling services that are there to help you consolidate your debt. But more than that, they will ask, even demand, that you alter your spending habits, your lack of savings initiative, your cavalier attitude regarding the use of credit cards. It's more than one lower monthly payment—it's a change in lifestyle. And it's not easy. But if you carry more debt than you should, then you know exactly what Emerson is talking about. And he seemed to recognize it a century and a half ago.

Let me tell you that I know the meaning of debt, and of living from paycheck to paycheck. It's scary. You worry what will happen if you lose your job or become disabled. You want so badly to give your children some of the things that you never had, that you rationalize that you are actually doing a good thing, a noble thing, a loving thing, by overextending yourself in order for them to enjoy these gifts. But if you end up leaving your children your debts, what actually have you accomplished? My goal right now is to leave my children no debts. I would certainly love to leave them an inheritance, but we take one step at a time. We know how debt can alter, even destroy our lives. We don't need a reminder…or do we? For me, to hear Emerson say, "…you must pay at last your own debt…," it resonates far more than reading the same suggestion in an article or listening to a financial wizard. Emerson possessed such great insights on how to lead a more fulfilling life, that when he offers a tip on money matters, I'm all ears.

WONDER

> "O Day of days when we can read! The reader and the book, either without the other is naught."
>
> Ralph Waldo Emerson
>
> (from "Books," *Society and Solitude*, 1870)

In the past few years I have rediscovered reading. When I was young I was a television fiend. The only books I read were comic books and those required by teachers. I rarely if ever just picked up a novel for the pure enjoyment of reading. At the time I didn't know what I was missing. In high school it was more of the same—I read what was required. In spite of this deficiency, I was a strong student. I read and re-read textbooks. I was all over assigned readings. But reading for the sake of reading just wasn't happening. I will say that some of the selections I was forced to read for English classes actually turned out to be some of my favorite books which I have since re-read. But even those positive experiences weren't motivation enough to pick up a book that wasn't mandatory reading. I have always been about productivity. I could see a clear upside for religiously poring through assigned readings but where was the payoff for non-assigned books? This trend continued through college.

Following graduation, I became an avid reader—of newspapers, magazines, trade journals, wire service copy. As the producer of a talk radio program, it was critical to stay on top of current events as well as researching show topic ideas. But novels and non-fiction choices were still very rare. When I left commercial radio and entered academia, my reading habits changed again. In order to prepare for classroom instruction, I needed to scrutinize textbooks and scholarly articles. Again, I had no problem with reading material with practical applications. Occasionally my kids would ask for homework help with books they were reading. If it had been assigned when I was in school, it was all good. If not, I was in the dark. It was bothersome at times, and I wanted to be more helpful, but I still wasn't motivated enough to answer the call and read for the sake of reading.

A few years ago, that all changed. We were in Florida visiting my parents who had retired to the Clearwater area sometime earlier. Each night would wrap up the same way. We'd join my folks at their condo for the evening. My mom, an incredible cook, would set out a spread like no other. After dinner, we would retire to the living room for a little baseball—or I should say, a lot of baseball. My dad was a baseball addict.

For Christmas, his grandsons had given him the MLB Baseball Package on cable. We'd watch hardball until it was time for bed.

It was during those baseball broadcasts that I couldn't help but notice something. While my dad and I stared at the tube, my wife and daughters had their noses buried in books. There was occasional conversation but when there was a lull, it was back to the books. I observed this dynamic night after night. I couldn't imagine why someone would choose to read when the national pastime, fifty-five inches of it, was ten feet away. I just didn't get it, and that was starting to bother me. The more I witnessed their voracious appetites for reading, the more I wondered what I was missing. I began asking them about what they were reading and why. I had to know more about this obsession.

On the flight home that year, I made a decision. I wanted to know if I was indeed missing something. I thought back to some of my favorite book experiences and how I felt following the lives of various characters. It began to bring back some pleasant memories. Before we landed, I had made a vow. I was going to investigate this reading addiction that was plaguing my family. I guess I also wanted to connect with my wife and kids on another level. Since I had been bugged incessantly by my youngest daughter to read Harry Potter (the first novel in the series had just come out), I decided to begin there. I made the decision to read every day as if the book had been assigned. I would read a specific number of pages each day, and find out for myself exactly what I had been missing. And then I remembered something that I once read in a magazine years before had always bothered me. It was a quotation that went something like this: a person who does not read is no better than a person who cannot read.

Well, I'm happy to report that I have joined the ranks of addicts. I discovered Harry Potter — the entire series. I've now joined the untold millions who have done so. I can't believe what I had been missing for so long. Newspapers, magazines, professional journals, textbooks, etc., are fine for maintaining an edge on current affairs and staying up to date on the changes in your own profession, but they sure don't offer the excitement and escape of a novel. I no longer care about how practical or impractical it may be to read a book for the sheer enjoyment of doing so. I've gotten to the point where I can't retire each night without having read an installment in my current self-assigned text. And now, before I finish a book, I know exactly what I'll read next. In fact, I have to have the next book in my possession before I finish the last one. I want to be ready. I can't imagine finishing a book and not having a new one ready to take its place the next day. I may have gotten a little obsessive about all of this, but this is one obsession of which I would choose not to be cured.

When I spotted this Emerson quotation, I knew that I wanted to include it, and the section on *Wonder* seemed the perfect fit. If you haven't yet discovered the wonder of reading, I cannot say enough to convince you to join the legions of satisfied customers. If you are an avid reader, and have been so for years, I can only say that I envy you. I envy the fact that while I was on the dark side, you were experiencing the unfolding of mysteries and adventures each and every day. And if I can't convince you join the ranks or to stay the course, perhaps Emerson can. "O Day of days when we can read! The reader and the book, either without the other is naught."

> **"What is a weed? A plant whose virtues have not yet been discovered."**
>
> Ralph Waldo Emerson
>
> (from "The Fortune of the Republic," *Miscellanies*, 1878)

Had there been a section in this book on *Tolerance*, the above quotation would have fit in nicely. Why include it then in the *Wonder* section? Well, when we discover the essence of what Emerson's message is all about, there is a certain feeling of awe and wonder, and a question of why it has taken us so long to see the light. We all come into this world wide-eyed and accepting. We will enthusiastically believe what we are told. These teachings become our own personal set of standards. If someone, therefore, teaches us that all weeds are bad, that they compete for sunlight and moisture with plant life, and can strangle flowers and crops and the greenest of grasses, it's fairly certain that we will want to see all weeds snuffed out.

But have you ever picked a weed from a flower bed or lawn, and then wondered if it was a weed at all? I was raised in a traditional middle-class family with relatively conservative ideals. I was taught right from wrong. I was taught that there will be consequences for my actions. And my parents instilled in me a strong work ethic. They were never ones to cheat their employers out of a hard day's work for even a minute, and made sure that I followed that example. Family values were especially important to them, and they have preached that to this very day. My dad was a World War II vet, and he was respectful of the sacrifices that service men and women have made and continue to make for our country. And I don't mean for this to sound negative, but with a traditional mainstream upbringing, comes a certain stereotyping of individuals. Although things seem much different today than when I was younger, we were taught to be wary of certain people and places. There were specific types of individuals and specific locations for a child to avoid. And there is nothing wrong with that.

But as we grow older we learn more about human nature and have a better understanding of why people act the way they do. Someone who we may have labeled *odd* forty years ago might simply have been a person with a learning disability. Today we have a better handle on these things. We realize that just because some people act differently doesn't mean that there is anything wrong or odd about them. And those people who choose to express themselves in a more outward manner (piercings, tattoos, unusual hair styles) means no more than the fact that they prefer these choices over others. When I was young, *different* meant something other than what it means today. It had negative connotations. We stereotyped people more often and made connections between someone's appearance and his or her character.

We know better now. A student of mine from a few years back helped enlighten me. It was the early 1980's, and I was a young instructor. I distinctly remember an incoming freshman who first appeared in my Mass Media & Society class. The thing that I remember most about him was his appearance, specifically his hair. It wasn't especially long, but it was purple…and pink…and a little blue. It was difficult not to notice him in class or anywhere else. Without knowing anything about him but his choice of hair color, I immediately felt that this young man was probably not college material. If he had been, he would have come to class in a more appropriate manner. I had little to base this on other than the fact that when I was that age, it was virtually unheard of for a male to color his hair. It was acceptable for women to do so, but the only males who would put dye to their hair were either aging older men trying to hide the gray, or oddballs.

I couldn't help notice that his hair colors would change each week. Every Monday there was an unveiling of sorts. I wasn't certain why he chose this way to express himself because he was proving himself to be a very capable student. He would turn in assignments of high quality, always met deadlines, and never failed to be anything but fully prepared for lively classroom discussion. His papers and exams were above average…so why the statement with the hair? Within a short time, this young man became one of my favorites. I became comfortable enough to discuss his hair color choices in class. I began trying to guess what the next combination might be, and went so far as to request a specific array of colors for the next week. He was more than happy to accommodate. He seemed to like the attention.

I remember mentioning this young man to some of my friends. When they heard about his hair, they immediately assumed he was some sort of nonconformist trying to disrupt class. Months before I might have thought the same thing. But something had changed. I had learned who this young man was on the inside. I suddenly found myself defending him. I tried to explain to the others that his hair was merely a form of personal expression and that he was a great kid. I explained that he was no different than any of the other students. Well, that's not true—he was different—he was stronger academically than many of the others. And then I thought about how we stereotype people—how I had stereotyped in the past—and how wrong it was to draw any conclusions about someone based simply on appearance. This had been my wake-up call.

Following graduation I had lost track of him. Then a few years ago, I received an envelope in the mail. In it was a letter and a check. The letter was from this young man's sister. She was informing me that her brother had recently passed away. He was still in his twenties. She didn't elaborate on the cause of death, and I didn't pry. She told me that she was sending a gift to the campus radio station (which I manage) in her brother's memory. She indicated that it was only fitting to do so because while he was in college, he so loved the time he had spent there. I think about him often, and about how he changed my life. This young man opened my eyes to tolerance and acceptance. He may have been one of my *students*, but to be more accurate, he was the *teacher*—he had taught me a valuable lesson about understanding, compassion, and human nature.

> "Men love to wonder, and that is the seed of our science."
>
> Ralph Waldo Emerson
>
> (from "Works and Days," *Society and Solitude*, 1870)

Curiosity may have undone the feline, but it has always been a lightning rod to discovery for man. Have you ever wondered why and how certain inventions came to be? It all began with a need, followed closely by wonder. First we have the problem or the need. Then the seed of an idea takes shape. Before long research and experimentation begin. And ultimately we are presented with the latest innovation. It is either something we can't live without, or the misguided efforts of a would-be inventor who zigged when he should have zagged.

Most of us never expect to invent or discover anything of substance in our lives, and for the most part, we would be right. But it doesn't mean that we should ever stop wondering, or displaying curiosity, or asking why? Each day when we awake, we open our eyes to a new world. We can learn something new every day without even trying. There have been thousands of discoveries, inventions and innovations in our lifetime alone. Imagine what the future will hold. Will you be part of that? Will you play a role in unearthing something — anything — that might change our lives as we know it? This can only happen if you are aware of what's going on around you. It is important to be tuned in to the problems that society faces. Someone, maybe you, will ultimately solve them.

A lot of you are probably thinking right now, "Even if I thought of something that might benefit society, I don't have the chemical or computer or medical or engineering or business or whatever type of knowledge necessary to bring it to fruition." But all the knowledge in the world is meaningless unless you're the type of person who is aware of your surroundings, aware of the needs of mankind. There are a lot of highly intelligent people out there — you might know some of them — who live in a vacuum, who are socially inept, who are not tuned in to the world around them. If you are the type of person who notices things that others seem to miss, then you possess the necessary trait of *wonder* that is a requirement for those seeking to change the world.

You have to believe — you have to continually tell yourself — that you are capable of great things. Think of every technical innovation that has evolved in the last ten years, the last twenty years, the last half century. Someone had to think of those things. Someone who wondered why there wasn't an easier way to do something. Look at the volumes of books at your local bookstore or library. Someone — someone like you — wrote each one. Someone thought up the premise, did the necessary research, then sat down and cranked it out. Are you capable of writing a book? What's stopping you? If you are an avid reader, you know what interests you, what stirs your emotions, what causes you to stay up all hours of the night fully engrossed in the latest mystery, supernatural thriller, science fiction story, or romance novel. Someone like you, with the same initial doubts, with the same yearnings, with the same hunger to accomplish something significant, wrote those books.

Walk down the streets of your local community. Glance at the businesses around you. Some are franchises; others are independent merchants. But they have something in common: both types of retail outlets were begun by individuals who sensed a need, and wondered how to satisfy it. You may be the type of person who thinks about things like that all the time. "What this town needs is a good _____." But maybe the investment necessary to make a plunge like that is a bit scary. What about an online business instead? It requires less capital and may help determine the market and the interest level in a particular type of business endeavor that may ultimately lead to a brick and mortar outlet.

Throughout the pages of this book, we've talked about people who *talk* and people who *do*. Now is the time to start doing. It may start out in the form of research, then evolve into the implementation of an actual idea. Are you afraid you've waited too long to undertake such an endeavor? In 1954, fast food giant, Ray Kroc, may have initially thought the same thing but he had the confidence in himself to take a risk and see it through:

> "I was 52 years old. I had diabetes and incipient arthritis. I had lost my gall bladder and most of my thyroid gland in earlier campaigns, but I was convinced that the best was ahead of me."

Emerson recognized that wonder is the seed of success. When Ray Kroc saw this modest hamburger stand operated by the McDonald brothers in San Bernadino, California, he wondered about the possibility of expanding on this idea. The rest of the story is a blueprint for entrepreneurial wizardry. There are great things waiting for you. Are you interested in discovering them? Are you ready? Are you tired of talking, and anxious to put the wheels in motion? If so, here is your charge: Continue to wonder, and then go out and create something wonder-ful.

"Nothing can bring you peace but yourself. Nothing can bring you peace but the triumph of principles."

Ralph Waldo Emerson

(from "Self-Reliance," *Essays, First Series*, 1865)

Here you have it—the one-hundredth Emerson principle, and one of the best. Simple, direct, uncomplicated. For centuries mankind has searched for peace—not global peace, mind you—but the peace within. We would all love to live on a planet where nations exist in a harmonious state, but since that appears to be a long time in coming, we desire the next best thing, and one in which we have some control—peace within. To be at peace suggests that you are comfortable and satisfied with who you are, with what you have accomplished, with how you are perceived by others, with your priorities. Personally I know very few people, if any, who are at peace, if we follow this definition. And it's not to say that we have defined the term incorrectly, it simply means that very few people are completely satisfied with where they are in life. The key word here is *completely*. There are certainly some people, perhaps many of us, who are relatively content with certain aspects of our lives, although we might like to make a few slight adjustments in some areas.

In order to discover complete peace, Emerson is issuing us a challenge. He is asking us to identify our principles, to determine if we are indeed following our moral compass, and in a nutshell, to stay the course. He's not around to monitor us, to keep track of our progress, to pick us up when we stumble. We have but his words—his powerful words. Therefore, we must set standards. Then we must maintain them. We must identify personal goals. Then we must do everything in our power to realize them. We must be relentless in our pursuits. We must do all of this and at the same time treat others with compassion and respect. This is a tall order. But if we try, really try to make this our mission, then we will achieve inner peace. And it won't matter how long it takes for us to meet our goals, because along the way, if we live by a set of moral laws, we will have met the most important goal of all—we will have maintained our integrity.

When Emerson says, "Nothing can bring you peace but yourself," he is encouraging us not to rely on the crutches that some people use to find peace. He is, in a sense, warning us of the dangers of alcohol, drugs, sex, abuse of power, etc., the vices that will appease us for short spurts, but in the long term will prove self-destructive. He is imploring us to resist these dangers not only because of the negative effects they will have on us both physically and mentally, but because they will deter us and sidetrack us in our quest for peace, leaving us further from our goal than when we first set out. We will then have to pick up the pieces and start over again.

In the second part of this quotation, Emerson presents us with a treasure map. With it, he identifies the path to peace. It's as if we're looking at a torn, yellowing, crumpled piece of parchment with hand-drawn locations, and a squiggly dotted line leading to a spot with an "X". "Nothing," he says, "can bring you peace but the triumph of principles." Notice that he's not saying that you must *identify* principles, or *set* principles for yourself. He clearly states that inner peace will be achieved through the *triumph* of principles. So, although we have the map, there is still a journey ahead. And the beauty is that we really don't have to sit down and list the principles that must be maintained in order to live a prudent life. We already know what they are. We've known about them since we were youngsters — right vs. wrong, good vs. evil, love your neighbor, etc. But we also know about the temptations that we will undoubtedly encounter on our journey — the same temptations that will prevent us from living a principled life.

There are no surprises here. We know precisely what it will take to win the prize — inner peace. It's time to begin packing, to map out your travel plans, and to set a destination. Then you must decide when to embark on this journey. And considering the payoff — the sooner the better. Godspeed.

EPILOGUE

"I hate quotations. Tell me what you know."

Ralph Waldo Emerson

(from a May, 1849 entry in Journal XL)

After having shared 100 of Emerson's most insightful quotations, I couldn't resist ending with a most unlikely choice. But don't for a minute think that this gifted author and philosopher is denigrating his own quotations. Actually he was referring to how writers approach the topic of *immortality*.

> "I notice that as soon as writers broach this question they begin to quote. I hate quotations. Tell me what you know."

Well, let me tell you what *I* know, or rather what I have learned through this experience. Writing this book has been pure joy. I have found guidance and inspiration with each quotation. But it's not without its frustrations. When I began researching this text, I made the mistake of searching for Emerson quotations on the Internet. There you will find hundreds of them…thousands of them. But when you take the time to research each quote to identify its origin, you soon learn that many of the quotations attributed to Emerson were either written or spoken by someone else, or never existed in the first place. I can comfortably say that at least 30% of the Emerson quotations online were incorrect. It was at that point that I abandoned online research and focused on hardbound selections—a choice I should have made from the onset.

I don't want to indict all of the online sources—just most of them. I found an absolutely brilliant online database of The Complete Works of Ralph Waldo Emerson hosted by the University of Michigan. This site was accurate, easy to navigate, and an absolute researcher's paradise. You can find it at http://quod.lib.umich.edu/e/emerson. It is simply wonderful. I can't imagine writing this text without having had access to it. In addition I would like to thank the Indiana University School of Journalism for granting permission to reprint one of the cases from their "Journalism Ethics Cases Online" website (http://journalism.indiana.edu/resources/ethics). A special thank you is extended to many of the inspirational writers and lecturers who have been personal favorites of mine over the years—Dr. Wayne W. Dyer, Denis Waitley, Brian Tracy, and Zig Ziglar. I also want to recognize a number of other references that provided me with accurate data and helpful background information for many of the topics discussed here. They are noted in the next section ("References").

The more deeply I delved into the works of Emerson, the more amazed I was at the intellect, the insightfulness, the depth, and the compassion of this man. He seems to have something to say about virtually every topic. And although that might seem like a negative statement, it is anything but. Emerson was so gifted that he was able to opine on a plethora of subject matter — and not just share an opinion, mind you — his comments were thought-provoking and inspirational. I have attempted to include the 100 Emerson principles that I felt provided a road map for daily living. All one need do is preview the table of contents, locate a particular area of interest or need, and then follow it to four quotations and reflections that hopefully will help you tackle whatever problem it is that you are currently facing.

Throughout this book, I have tried to share personal experiences that I hope help illustrate the ways in which we can apply these precepts to our daily lives. In some cases, I offered details regarding certain critical moments in my life that I might have handled differently had I owned this text. I have also drawn upon news stories that featured individuals who seem to have lived their lives according to the master. I have shared reflections and opinions of others who, whether they realized it or not, were following the suggestions of Emerson. I hope you found these helpful, and through them, were able to see how you might be able to apply these principles to your life. I am hopeful that you will keep this book in an accessible area. Depending on the situation, you may find yourself referring to it time and time again.

Finally, thank you so much for choosing this particular collection. It has taken me the better part of a year to research and write this book. And during that time, I have been greatly affected by the words of Emerson. Each reflective essay that follows the quotations has been therapeutic. As I searched for examples of how readers might apply the Emerson principles to their own lives, I found myself imagining how each particular phrase had assisted me and had changed my life for the better. My intentions are to assist those looking for answers. By working on this project, I managed to better understand myself. I come away from this experience with a commitment to preach the Emersonian gospel to all who will listen. Thanks for listening.

REFERENCES

"Accord in Death of Girl Who Made Peace Trip." *The New York Times* 18 January 1989: 13.

Adams, Douglas. *Dick Gently's Holistic Detective Agency*. New York: Simon & Shuster, 1987.

Asante, Molefi K., Ama Mazama. *Encyclopedia of Black Studies*. Los Angeles: SAGE, 2005.

BBC News. "Exxon Valdez Creates Oil Slick Disaster." News.BBC.co.uk. March 24, 1989. http://news.bbc.co.uk/onthisday/hi/dates/stories/march/24/newsid_4231000/4231971.stm

BBC News. "The Kursk Disaster: Day by Day." News.BBC.co.uk. August, 24, 2000. http://news.bbc.co.uk/2/hi/europe/894638.stm

BBC News. "Friends Help People Live Longer." News.BBC.co.uk. June 15, 2005. http://news.bbc.co.uk/2/hi/health/4094632.stm

Bio.True Story. "Andrew Carnegie Biography." Biography.com. April 7, 2009. http://www.biography.com/search/article.do?id=9238756

"Butt Out: The Life and Death of Cigarette Advertising on TV." Time Machine with Jack Perkins." Arts & Entertainment Network. 11 December 1992.

Carmichael, Evan. *"The Burger King: Ray Kroc is Born."* Famous Entrepreneurs. 28 July 2009. < http://www.evancarmichael.com/Famous-Entrepreneurs/756/The-Burger-King-Ray-Kroc-is-Born.html>.

Carnegie Corporation. "Andrew Carnegie Biography." Carnegie Corporation of New York. April 7, 2009. http://www.carnegie.org/sub/about/biography.html

Chapin, Harry. "Cat's in the Cradle." Author: Sandy Chapin. <u>Verities and Balderdash</u>. Elektra, 1974.

Dyer, Wayne W. *Real Magic: Creating Miracles in Everyday Life*. Harper Collins, 1992.

Dyer, Wayne W. *What Do You Really Want for Your Children?* New York: Harper Collins, 2001.

Eliot, Charles W. (editor). *The Harvard Classics – Essays and English Traits by R. W. Emerson*. New York: P. F. Collier and Sons Company, 1909.

Emerson, Edward Waldo, editor. *The Complete Works of Ralph Waldo Emerson*. University of Michigan. http://quod.lib.umich.edu/e/emerson, 2006.

Emerson, Ralph Waldo. *The Conduct of Life*. Whitefish, MT: Kessinger Publishing, 2004.

Emerson, Ralph Waldo. Emerson, Edward Waldo. Forbes, Waldo Emerson. *Journals of Ralph Waldo Emerson.* Wilmington, MA: Houghton Mifflin Company, 1911.

Emerson, Ralph Waldo. *Essays: First Series*. Cambridge, MA: Henry Altemus, Harvard University Publishers, 1895.

Emerson, Ralph Waldo. Edited by Frome, Keith. *Hitch Your Wagon to a Star – and other Quotations from Ralph Waldo Emerson*. New York: Columbia University Press, 1996.

Emerson, Ralph Waldo. Perry, Bliss: contributor. *Heart of Emerson's Journals*. Whitefish, MT: Kessinger Publishing, 2003.

Emerson, Ralph Waldo. Edited by Porte, Joel. *Emerson: Essays and Lectures*. New York: Literary Classics of the United States, Inc., 1983.

Goldman, Russell. "U.S. Airways Hero Pilot Searched Plane Twice Before Leaving." ABCNews.com. January 15, 2009. http://abcnews.go.com/US/story?id=6658493&page=1.

Internet Movie Database Pro. "Dick Elliott." 26 May 2009. <http://pro.imdb.com/name/nm0254424/>.

Johnson, Dirk. "Ryan White Dies of AIDS at 18; His Struggle Helped Pierce Myths."
New York Times 9 April 1990: *The New York Times Online* 7 May 2009 <http://www.nytimes.com/1990/04/09/obituaries/ryan-white-dies-of-aids-at-18-his-struggle-helped-pierce-myths.html>.

Kasindorf, Jeanie. "Six Degrees of Impersonation." *New York Magazine*. March 25, 1991: 40-46.

Kateb, George. *Emerson and Self-Reliance*. Lanham, MD: Rowman & Littlefield Publishing Group, 2002.

Lazarus, Arnold A. *In the Mind's Eye: The Power of Imagery for Personal Achievement*. New York: Guilford Press, 1984.

Luecke, Richard. Barton, Larry. *Crisis Management: Master the Skills to Prevent Disasters*. Boston, MA: Harvard Business Press, 2004.

"Millard Fuller—Habitat for Humanity International Founder." Habitat for Humanity. 22 July 2009.
<http://www.habitat.org/how/millard.aspx>.

MSNBC.com staff. "N.Y. Jet Crash called 'miracle on the Hudson.'" MSNBC.com. January 15, 2009. http://www.msnbc.msn.com/id/28678669.

The New Oxford Annotated Bible. Michael D. Coogan, editor. Luke 18:9-14. New York: Oxford University Press, 2001.

National Do Not Call Registry. https://www.donotcall.gov. 5 July 2009.

Newman's Own. "Newman's Own—Shameless Exploitation in Pursuit of the Common Good." April 1, 2009. http://www.newmansown.com/index.aspx.

Ojanpa, Brian. "When Journalists Play God..." Journalism Ethics Cases Online. School of Journalism, Indiana University. 2009. http://journalism.indiana.edu/resources/ethics/ sensitive-news-topics/when-journalists-play-god.

"Plot Summary for 'Pay it Forward.'" *Internet Movie Database (IMDB).* 2000. 22 July 2009. <http://www.imdb.com/title/tt0223897/plotsummary>.

Rosen, Jeffrey. "The Hopeless Moralist." *The New York Times.* November 2, 1997. *The New York Times on the Web.* http://www.nytimes.com/books/97/11/02/reviews /971102.02 rosent.html?_r=2

Sernett, Milton C. *African American Religious History: A Documentary Witness.* Durham, NC: Duke University Press, 1999.

"Star." Microsoft Bookshelf '95. 1st edition. 1995. 8 July 2009.

Stedman, Edmund Clarence & Hutchinson, Ellen MacKay (editors). *A Library of American Literature from Earliest Settlement to the Present Time.* New York: W. E. Benjamin, 1894.

St. Jude Children's Research Hospital. "All About Danny Thomas." May 6, 2009. http://www.stjude.org/stjude/v/index.jsp?vgnextoid=3f08fa2454e70110VgnVCM1000001e0215acRCRD&vgnextchannel=8be01e251b7f1110VgnVCM1000001e0215acRCRD

Teuber, Professor Andreas (editor). Ralph Waldo Emerson Biography. Brandeis University, Department of Philosophy course description: "Coming Into One's Own." http://people.brandeis.edu/~teuber/usem.html#description.

Twohey, Megan. "Linguist jumped at every opportunity." Chicago Tribune 3 May 2009, Section 2, Chicagoland, p. 1.

About the Author

John Madormo is an author, screenwriter, and college professor. He is the author of a mystery series with Penguin-Random House titled Charlie Collier Snoop for Hire. The books in the series include "The Homemade Stuffing Caper," "The Camp Phoenix Caper," and "The Copycat Caper." John also sold a comedy screenplay to a producer in Los Angeles. It is currently in pre-production. When he isn't writing, John is a college professor at North Central College in Naperville, IL. You can reach him at john@johnmadormo.com.

Made in the USA
Monee, IL
28 November 2021